A "MOST TROUBLESOME SITUATION"

A "MOST TROUBLESOME SITUATION"

THE BRITISH MILITARY AND THE PONTIAC INDIAN UPRISING OF 1763-1764

Timothy J. Todish

Todd E. Harburn

PURPLE MOUNTAIN PRESS
Fleischmanns, New York

This has been, and is Like to Continue, the most troublesome Situation I was in with Such Inconveniencys but we must withstand them by all perseverence. . . .
Letter from Lieutenant Colonel William Browning to Sir William Johnson, October 22, 1763

A "Most Troublesome Situation": The British Military and the Pontiac Indian Uprising of 1763-1764
First Edition 2006

Published by
PURPLE MOUNTAIN PRESS, LTD.
P.O. Box 309, Fleischmanns, New York 12430-0309
845-254-4062, 845-254-4476 (fax), purple@catskill.net
www.catskill.net/purple

Library of Congress Control Number: 2006901362

ISBN 1-930098-72-3

Front cover:
Fort Pitt Under Siege (detail), painting by Robert Griffing
Courtesy of Paramount Press

Frontispiece:
Rogers Meets Pontiac (detail), drawing by Gary Zaboly

Back cover:
The portrait of Captain James Dalyell is used with the permission of
The Honorable Tam and Kathleen Dalyell of Linlithgow, Scotland

Cover typography by Janet Atkin, Hinterland Design, Coxsackie, New York

Manufactured in the United States of America
5 4 3 2 1

To our longtime friend and mentor,
Dr. David A. Armour,
recently retired Deputy Director of
Mackinac State Historic Parks

Epigraph

Our Empire now is large, our Forces strong,
Our Chiefs are Wise, our Warriors valiant Men;
We are all furnish'd with the best of Arms,
And all things requisite to curb a Foe;
And now's our time, if ever, to secure
Our Country, Kindred, Empire, all that's dear,
From these Invaders of our Rights, the *English*. . . .
The *French* familiarized themselves with us,
Studied our Tongue, and Manners, wore our Dress,
Married our Daughters, and our Sons their Maids,
Dealt honestly, and well supplied our Wants,
Used no One ill, and treated with Respect
Our Kings, our Captains, and our aged Men;
Call'd us their Friends, nay, what is more, their Children,
And seem'd like Fathers anxious for our Welfare.
Whom see we now? Their haughty Conquerors
Possess'd of every Fort, and Lake, and Pass,
Big with their Victories so often gained;
On us they look with deep Contempt and Scorn,
Are false, deceitful, knavish, insolent;
Nay think us conquered, and our Country theirs,
Without a Purchase, or ev'n asking for it.
With Pleasure I wou'd call their King my Friend,
Yea, honour and obey him as my Father;
I'd be content, would he keep his own Sea,
And leave these distant Lakes and Streams to us. . . .

Chief Pontiac
from *Ponteach: Or the Savages of America—A Tragedy*
by Major Robert Rogers, London, 1766, p. 201

Contents

Foreword

FROM THE BEGINNING of the European colonization of North America, the West beckoned as a land of opportunity and expansion. Immigrants, native-born colonists, and European administrators could look to the seemingly endless forests and plains and visualize the wilderness eventually transformed by farms and cities. But this westward movement was an enterprise marked by danger, conflict, and tragedy as the new arrivals competed with indigenous peoples who occupied what was too often seen as empty land. The English-speaking American frontier, from seventeenth-century Virginia and New England to the late-nineteenth-century Great Plains, was marked by clashes of arms and of cultures that were most visibly apparent in periodic, open warfare.

For a variety of reasons, it is the final fifty years of these three centuries of frontier turmoil that have seized and held the modern, popular imagination. Events and characters of the settlement of the trans-Mississippi West have become enshrined in American culture through the influence of literature, photography, and cinema. It had taken much of the preceding two and one-half centuries, however, for the frontier to cross the Mississippi River. Fighting between competing European powers and conflicts between their colonists and diverse Native American groups marked those years. For anyone interested in the history of this "old" West, there is no more colorful or engaging event than the great Indian uprising that took place west of the Appalachian Mountains in the years 1763 and 1764, a conflict that has become firmly associated with the Ottawa leader, Pontiac.

"Pontiac's War" has been a popular subject since at least the early years of the nineteenth century. Historians have explored the uprising in its military, political, and cultural contexts and in relation to the colonial "French and Indian War" and the much broader international conflict known as the Seven Years' War. Specialized monographs have treated its sieges and battles and the material culture of the participants. Now Tim Todish and Todd Harburn offer a concise narrative of the military events of "Pontiac's War" as they unfolded for the British soldiers who served on the front lines.

The "British" forces of this conflict included regular soldiers from Europe, provincial troops from the colonies (including the newly acquired former French possession of Canada), and Native Americans whose interests or loyalties cast them as allies of King George III. The brunt of the fighting, however, was borne by the soldiers of the regular army, particularly during the critical year of 1763. Many of these men were veterans of the recent war against the French and Indians as well as of campaigns in the warmer climate of the Caribbean. Despite their previous American experience, the Indian war of 1763-1764 proved to be a new and often daunting experience that the British military met with varying degrees of success. The lessons learned during "Pontiac's War," fought across the vast wilderness of the Great Lakes and the Ohio country, would influence British policies and tactics in the West for the rest of the eighteenth century.

The life and duties of the British "redcoat" in America have been the subject of several recent scholarly works, notably Stephen Brumwell's *Redcoats* and Michael N. McConnell's *Army & Empire*. Tim Todish and Todd Harburn present a straightforward narrative account of these soldiers' activities in the field against an elusive and resilient opponent. Readers of all sorts will find a useful guide to "Pontiac's War" in the details the authors present on the military actions, organization, and locales of the fighting.

BRIAN LEIGH DUNNIGAN
CURATOR OF MAPS, WILLIAM L. CLEMENTS LIBRARY

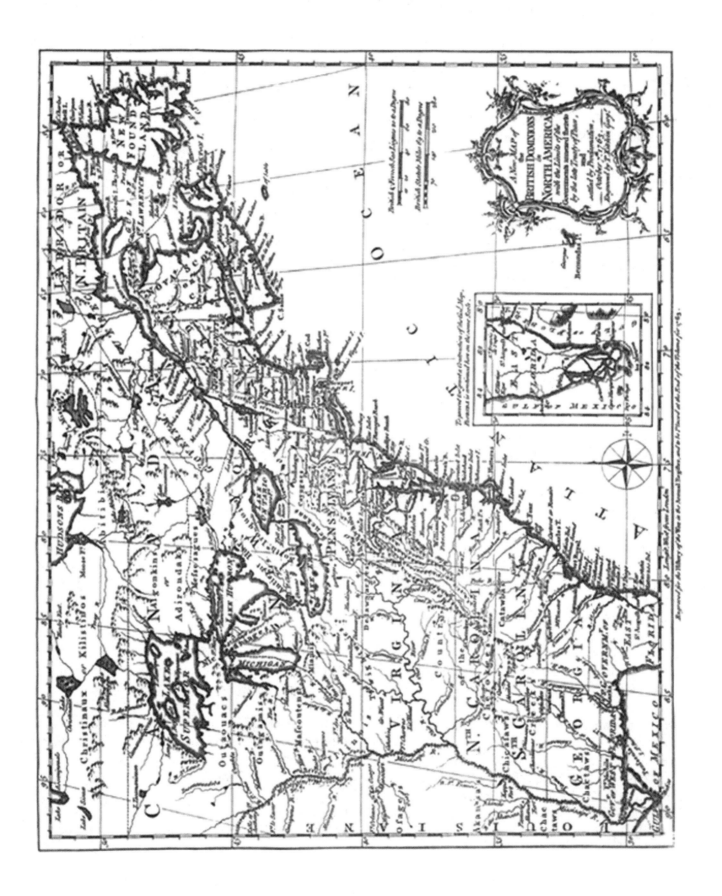

Preface

AT THE CONCLUSION of the French Indian War, the triumphant British took possession of a vast area west of the Appalachians in the Great Lakes region that was not only replete with a lucrative fur trade and almost infinite colonization possibilities, but also hostile Indians harboring lingering loyalties to their former French allies. It was not long before overly strict British regulation of the fur trade, coupled with a perceived arrogance, further fueled Indian resentment of colonial expansion into their territories. Pontiac's Uprising, or Pontiac's Conspiracy, of 1763, named after the Ottawa chief generally recognized as one of its main catalysts, was the violent, sometimes horrifying tribal reaction against two short years of controversial British military rule.

Several prominent historians and authors have examined the story of Pontiac's Uprising. The definitive work on the subject, as Clements Library Director John C. Dann eloquently points out in his Foreword to the 1994 reprint, is still Howard H. Peckham's 1947 *Pontiac and the Indian Uprising*. Serious students of this period are no doubt also familiar with the works of Francis Parkman, Lyman C. Draper, Charles Moore, Clarence Burton, Clarence Walworth Alvord, Clarence Edwin Carter, Milo Quaife, Reuben Thwaites, Raymond McCoy, and David A. Armour. More recently, Fred Anderson, Gregory Evans Dowd, Brian Leigh Dunnigan, Kerry A. Trask, William R. Nestor, Edward W. Ahrens, and David Dixon have added significant contributions. Despite this substantial body of material, this fascinating conflict remains relatively unknown to most people today. It is for this reason that the current work was undertaken.

The idea for the book was conceived in 1997 while we were on a train trip to a historical reenactment in Texas, and also during our involvement in the History Channel series *Frontier: Legends of the Old Northwest,* later that year. We both have a longstanding interest in this era, and we decided that we would produce this work as a sequel to Tim Todish's previous book, *America's FIRST First World War, The French and Indian War, 1754-1763*. To make our work different from that of other authors, we decided to approach the story from the viewpoint of the British army officers involved in the uprising. We have included excerpts from numerous primary sources to give the reader a sense of witnessing the events through the eyes of the participants. Although our story is told from the British perspective, we have made every effort to also accurately present the feelings and interests of the Indian and French habitants. As the reader will see, and contrary to what is often believed, at least some British officers worked hard to treat the Indians honestly and fairly.

The story we tell is sometimes touching and at other times cruel and gruesome. We have attempted to show the good and bad on both sides as it actually happened. We ask our readers to keep in mind that those involved were all human beings with strengths and faults like the rest of us. They also came from a different time and culture, and many actions that were acceptable in their day are looked upon with horror today. The term "anachronistic consciousness" best describes this dilemma, which the writers first encountered in the work of Texas historian Jesus de la Teja.*

Simply put, it means that it is unfair to apply our twenty-first-century sense of morality to people from earlier eras. Most of the people in the 1760s were trying to live their lives and provide for their families according to the rules of their society at that time, and it is by those rules that they should be judged. We hope that you enjoy our story.

TIMOTHY J. TODISH
GRAND RAPIDS, MICHIGAN

DR. TODD E. HARBURN
OKEMOS AND MACKINAW CITY, MICHIGAN

A Revolution Remembered: The Memoirs and Selected Correspondence of Juan N. Seguin. State House Press, Austin, 1991, p. ix.

Acknowledgments

THE AUTHORS are especially indebted to the following organizations and individuals. Without their unselfish help and encouragement this book would not have been possible.

The William L. Clements Library at the University of Michigan, Ann Arbor. The authors are especially indebted to Director Dr. John C. Dann and Curator of Maps Brian Leigh Dunnigan for their many years of invaluable assistance and support. We are also thankful for the always friendly and cheerful assistance of staff members Anna Casey, Laura Daniel, Barbara DeWolfe, Clayton Lewis, Valerie Proehl, Don Wilcox, and the late John Harriman.

Mackinac State Historic Parks, Mackinac Island, Michigan: Director Phil Porter and Chief Curator Steve Brisson, as well as two retired administrative staff members, former Deputy Director Dr. David Armour and former Curator of History Dr. Keith Widder have all given us invaluable assistance and support over the years.

Fort Ticonderoga, Ticonderoga, New York: We are grateful to Executive Director Nick Westbrook and Curator Chris Fox for their personal assistance and encouragement as well as for sharing the resources of the Thompson-Pell Research Center with us over a period of many years.

For the beautiful artwork that is such a valuable addition to our text, we thank Robert Griffing of Gibsonia, Pennsylvania, and his publishers Jerry and Cathy Seymour of Paramount Press, of Stow, New York.

We also are indebted to our good friend Gary Zaboly of New York City, not only for the use of his wonderful artwork, but also for sharing his incredible knowledge of colonial history with us for many years..

Honorable Tam and Mrs. Kathleen Dalyell of Linlithgow, Scotland, graciously allowed us to reproduce the portrait of Captain James Dalyell.

William Reese of New Haven, Connecticut, kindly permitted us to reproduce the portrait of Colonel John Bradstreet.

Dr. Seymour I. Schwartz, M.D., of Rochester, New York, generously granted us use of his extensive collection of period maps and prints.

Robert Andrews of Ganaoque, Ontario, Canada, and John Houlding of Ruckersdorf, Germany, selflessly shared their ongoing research on the British army in North America, and provided many new and obscure details for our story.

We are especially indebted to our friend, fellow reenactor, and Emmy winning screenwriter Eleanor Labine-Mancusi, of Long Island, New York, for accepting the daunting task of reviewing our text. Her effort helped us to blend our different writing styles into what we hope is one smooth narrative.

We are also very grateful to the following people and organizations for the invaluable assistance they gave us during the preparation of this book:

Abraham Lincoln Presidential Library, Springfield, Illinois (Illinois State Historical Library Collections): Debbie Hamm, Cheryl Schnirring and Glenna Schroeder-Lein)
George A. Bray III, Rochester, New York
Colonial Cahokia State Historic Site, Cahokia, Illinois (Andrew Cooperman)
Dr. Stephen Brumwell, Amsterdam, the Netherlands
Detroit Institute of Arts, Detroit, Michigan (Sylvia Inwood)
Detroit Public Library, Burton Historical Collections, Detroit, Michigan (Mark Patrick)
Elmwood Historic Cemetery, Detroit, Michigan (Allen and Cheryl Barksdale, Joseph Malburg, and Chauncey Miller)
John Fenner, Green Bay, Wisconsin
Fort Ligonier, Ligonier, Pennsylvania (Director Martin West)

Fort St. Joseph Museum, Niles, Michigan (Director Carol Bainbridge)

Johnson Hall State Historic Site, Johnstown, New York (Wanda Burch, Bonnie Pulis and Wade Wells)

Christopher Matheney, Ohio Historical Society, Columbus, Ohio

McCord Museum, Montreal, Quebec, Canada (Shiri Alon)

Lt. Col. Ian McCulloch (Canadian Forces), Virginia Beach, Virginia

The late "Captain" Ron Meesig, Rush, New York

Old Fort Niagara, Youngstown, New York (Director Robert Emerson)

Roland "Bud" Miner, Herkimer, New York

Jerry Olson, Dearborn, Michigan

The late Dr. Joseph Peyser, Professor Emeritus of French, Indiana University-South Bend, South Bend, Indiana

Purple Mountain Press, Fleischmanns, New York (Wray and Loni Rominger, publishers; Aileen Weintraub, copy editor)

Robert J. Rogers, St. Albert, Alberta, Canada

Royal Green Jackets Museum, Winchester, England (Maj. Kenneth Gray, ret., Col. I. H McCausland, ret., Maj. Gen. Giles Mills, ret., Lt. Gen. Sir Christopher Wallace)

Dr. R. Scott Stephenson, Wilmington, Delaware

Charlie Sum, Orlando, Florida

University of Michigan Hatcher Graduate Library microfilm staff, Ann Arbor, Michigan

U.S. Geological Survey/Upper Midwest Environmental Sciences Center, La Crosse, Wisconsin (Mike Caucutt and Carol Lowenberg)

Lee White, Richland, Mississippi

Yale University Center for British Art, New Haven, Connecticut (Corey Myers)

Chapter I
A Bold and Successful Expedition: The British Empire Reaches West 1760

He [Pontiac] assured me that he was inclined to live peaceably with the English while they used him as he deserved, and to encourage their settling in his country. . . .
Major Robert Rogers

WHEN QUEBEC FELL to the combined British and Provincial army under General James Wolfe on September 13, 1759, it was the beginning of the end for New France. For the 1760 campaign, British commander in chief General Jeffery Amherst designed a three-pronged attack on the remaining French stronghold of Montreal. When the three armies finally converged at the end of the summer, the outnumbered and beleaguered French troops had no choice but to surrender, which they did on September 8. Under the terms of capitulation, the British found themselves masters not only of Canada, but also all of the French posts in the Midwest and Great Lakes areas. This was a land of great promise, but few if any British subjects had ever seen it.

Command of the expedition to take possession of the western French posts would require more than just a soldier's skill and courage. The leader would have to guide his men successfully through new and dangerous country late in the season, when the treacherous weather could easily spell death and failure. It would require diplomatic skill to deal successfully with the French and Canadian settlers in the region. It would require an even greater understanding to deal successfully with the many different Indians tribes that would be encountered along the way.

The primary objective of the mission was to take possession of Fort Detroit, which was the gateway from Lake Erie to the western Great Lakes. The British would also claim several smaller French posts in the region. To lead this important and dangerous expedition, Amherst needed a man he knew could accomplish the job—so, he chose the intrepid Ranger leader Major Robert Rogers. During a time when British and other Provincial soldiers were struggling to learn how to fight the French and their Indian allies on their own terms, Rogers had thoroughly mastered the art of wilderness warfare. Commanding his famous corps of Rangers, Rogers took the fight deep into the enemy's territory, capturing prisoners, gathering intelligence, burning villages and crops, and otherwise keeping his adversaries off balance. Even in his rare defeats, he had shown the strength and resourcefulness to bring as many of his men back to safety as possible.

In his written orders to Rogers, Amherst directed him to require the French habitants to take the oath of allegiance to King George, after which "they shall be protected in the peaceable and quiet possession of their properties and so long as they behave as becometh good and faithful subjects, shall partake of all the other privileges and immunities granted unto them by the said capitulation."[1]

Rogers was also ordered to explore the country as much as he could without losing unnecessary time, and in that regard, Lieutenant Diedrich

Niagara Falls 1762, detail, by Captain Thomas Davies of the Royal Artillery. Davies was not only a competent soldier, he was also a very gifted artist who captured the beauty of early America in his many landscape paintings.
LAC

Brehm, an engineer, and Lieutenant Thomas Davies of the Royal Artillery were sent along to assist. In his journal, Amherst noted that he had ordered Davies, an accomplished artist, to "take a view of Niagara Falls" for him.[2]

According to Rogers, the expedition was "to be kept a profound secret for fear the march should be impeded by the enemy Indians through whose country I was obliged to march."[3]

The party left Montreal about noon on September 13, in fifteen whaleboats and two birchbark canoes. It consisted of two companies of Rangers, about two hundred men, plus Davies, Brehm, and one Joseph Poupao, also known as La Fleur, a French guide who was from Detroit. They traveled up the Saint Lawrence River, their progress slowed at times by unfavorable winds. When they reached the site of Fort Frontenac about September 24, they were forced to lay-over due to an early season snowfall.[4] Here, as he would do at every opportunity, Rogers advised the local Indians of the French surrender. The Indians usually welcomed the

British victors, who often received food supplies either as gifts or through purchase.

Able to travel again on the twenty-fifth, the party continued along the north shore of Lake Ontario until October 1, when, from the site of modern Toronto, they veered due south across the lake. By evening, they had reached the south shore about five miles west of Fort Niagara. The boats had taken a beating, and some were leaking dangerously. By keeping the flotilla close together, disaster was averted when the boat commanded by Lieutenant Caesar McCormack filled with water and sank. No lives were lost, only the Rangers' packs.

At Fort Niagara, the party drew blankets, clothing, shoes, and moccasins from the fort's stores, as well as eighty barrels of provisions. Two of the whaleboats were exchanged for bateaux, which also proved leaky. While the majority of the party began the arduous task of transporting the boats and supplies over the Niagara Portage, Lieutenant Brehm and Lieutenant Davies "took a survey of the great cataract of Niagara" as ordered by General Amherst.[5]

Rogers had orders to meet with Brigadier General Robert Monckton at Fort Pitt (Pittsburgh, Pennsylvania) for further orders. Accordingly, on October 5, he set out with Lieutenant Brehm, Lieutenant Robert Holmes of the Rangers, and eight men in a birchbark canoe, leaving the rest of the party to follow under the command of Captain Jonathan Brewer. On the eighth, Rogers and his advance group arrived at Fort Presque Isle (Erie, Pennsylvania), where Colonel Henry Bouquet of the 60th Regiment held command. They brought him his first news of the surrender of Canada.

After only a few hours rest, Rogers, Brehm, Holmes, and three Rangers headed south by canoe for Fort Pitt, some 120 miles distance. They followed French Creek to Fort Le Boeuf (Waterford, Pennsylvania), reaching it about ten o'clock in the morning on the ninth. After three hours rest, they continued on, arriving at Fort Venango (Franklin, Pennsylvania) on October 12. On the seventeenth, they reached General Monckton at Fort Pitt, where Rogers delivered the orders from Amherst and received additional instructions for himself from Monckton.

Rogers' new orders included more details about how he was to handle the takeover of Fort Detroit and how he would deal with the French soldiers and habitants there. Monckton instructed him: "You will keep up the Strictest discipline in the Troops under yr Command, and not Suffer any of the Inhabitants to be disturbed or molested, as they are now become the Subjects of the King of great Brittain."[6]

Many of the French habitants were fearful of how they would be treated after the fall of Montreal, and, for the most part, they were very thankful for how little their lives changed under the British. At this point, Captain Donald Campbell and a detachment of Royal Americans destined to become the new garrison at Detroit joined the party.

The expedition was now divided into three groups. Captain Brewer and a small party were ordered to march overland to Detroit, driving forty oxen that were to be used as a supply of fresh meat. At the same time, Captain Joseph Waite was sent back to Niagara for more provisions. After he secured them, he was to sail along the north shore of Lake Erie, halting at a point just short of Detroit to await further orders. Rogers himself rejoined the Rangers waiting at Presque Isle, and on November 4, began sailing west along the south shore of Lake Erie.

Because of rough waters caused by its shallow depth, many consider Lake Erie to be the most hazardous of the Great Lakes for navigation. These dangers were not unknown to the party. Robert Kirkwood, a Highland soldier who joined Rogers for this trip, noted in his journal, "During our passage upon this Lake, we were wind-bound frequently six or seven days together, we never durst let our boats remain in the water at night, as they would have been dashed to pieces by the surf; so we were obliged to haul to shore every night and unload our boats. When you have got about one hundred miles up the lake, you meet with a long range of high-lands, which is very dangerous in passing, for if a storm should rise, your boats will inevitably be dashed in pieces, and every soul lost; because the shore is so rugged, that it is impossible for any person to climb it, being very steep, and straight as a stone-wall." Kirkwood noted a spot "Where the French lost an hundred men, and a great quantity of provisions, and in memorial to those who met this catastrophe, they have erected grave-stones with crosses, and the names of some of the most eminent among those who were drown'd"[7]

In his orders Rogers cautioned, "It is recommended to the soldiers as well as officers, not to mind the waves of the lake; but when the surf is high to stick to their oars, and the men at the helm to keep the boat quartering on the waves, and briskly follow, then no mischief will happen by any storm whatever."[8]

Ten of the best steersmen from the Rangers were assigned to the Royal Americans. Lieutenant Holmes and Ensign Benjamin Waite made up the

rear guard with their boats, and they were to quickly move to assist any of the others that found themselves in difficulty. If conditions became too rough, a red flag in the major's vessel would be the signal to immediately head for land. Lieutenant Brehm, the engineer, did not have to follow the order, but could "steer as is most convenient for him to make his observations."[9]

Although Rogers mentions Brehm's presence several times after leaving Fort Niagara, he never again mentions Lieutenant Davies. This raises the question as to whether Davies continued with the expedition. Even though he was a prolific artist, no scenes by him from west of Niagara are known to exist, and it is uncertain whether he accompanied the party beyond that spot.

Rogers' attention to detail was evident when the expedition made camp. Lieutenant Holmes' division was to make up the right wing along with the members of the Indian department under George Croghan. Croghan, who had joined the party at Fort Pitt, was the deputy northern superintendent of Indian affairs. Lieutenant McCormack's men were to cover the left wing, while the Indian Rangers were to encamp in front of the main body, forming a picquet guard. No men were to wander beyond the outer sentries. The officers were to inspect the men's arms daily, and no guns were to be fired without permission, except to signal an emergency.

On November 7, a delegation of Ottawa Indians from Detroit met the party. Rogers informed them of the fall of New France and of his mission to take possession of the region for the king of England. He gave the Indians a belt of wampum and offered to allow them to accompany him to Detroit to witness the truth of his words. The Indians held a conference to weigh Rogers' claims, and the next morning advised him that the young warriors would accompany him, while the older ones would stay to hunt for their families. Bad weather prevented them from resuming their march until the twelfth, and while they were waiting, "the Indians held a plentiful market in our camp of venison and turkies."[10]

Rogers claims that one of the Indians he met with about this time was Pontiac, who was not yet a well-known chief.[11] Rogers later wrote that Pontiac "Puts on an air of majesty and princely grandeur, and is greatly honoured and revered by his subjects."[12] Very little is known about Pontiac's early life. He was born among the Ottawas, but is believed to be half Chippewa. It is not known for certain which parent was Chippewa. He was raised around Detroit and developed an early animosity toward the British.

There is no known authentic portrait of Pontiac, and perhaps Rogers gives the most accurate verbal description of him. He was proud and intelligent, with a commanding and intimidating presence. Deputy Indian Agent George Croghan described him as "a shrewd, sensible Indian of few words, and commands more respect amongst these nations that any Indian I ever saw."[13]

However, Pontiac could be ruthless at times and also hypocritical. More than once he exhibited a lack of integrity by not keeping his word. General Thomas Gage would later remark that "there is Reason to Judge of Pondiac, not only as a Savage, possessed of the most refined Cunning and Treachery natural to the Indians, but as a Person of extraordinary Abilities."[14]

Rogers is not perfectly clear on just when their alleged meeting took place, saying, "At the first salutation when we met, he demanded my business in his country, and how it happened that I dared to enter it without his leave?[15]

Rogers explained that he meant no harm to the Indians, but was there to take over the French posts that had been won with the capitulation. Pontiac replied that the British must advance no farther without his permission, and then he

Facing page. *Rogers Meets Pontiac* by Gary Zaboly depicts the Lake Erie meeting between Major Robert Rogers and Pontiac in 1761, during Rogers' expedition to Detroit. Although no original portraits or sketches of Pontiac are known to exist, this illustration is based on Rogers' written description of the Ottawa chief. Courtesy of Terry Todish and Gary Zaboly.

inquired if the party needed anything. When the chief returned the next day, he brought provisions, which the Indians were paid for. He and Rogers then smoked a pipe of peace. Pontiac declared that the party might proceed, and "he would protect me and my party from any insults that might be offered or intended by the Indians; and as an earnest of his friendship, he sent 100 warriors to protect and assist us in driving 100 fat cattle. . . ."[16] After several meetings with Pontiac, Rogers declared that he had shown:

> great strength of judgement, and a thirst after knowledge. He endeavored to inform himself of our military order and discipline. He often intimated to me, that he could be content to reign in his country in submission to the King of Great Britain, and was willing to pay him such annual acknowledgment as he was able in furs, and to call him his uncle. He was curious to know our methods of manufacturing cloth, iron, &c. and expressed a great desire to see England, and offered me a part of his country if I would conduct him there. He assured me he was inclined to live peaceably with the English while they used him as he deserved, and to encourage their settling in his country; but intimated that, if they treated him with neglect, he should shut up the way, and exclude them from it; in short his whole conversation sufficiently indicated that he was far from considering himself a conquered Prince, and that he expected to be treated with the respect and honour due to a King or Emperor, by all who came into his country, or treated with him.[17]

The party eventually continued their journey westward, fighting the ever-increasing bad weather until on or about November 20 they encamped several miles west of Sandusky Bay. From there, Rogers sent Lieutenant Brehm ahead to Detroit with a letter for its commandant, Captain Francois-Marie Piquote de Belestre. He advised Belestre not to be alarmed at his approach, and that he would "encamp the troops I have with me at some distance from the fort, till you have reasonable time to be made acquainted with the Mar-

quis de Vaudreuil's instructions, and the capitulation, a copy of which I have with me. . . ."[18]

When Rogers followed Brehm with the main party, several Huron sachems met Rogers and advised him that they had been sent to determine whether or not Canada had really surrendered. They also advised him that four hundred warriors waited farther on to prevent him from taking Detroit. With his typical diplomacy, Rogers presented them a large belt of wampum and told them Canada had indeed fallen. The Indians were to return to their villages, and he would meet with them as soon as he dealt with the French garrison at Detroit. He said that the Indians should:

> live happily in your own country. . . . Tell your warriors to mind their fathers [the French] no more, for they are all prisoners to your brothers [the English], who pitied them, and left them their houses and goods, on their swearing by the Great One who made the world, to become as Englishmen for ever. They are now your brothers; if you abuse them, you affront me, unless they behave ill. Tell this to your brothers the Indians. What I say is truth. When we meet at Detroit I will convince you it is all true.[19]

Rogers reported that the sachems departed on good terms on the morning of the twenty-first, but because of high winds, his party remained in camp for one more day. On the twenty-third, they had reached Point Cedar (Cedar Point, Ohio) and set up camp when some of the Indians from the council a few days earlier reappeared. They advised Rogers that Captain Belestre intended to resist him. These Indians joined the party as it continued toward Detroit, and on the evening of the twenty-fourth, sixty more from Detroit joined them. They told Rogers that Brehm and his party had been confined, and that Belestre "had set up an high-flag staff, with a wooden effigy of a man's head on the top, and upon that a crow; that the crow was to represent himself, the man's head mine, and the meaning on the whole, that he would scratch out my brains. This artifice, however, had no effect; for the Indians told him (as they

Rogers at Detroit by Gary Zaboly. Major Robert Rogers as he probably appeared during the takeover of Fort Detroit on December 29, 1760. Courtesy of Tim J. Todish and Gary Zaboly.

said) that the reverse would be the true explanation of the sign."[20]

The party spent November 25, and November 26, camped a short distance from Detroit, and Rogers spent the time "conciliating their [the Indians'] minds to peace and friendship."[21]

On the morning of the twenty-seventh, the party received a message from Captain Belestre. He acknowledged receipt of Rogers' earlier dispatches and asked him to halt at the entrance to the Detroit River and send ahead a copy of the terms of the capitulation and the letter from Governor Vaudreuil. He also commented that he was surprised that no French officer had accompanied the party, as was customary on such occasions. A second letter a short time later advised Rogers that he might find the local inhabitants on their guard, "as it was told them you had several Indian nations with you, to whom you had promised permission to plunder. . . . I have therefore allowed the said inhabitants to take to their arms, as it is for your safety and preservation as well as ours; for should these Indians become insolent, you may not perhaps, in your present situation, be able to subdue them alone."[22]

On November 29, the party encamped five miles farther up the river, and Captain Campbell and a small party were sent to the fort with the capitulation and Vaudreuil's letter. Rogers advised that he would stop his men at the far end of the town until 4:00 p.m., at which time he expected Belestre's answer. He added, "I can assure you sir, the inhabitants of Detroit shall not be molested, they and your complying with the capitulation, but be protected in the quiet and peaceful possession of their estates; neither shall they be pillaged by my Indians, nor by yours that have joined me."[23]

Rogers drew his detachment up in a grassy field a half-mile from the fort and Captain Campbell and a French officer soon joined him. The officer advised Rogers that the French garrison was prepared to surrender. Lieutenant William Leslie of the Royal Americans, Lieutenant McCormack of the Rangers, and thirty-six men were sent to take

possession of the fort. The French colors were lowered, the flag of Great Britain was raised, and "700 Indians gave a shout, merrily exulting in their prediction being verified, that the crow represented the English." Rogers further noted, "They [the Indians] seemed amazed at the submissive salutations of the inhabitants, expressing their satisfaction at our generosity in not putting them to death, and said they would always for the future fight for a nation thus favoured by Him that made the world"[24]

By noon on December 1, Rogers had received a plan of the fort, (which was more of a fortified village than a true military fortification), as well as a list of its stores. The local militia had also been disarmed, and the inhabitants had been administered the oath of allegiance, by which they promised in part that "I Shall behave my Self honestly, toward His Sacred Majesty George the Second. . .and that I will defend him, and his in this Country, with all my Power against his or their Ennemies. . . ."[25]

Although the takeover was accomplished without incident, there is some evidence to substantiate the warning that the Indians had delivered to Rogers about Belestre initially planning to resist. John Porteus, a Scottish fur trader, later wrote to his parents, "Capt. Belletre the French commandant here bribed & sent all the Indian Nations about this place to cut off the English upon the lake, altho' they no sooner met Major Rogers who commanded the troops for said purpose, than they came & made an alliance with him & came along with him to Detroit & would have willingly sacrificed every French soul in the settlement if he had not strictly forbid them."[26]

Belestre himself also later admitted that on November 28, the day before he surrendered the fort to the British, he held a council with the local Indians. He promised to deliver an Indian calumet to the king of France and relay their request that he (the king) not abandons them to the English. Belestre assured the Indians that the king would not forget them.[27]

Captain Campbell and his Royal Americans were to become the new garrison of the fort.

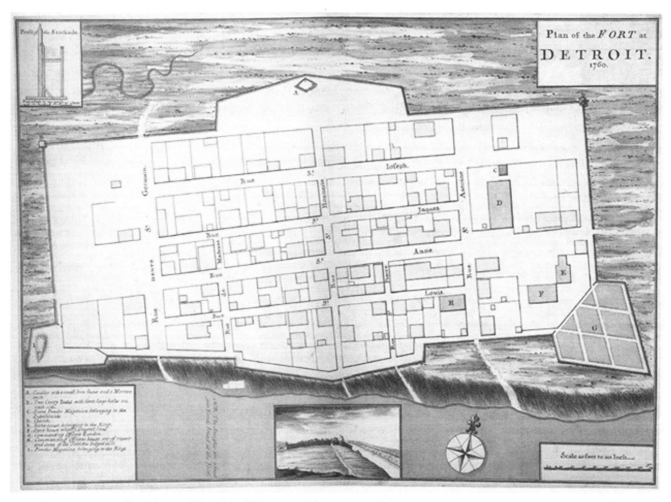

Plan of the Fort at Detroit 1760 by Lieutenant Dedrich Brehm is the earliest known British map of Fort Detroit. Courtesy of the Detroit Public Library, Burton Historical Collection.

Campbell described the fort this way in a letter to Colonel Bouquet:

> The Fort is very large and in good repair, there are two Bastions towards the water, and a Large flat Bastion towards the Land in the point of the Bastion is a Cavalier [a defensive work built on a bastion and rising above the rampart to command rising ground and to prevent the walls between bastions from being enfiladed] of wood on which there are mounted three three pounders and three small Mortars, or Coehorns.
>
> The Palisadoes are in good order. There is a Scaffolding round the whole, which is only floored towards the land for want of Plank, it is by way of a Banket [banquette, a step behind the parapet allowing defenders to fire over the crest].
>
> There are Seventy or eighty houses in the Fort laid out in Regular Streets. The Country is inhabitated ten Miles on each side of the River, and is a most Beautifull Country, the River is here about nine hundred yards over and very deep, and every Thing in great Plenty before this last year.[28]

Lieutenant Holmes and thirty Rangers were detailed to escort Captain Belestre, his officers, and the thirty-eight privates of the Detroit garrison to Philadelphia. A number of redeemed white captives also accompanied them. From Philadelphia, the French soldiers were taken to New York and then transported home to France.

During this time, Rogers and Croghan met with the local Indians, attempting to gain their loyalty by giving them gifts. Highland soldier Robert Kirkwood noted in his journal, "We delivered them the peace belt, and what other presents we had with a gallon of rum to each family; they then got drunk, and committed a great many excesses; they also had several war-dances,—we were very careful to let them have their own way, for if they had a mind for cross purposes, we were only a handful among them."[29]

Lieutenant John Butler and Ensign Waite, with a party of twenty Rangers, were sent to take possession of the smaller French forts of Miami (Fort Wayne, Indiana) and Ouiatenon (West Lafayette, Indiana), following the same general procedures that were used at Detroit. They were to proceed first to Fort Miami, where Waite and a portion of the party were to serve as the new garrison. Butler and the rest of the men would continue on to Ouiatenon, where they would take over and garrison the fort. Captain Brewer would lead the bulk of the Rangers back to Fort Niagara, while Rogers, Lieutenant McCormack, and thirty-seven Rangers would attempt the most difficult remaining task, the takeover of Fort Michilimackinac.

After meeting with several of the local Indian tribes, Rogers and his party left for Michilimackinac late on December 10. Located at the Straits of Mackinac (Mackinaw City, Michigan), Fort Michilimackinac was one of the largest and most important of the interior French posts. Although it saw no hostile action during the war, many of its local inhabitants, both French and Indian, had traveled east to take part in the fighting. Its strategic location controlled access to the western fur trade. Not surprisingly, the weather was rapidly turning worse, and on the sixteenth, after reaching Saginaw Bay, ice on the lake made farther northward travel impossible. It was one of the few times in his life when Robert Rogers was forced to turn back from an objective, and it was only with great difficulty that the party was able to make it back to Detroit on December 21. On the twenty-second, leaving Captain Campbell in command at Detroit, Rogers, Lieutenant Brehm, and the last of the Rangers headed by land for Fort Pitt, where they arrived on January 23, 1761.

Rogers' bold and successful expedition to Detroit is important for a number of reasons. He completed the very difficult mission of taking possession of the French forts late in the season and in the face of very inclement weather. In only four months, his small but hearty party covered over sixteen hundred miles by sea and by land—farther than Lewis and Clark traveled during the entire first year of their famous expedition forty years later.[30]

As he did so, Rogers accumulated invaluable information about the newly won territory. He also dealt successfully with the Indians that he met along the way and laid the groundwork for what could have been friendly future relations, if not for the attitudes of many other British military officers and civil authorities. He did it all with the loss of only one man—one of the Royal Americans who fell overboard and drowned.

Chapter II
Peaceable Possession of the Forts:
Early Trouble Averted
1761

Lieut. Leslye writes me, they arrived [at Michilimackinac] *Just in time to Save*
The Traders from the Indians, who threatened to destroy them. We have got Peaceable
Possession of the Fort, and everything is now quiet. . . .
Captain Donald Campbell

The Balfour Expedition

THE EXPEDITION under Major Robert Rogers in the fall of 1760 resulted in British possession of three former French forts at Detroit, Miami, and Ouiatenon. To successfully follow up on Rogers' accomplishments, General Amherst wrote to Secretary of State William Pitt, "I think it will be necessary to send a small body of Troops that way in the Summer [of 1761], that all the Out-Posts of the French may be called in, the country may be thoroughly explored, some small Craft built on the Lakes, and Posts fixed for a quiet Possession of the whole."[1]

There were still three significant posts to be occupied—Michilimackinac, La Baye (Green Bay, Wisconsin), and Saint Joseph (Niles, Michigan). Possession of these posts would remove the French military threat from the region and also ensure British control over the lucrative Great Lakes fur trade. This time, Robert Rogers was not available to command the effort. He was enjoying a well-deserved furlough, much of which was spent trying to settle his financial accounts from the war years. He also took time to court and marry Elizabeth Browne, the twenty-year-old daughter of a prominent Portsmouth minister.

Initially, command of the 1761 expedition was given to steady and capable Captain Henry Gladwin of the 80th (Gage's or Wilmot's) Light Infantry Regiment, but illness forced him to remain at Detroit.[2] Captain Henry Balfour, also of the 80th, succeeded him as commander of the expedition. Balfour too was a seasoned officer, having first been commissioned in the prestigious 1st Regiment of Foot in 1755. On September 9, more than 170 men headed north from Fort Detroit. Lieutenant Brehm, the engineer from the Royal American Regiment and veteran of Rogers' 1760 expedition, also went along. The route followed can be traced on a map most likely drawn by Brehm, or at least done under his supervision. This map became the first British cartographic record of their newly won territory.[3]

On September 28, Balfour and his men reached their first objective, Fort Michilimackinac, the important fur-trading center at the Straits of Mackinac. A few hardy British traders had already arrived ahead of them, and the French garrison had vacated the post and gone down to Fort de Chartres on the Mississippi River in the fall of 1760. The commandant, Captain Louis Lienard Beaujeu de Villemonde, had left the fort in the care of the noted partisan officer Charles-Michel Mouet de Langlade, who formally turned it over to Balfour. Lieutenant William Leslie and twenty-eight men of the Royal Americans were detailed to remain as the new garrison, and they were left with ten-months provisions. As a premonition of things to come, Lieutenant Leslie sensed that the Indians were not completely happy with the British occupation. From Detroit on November 8, 1761, Captain Campbell wrote to General Amherst, "Lieut Lessley likewise writes that the Indians Seem not quite reconciled with the change of Government, that he has done all in his power to please them, and was obliged to give them Ammunition before they went to their Hunting where they continue 'till Spring."[4]

With Michilimackinac now in British hands, on October 1, Balfour and about half the remaining force proceeded on to Fort La Baye, while the rest returned to Detroit. Again breaking new ground for a British military party, the expedition crossed the straits and followed the north shore of Lake Michigan to Green Bay. They reached the fort on October 12, and found that the French had also abandoned this post. Ensign James Gorrell and seventeen of the Royal Americans were assigned to garrison the site. A French interpreter and two English traders also remained. The small post, whose name was changed to Fort Edward Augustus, was in a bad state of repair. Gorrell noted in his journal, "the fort quite rotten, the stockade ready to fall, the houses without cover, our fire wood far off, and none to be got when the river closed."[5]

Gorrell also recorded a concern that was on the mind of every British officer assigned to the Great Lakes region—whether the French traders and inhabitants would incite the Indians against the British. He wrote that French traders who were licensed by General Gage to trade in the country "did all that laid in their power to persuade the Bay Indians to fall upon the English on their way, as they heard of our coming, and telling the Indians that the English were very weak, and that it could be done very readily."[6]

After two days of rest, Balfour and the rest of his force departed for Fort Saint Joseph on October 14, a journey that would take twenty-six days to complete. They traveled south along the west shore of Lake Michigan then east around the bot-

A private of the 80th (Gage's) Regiment of Light Armed Foot by Gary Zaboly. This regiment played a major part in the British occupation of the Great Lakes and in the Pontiac Uprising. In 1763, Colonel Montagu Wilmot commanded the regiment. The figure here wears the brown 1758–1759 uniform. The exact colors of the Pontiac War uniform are uncertain; it is possible that the coats were brown with white or plumb facings or scarlet with red-orange facings. Courtesy of James Butler Jr. and Gary Zaboly.

tom of the lake past the site of present-day Chicago. As the shoreline turned north again, they followed it until they reached the Saint Joseph River, which they followed several miles east until they reached the site of the small fort. This French garrison had also long since departed, and Ensign Francis Schlosser and ten men of the Royal Americans were left as a garrison.

It was too late in the season for Balfour to return to Detroit by water, so he marched most of his remaining men overland following an old Indian trail, arriving on November 22. This was the first time a British party had traversed southern Michigan by foot. The party left Detroit by boat, but bad weather forced them to travel overland after they reached Sandusky. They arrived at Fort Pitt on December 28, and after a short rest, continued on to New York, where they arrived in mid-February 1762.

As Balfour trekked to Detroit, Lieutenant Brehm and five men marched to Fort Miami and then paddled a canoe down the Wabash River to Fort Ouiatenon, making further notes on the country as they traveled. By the time Brehm was sent on this mission, Major Gladwin had already sent Regular troops to relieve the Rangers that had initially garrisoned Forts Miami and Ouiatenon. From Ouiatenon, Brehm's party proceeded to New York, where he made his report to General Amherst.

Even as these first British troops were taking over the former French forts, there were hints that the Indians were dissatisfied with the new regime. On October 12, Captain Donald Campbell at Detroit wrote Colonel Henry Bouquet about a report he had received from Michilimackinac: "Lieut Leslye writes me, they arrived Just in time to Save The Traders from the Indians, who threatened to destroy them. We have got Peaceable Possession of the Fort, and every thing is now quiet, tho I am certain if the Indians knew General Amherst Sentiments about keeping them Short of Powder it would be impossible to keep them in temper."[7]

Early Trouble Averted

Indian hostility very nearly erupted into violence at the very onset of British occupation in late 1760 and early 1761. There is proof showing that the Senecas proposed an insurrection against the British at that time. To air their grievances, two Seneca chiefs, Kiasutha and Tahaiadoris journeyed to Detroit in June 1761, where a council was held with the Ottawas and Wyandots to propose a general revolt. The Senecas encouraged an attack on the garrison there, while other war belts were sent to the Delawares and Shawnees in the Ohio Valley and Pennsylvania frontier. Similar belts were sent to the Potawatomies and Weas in the Illinois Country, urging them all to fall on their local posts in coordination with the Seneca attacks. Captain Donald Campbell, the commandant at Fort Detroit, documented the information that Indian interpreters and other inhabitants at the post relayed to him:

I have been a little allarmed by the reports of the discontent & bad designs of the Indian Nations, which as they carried some oppearance of truth, put me upon my guard & made me at pains to find out the true cause of their discontent, it was first told me it proceded from the Northern Indians but I now find it comes from the Six Nations, and for your information I give you the intelligence I had from my Indian interpreters & several other people of Character whom I can depend upon.

The Six nations have sent deputies & large belts of Wampum, to all the Indians from the Bay of Gaspie to the Illinois [in effect, all of French Canada from the mouth of the Saint Lawrence down to Fort de Chartres on the Mississippi] inviting them to take up the Hatchet against the English two of their deputies (Seneca Cheiffs) came here two days agoe to propose it to the Nations here & to invite them to a grand Council at the little Lake [Sandusky Bay], with the Delewars and Shawanies, whose cheiffs are already there amongst whom is the Baver [Beaver]. . . .

The Scheme laid, is that the Indians in general, shall at one time cut of all the Communications & stop the roads, at Niagara Fort Pitt & here, and at the same time Sease upon all the goods & Horses of the traders at Sandusky, in order to prevent their taking the Advantage of the powder & Indian goods at Sandusky. . . .[8]

His letter of the following day to Major William Walters, commandant of Fort Niagara, further read:

I have sent you an Express with a very Important piece of Intelligence, I have had the good fortune to discover, I have been lat'ly alarmd with Reports of the bad Designs of the Indian nations against his place and the English in General, I can now Inform You for certain it comes from the Six nations and that they have Sent belts of wampum and deputys to all the nations from nova Scotia to the Illinois to take up the Hatchet against the English and have employd the Messagues [Missisaugas] to Send belts of wampum, to the northern nations, there are now two chiefs of the Senecas in the Wyandat town privately to Invite the nations here to a Councel at the Little lake or San-

duskey, I had a past Information of all their Designs before they had time to hold a Councel with the nations and have prevented it So far that I called the nations to a councel this day and told of the bad Intention of the Senaca nation against us—which I hope will have good Effect as they promised to have no concern with them. their project is as follows the Six Nations at least the Senecas, are to Assemble at the head of french creek within five and twenty Leagues of PresquIsle, part of the Six nations the Delawars and Shawnees are to Assemble on the Ohio, and all at the same time About the Latter End of this month to Surprise niagara and Fort Pitt and cutt of the Communication Every where I hope this will come time Enough to put You on Your Guard and to Send to Oswego and all the posts on that Communication they Expect to be Joyned by the nations that are come from the north by Toronto. You have certainly a great many of them at present at niagara You cannot use to much precaution against them, I hope when they find the whole plot is Discovered they will desist from their attempt. . . .[9]

Historian Gregory Dowd discounts that it was a Seneca plot alone, suggesting, "The evidence for the 'Seneca plot' in short, points as convincingly to the Anishinabeg [Ottawas, Chippewas, and Potawatomies] as to the Iroquois." He relates that the Indians told the French in 1760 that they would rise up against the British and that further discussions between Indians and inhabitants in those regions took place. Although he admitted definitive documentation is lacking.[10]

Much later during the uprising, the Delawares at Fort Pitt admitted that some of the fuel for the uprising originated from the Illinois Country tribes, as well as from the French. Nonetheless, at Campbell's conference on July 3, the Wyandots, Potawatomies, Ottawas, and Shawnees declined to join the Senecas, possibly because of Campbell's

assurances that they would "be Constantly treated as our Friends and Allies."[11] At the same time, he warned them against joining the plot.

Alexander Henry was one of the first British traders to enter the Great Lakes. He arrived at Michilimackinac ahead of Balfour's troops and gives a vivid account of his first trip from Montreal. Because of the danger of being killed, he had to disguise himself as an Indian. When he arrived at the fort, French traders betrayed his identity, and Minavavana (the Grand Saulteur), a Chippewa chief, confronted him. Minavavana delivered a threatening speech, openly admitting allegiance to the French and saying that the local tribes did not consider the British king as their father. He further warned that they anticipated that the French would return to power. However, since Henry had come unarmed to trade among the Indians, they would "regard you, therefore, as a brother; and you may sleep tranquilly, without fear of the Chippewa. . . ."[12]

Their promises aside, Henry would eventually be engulfed in the attack on the fort some nineteen months later. The following day, Henry related further threats with the arrival of a large band of Ottawas from nearby L'Arbre Croche (Cross Village), where their village and the Jesuit mission of Saint Ignace were located. Henry's description of these dangers clearly demonstrate the general animosity toward the British:

> The new dangers which presented themselves came from this village of Ottawa. Everything as I have said was in readiness for the departure of my goods when accounts arrived of its approach; and shortly after, two hundred warriors entered the fort and billeted themselves in the several houses among the Canadian inhabitants. The next morning they assembled in the house which was built for the commandant, or governor, and ordered the attendance of myself and of two other merchants still later from

Facing page, left. Private, 60th or Royal American Regiment of Foot, by Dirk Gringhuis. The 60th was one of the primary units serving on the frontier during Pontiac's Uprising. It was a unique British regiment with many Swiss and German officers, while most of the rank and file were enlisted in North America. While it was a "royal" regiment, with traditional blue facings on its uniforms, lace was deliberately omitted for better concealment in forest warfare. Right. Ottawa Indian warrior, by Dirk Gringhuis. Both courtesy of Mackinac State Historic Parks

Sir William Johnson, the northern superintendent of Indian affairs. Portrait by John Wollaston, ca. 1750. Courtesy of King's Arms Press. Signature from Benson Lossing's *Field Book of the American Revolution*. Tim J. Todish collection.

Montreal, namely Messrs. [James] Stanley Goddard and Ezekiel Solomons.[13]

The Ottawas demanded most of the trade goods, which they believed should have been brought for their benefit, as had been the custom of the French traders. Henry and his fellow traders realized that complying with the demand would cost them nearly all of the goods, and they attempted to buy time by informing the Ottawas that they would give them an answer in the morning. French trader and interpreter Jacques Farley (Farli), who was a confidant of the Indians, told

them that the Indians were considering killing them that very night. Fearful for their lives, the traders armed themselves in the house:

> [F]or a long night was to be passed, and our fate might be decided before the morning. To increase our apprehensions, about midnight we were informed that the Ottawa were holding a council, at which no white man was permitted to be present, Farley alone excepted; and him we suspected, and afterward positively knew to be our greatest enemy. We, on our part, remained all night upon the alert; but at daybreak to our surprise and joy we saw the Ottawa preparing to depart. . . . By sunrise not a man of them was left in the fort; and indeed the scene was altogether changed. The inhabitants, who, while the Ottawa were present, had avoided all connection with the English traders, now came with congratulations. They related that the Ottawa had proposed to them that if joined by the Canadians they would march and attack the troops which were known to be advancing on the fort; and they added that it was their refusal which had determined the Ottawa to depart.[14]

The arrival of the British troops at noon on September 28, 1761, relieved their fears and assured their safety, at least for the time being.

Yet the Lake Erie Wyandots expressed another brief example of anti-British feeling when Fort Sandusky was built that same fall. One of the local chiefs proclaimed to the British officer in command there that "he would have it burnt down in the Spring."[15]

After previously admonishing the Six Nations for their part in the scheme, Sir William Johnson held a grand council at Detroit in September. The council was the result of the desire of both Amherst and Johnson to set trade regulations and quell the rumored regional unrest. Sir William's deputy, George Croghan, arrived on August 16, and held preliminary discussions with the Indians while awaiting Johnson.[16]

Trade prices and regulations were set for the posts, and the early uprising was averted. Regardless of who sent the initial war belts, there is no doubt that the Senecas were involved. Their actions, which in part were the result of land disputes at the Niagara Portage, incensed Amherst, who blamed them for originating the war when it did erupt in 1763. Captain Campbell wrote, "Sir William is fully convinced that the Conspiracy was Universal amongst the Indian Nations in this Part of the continent but General Amherst in his last letter to me quit discredits any bad designs of the Indian Nations, and thinks they are incapable of doeing us any hurt, and recomends it by all Means to keep them Scarce of Powder."[17]

Amherst's naivety would soon have grave consequences.

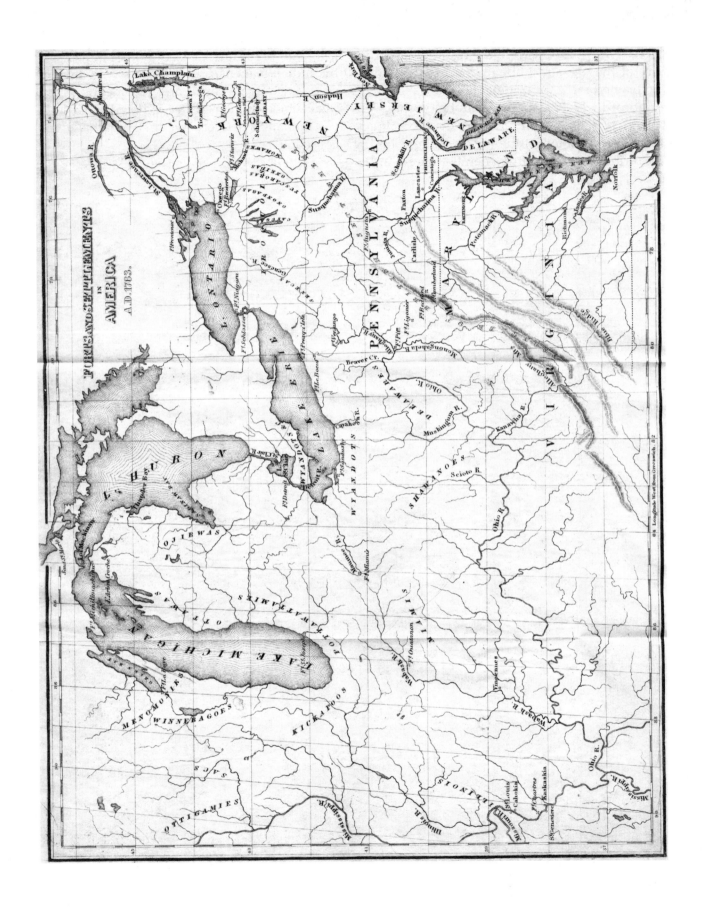

Chapter III
Early Signs of Discontent:
The Origins of the Uprising
1761–1763

By being too Saving of a few Presents to the Savages, which properly distributed would certainly have prevented it.
Colonel Henry Bouquet

HISTORIANS have debated the origins of the 1763–1764 Indian uprising for many years, focusing on factors ranging from Pontiac's role in the conspiracy to the specific restrictions on the fur trade and even socioeconomic and cultural factors. Some disagree as to Pontiac's specific organizational role in the conflict. Some have focused on the Indian perspective, examining cultural and spiritual contributions to the uprising, in contrast to the more traditional laying blame on British aggression. While these newer perspectives have valid points, many of the traditional analyses remain indisputable.

Perhaps the biggest disagreement has been over whether Pontiac was the sole architect of the general uprising. Recent historians have questioned whether the names "Pontiac's Uprising" or "Pontiac's Conspiracy," which some early historians have used, are valid. Howard Peckham's twentieth-century history is generally considered to be *the* definitive biography of Pontiac, and perhaps the best overall telling of the conflict. He discusses Pontiac's organizational involvement at length and concludes that he was *not* the sole architect of the entire conspiracy as Parkman and others believed. There is no conclusive evidence that Pontiac singularly planned the uprising of all the various Indian nations. On the other hand, those who allege that he did not issue directives or conspire to do so—that there was no conspiracy at all—are incorrect as well. The truth is that Pontiac was indeed a catalyst for the revolt and directed a conspiracy at least among the western tribes, inducing them to rise up against the British. Although some historians in recent years suggest that Pontiac had no influence with *all* the tribes, there certainly is evidence that he at least had power among the various regional tribes. This is true in spite of the fact that they had preexisting differences of their own over trade practices and particularly over the establishment of military posts in their areas. One example is that emissaries of the Ottawas around Detroit incited the Wyandots at Fort Sandusky to strike that post, which they admitted to the commanding officer at the time of the attack.

Numerous historians have debated the question of who the real architect of the uprising was. A Delaware, Neolin, known as "the Prophet," and also as "the Imposter," came to have much influence among the Delawares, Shawnee, and to some extent the Senecas in the early 1760s. With his messianic prophecy or *vision*, he advocated a new Indian cultural and religious doctrine. Neolin is reported to have lived among the the Tuscarawas on the Tuscarawas River in Ohio and at Cuyahoga Town near Lake Erie, which explains how the western tribes may have heard of his teachings.[1]

Facing page. *Forts and Settlements in America, A.D. 1763,* drawn ca. 1870. Mapmaker unknown. Tim J. Todish collection.

Late Arrivals by Robert Griffing. The lakes and rivers were the first highways through the North American wilderness. For Indians and whites alike, lightweight yet sturdy birchbark canoes were ideally suited for travel on these waterways. Courtesy of Robert Griffing and Paramount Press.

Both James Kenny, a young Quaker trader from Fort Pitt, and John McCullough, who had been a captive among the Delawares, described Neolin's doctrine in 1762. The vision, which Neolin claimed to have received from the Master of Life, directed the Indians to abandon the white man's ways and disassociate themselves from his society. They were to return to their native culture for self-determination and self-dependency. Within this doctrine there were some aspects of Christianity, which historians have shown were most likely the result of Neolin's interaction with white missionaries.[2]

There is also evidence that Neolin might have had a psychological or mental condition that would account for his personality and behavior, as evidenced by his "almost constantly crying and exhorting."[3]

Historians have written extensively about the Prophet's message. Rather than reiterate those studies in detail, period descriptions by James Kenny and John McCullough will be used to tell the story:

I think I have made mention before of the Imposter which is raised amongst the Delawares, in order to show them the right way to Heaven. This plan is portrayed on a dressed leather skin and some [times] on paper; [it] fixes the earth at the bottom and heaven at the top, having a straight line from one to the other by which their forefathers used to ascend to happiness. About the middle is like a long square cutting their way to happiness at right angles and stopping them, representing the white people. The outside is a long square-like black stroke circumscribing the whole within it, and joining on the left hand, issuing from the white people's place is cut many strokes parallel to their square of situation. All these strokes represent all the sins and vices which the Indians have learned from the white people through which now they must go, the good road being stopped. Hell being fixed not far off, there they are led irrevocably. The doctrine issued on this and the way to help it is said to be to learn to live without any trade or connections with the white people, clothing and supporting themselves as their forefathers did; it's also said that the Imposter prognosticates that there will be two or three good talks and then war. This gains amongst them so much that mostly they have quit hunting any more than to supply nature in that way.[4]

McCullough, who, like Kenny, never actually saw Neolin, described his teaching this way:

My brother has gone to Tus-ca-la-ways [Tuscarawas], about forty or fifty miles off, to see and hear a prophet that had just made his appearance amongst them. He was of the Delaware nation; I never saw nor heard him. It was said by those who went to see him, that he had certain hieroglyphics marked on a piece of parchment, denoting the probation that human beings were subjected to whilst they were living on earth, and also denoting something of a future state. They informed me that he was almost constantly crying whilst he was exhorting them. I saw a copy of his hieroglyphics, as numbers of them had got them copied and undertook to preach or instruct others. The first (or principle doctrine) they taught them was to purify themselves from sin, which they thought they could do by the use of emetics and abstainence from carnal knowledge of the different sexes; to quit the use of fire arms, and to live entirely in their original state that they were in before the white people found out their country; nay, they taught that the fire was not pure that was made by steel and flint, but that they should make it by rubbing two sticks together. . . . It was said that their prophet

taught them, or made them believe, that he had his instructions immediately from 'Keesh-she-la-mil-lang-up,' or a being that thought us into being, and that by following his instructions they should in a few years be able to drive the white people out of their country.[5]

As the Prophet traveled, his message spread among the various eastern tribes, including the Senecas, although not all of them accepted it. He also reached the western Potawatomies, Wyandots, Chippewas, and Ottawas, and certainly Pontiac himself.[6]

While all the tribes had grievances against the British, there has been some controversy as to the specifics of the Prophet's message and its role in inciting the combined uprising. Peckham argues that Neolin was not advocating violence against the British, while Pontiac was. Other historians have argued that after hearing Neolin's message, Pontiac distorted the doctrine in several ways, but some recent studies suggest that there is evidence to the contrary. Dowd and Dixon discuss this in their recent books, arguing that Pontiac indeed followed the Prophet's message, and that it incited, or at the very least was interpreted to advocate, a violent uprising. Both historians discuss evidence that the message was more favorable to the French, who were to be spared the wrath of the Indians, as opposed to earlier interpretations advocating complete disassociation from *all* white men. Dowd does concede that there is still some evidence that Pontiac manipulated the Prophet's teachings. Among particulars of Neolin's message that both authors discuss are the use of the bow and arrow, discontinuing the use of firearms, and the avoidance of alcohol.[7]

Regardless of the disagreements over the Delaware Prophet's message, there is no question that it had a great influence on Pontiac. Moreover, it is undeniable that both Pontiac and Neolin were catalysts for the revolt, the latter albeit passively. Both significantly influenced the tribes to revolt against the British and remain loyal to the French. The first one to start the actual hostilities was clearly Pontiac. With the above facts in mind, the names "Pontiac's Uprising" and "Pontiac's Conspiracy" are certainly not inappropriate titles for the war.

While these factors are all interconnected, perhaps most important are the cultural connections that developed between the French and the Indians over time. Such ties could not simply be transferred to the British by mere treaty at the conclusion of the French and Indian War. Historian Kerry A. Trask writes that as a result of this gradual "French paternalism," they were becoming one people, a change that eventually was reflected in the language, with "the Indians referring to the French as their 'fathers' and to themselves as 'children'. . . . French paternalism was accepted by the Indians. . . ."8

French paternalism to the Indians was a fundamental reason for the latter's resentment against the British when they took over after the French and Indian War. This developed out of a respect and deep affection of each group for the other beyond the parameters of the economic system. That is not to say that the French traders never abused the Indians, but by and large the relations were cordial.

Some historians have argued that because the Indian view has been presented through surviving British and French written sources, it is biased, but it is also our main source of information because the Indians did not have a written language. While some white sources were biased, it is neither fair nor accurate to assume that all were. The Jesuits were widely known for accurately depicting Indian life. Captain Campbell for one valued their communications:

> The Jesuits of Mchillimakinac [Father Pierre du Jaunay and Father Marin Louis le Franc] writes the Recollet Priest of this Place [Detroit, Father Simple Bocquet] that their Indians were never more disposed against us, than this last winter, and that Monsr Langlaade [Charles Langlade], and some of their Chiefs, had much Trouble to prevent them coming to war against us here at Detroit, but at last they have prevailed upon them to come here, Monsr Langlade writes that they are peaceable enlined at present. . . .9

This is one more example that the Indians were inclined to revolt, but it still was to be seen who would initiate the hostilities. Clearly Pontiac was the one to do so.

While the early uprising was temporarily avoided, relations between the Indians and the British continued to deteriorate over the next two years, eventually leading to the uprising of 1763. In addition to the issues of land acquisition and British attitudes, there were specific problems, including regulation of the fur trade and ammunition, the distribution of alcohol, and alleged French involvement in the uprising.

By 1761, the crown had an enormous debt from the French and Indian War. During the war, the annual British military expenses swelled to £14.5 million sterling, more than double than what it was in the five years prior to the war, while total military debt nearly doubled to £140 million sterling by 1763.10

In an attempt to control expenses, presents and ammunition to the Indians were greatly reduced. In addition, trade, the supply of liquor, and access to the forts—all amenities, which the Indians were accustomed to under the French, were severely restricted. The cost reduction objectives were largely accomplished by the end of 1762 and even more so by the end of 1763.11

This economy unavoidably contributed to the hostilities that erupted in the spring of 1763.

General Jeffery Amherst, commander in chief of His Majesty's forces in North America and hero of the late war against the French, had the difficult task of maintaining the still-necessary British military while curtailing expenses. Although he was an extremely meticulous and capable administrator, he has been traditionally seen as the person most responsible for the events leading to the 1763 uprising. The main reason was, as Peckham correctly and flatly states, that "he never learned to understand them [the Indians] and he would not listen to the advice of his able subordinates."12

This is clearly evident in Amherst's stubborn stance on the elimination of presents to the Indians. Sir William Johnson and other British officers

General Jeffery Amherst by Sir Joshua Reynolds. Amherst was the British army commander in chief during most of the Pontiac Uprising. Courtesy of the William L. Clements Library. Signature courtesy of King's Arms Press.

had a more realistic view and repeatedly attempted to point it out. Johnson wrote:

Next to that [the behavior of the commanding officers at the posts] there's nothing can more Effectually Establish & preserve a good Understanding between us and them than a free and open Trade to be Carried on with them under proper Regulations & Restrictions. . .it is very necessary, and will always be Expected by the Indians, that the Commanding Officer of Every Post have it in his power to supply them in Case of Necessity with a Little Cloathing, some arms and ammunition to hunt with; also some provisions on their Journey homewards, as

well as a smith to repair their arms and working utensils, etc.[13]

Amherst actually was in agreement with Johnson on some of these ideas. Contrary to the belief of some historians, he did not advocate mistreating or cheating the Indians; rather, he supported free and fair trade, while at the same time protecting the traders and reducing costs. He specifically spelled this out in correspondence with Johnson:

Our Intercourse must be free & Safe: to make it more so and to improve all the Advantage that must of Necessity result from the possession of so valuable a Country, I propose, so soon as the Season will admit of it, not only to Garrison these Several posts properly but I propose to appoint a Person of knowledge, & probity to be Governor at the Detroit, with Direction to open a free and fair Trade between the subjects and Indians, giving to each such Advantages, as Shall make it their respective Interests to deal fairly & honestly by each Other, and at the same time to reap reasonable profits; I should there fore be much obliged to you for Such hints, as may Enable me to Establish this Trade upon a lasting & good foundation, by Acquainting me with what commodities it will be most proper to Send among the Indians: their value, and what profit, the Trader should have to Enable him to keep it up with a reasonable Gain, & without Imposing on the Indians, who, so long as they behave well, must not be Imposed upon, but receive a just Equivalent for their furrs. . . .[14]

The problem was the philosophical difference between "necessities" and "presents" as viewed by Johnson and some of the lower ranking British officers. Amherst's personal philosophy was made clear in his further correspondence with Johnson:

With regard to furnishing the latter [Indians] with a little Clothing, some arms and ammunition to hunt with, That is all very well in cases of necessity; but as, when the Intended Trade is once Established they will be able to supply themselves with these, from the Traders, for their furs, I do not see why the Crown should be put to that Expence. I am not either for giving them any Provisions; when they find they can get it on Asking for, they will grow remiss in their hunting, which should Industriously be avoided; for so long as their minds are Intent on business they will not have leisure to hatch mischief. . . . Services must be rewarded; it has ever been a maxim with me; but as to purchasing good behavior either of Indians, or any Others, [that] is what I do not understand; when men of whatsoever race behave ill, they must be punished but not bribed.[15]

In his analysis of the causes of the uprising, historian Gregory Dowd argues that the war *did not* result from the British failure to understand the Indian custom of gift giving. He holds that the British understood that such transactions were an "assurance of continued Indian allegiance" (what Peckham referred to as a "technique of maintaining friendship"), and that a lack of presents implied a lack of respect by the British toward the Indians.[16]

Dowd further argues that neither group viewed the practice as being without obligation, because the principle of gratitude was inherently involved in the reasons for gift giving.

While all of this is true, the issue of presents cannot be reduced to respect and gratitude alone. An economic component was also present—the need to reduce overall military expenditures was the main force behind the reduction of gifts. Dowd is correct that the British understood the "meaning attached to gifts," and the lack of gift giving was a major source of irritation to the Indians.[17] Sir William Johnson understood that gift giving was proof of the sincerity of words to the Indians. Some other British officials also believed this, including George Croghan, Donald Campbell, and eventually even Henry Bouquet. Johnson also understood that the Indians expected the act of gift giving itself. The British did continue to provide presents, if in a reduced capacity. There are numerous examples of British officers stating that even when the Indians received presents, they constantly complained that they did not receive enough. As one example, Ensign Robert Holmes, commander of Fort Miami, wrote, "as for the Indi-

King George III ascended to the throne of England at the end of the French and Indian War. He oversaw the British policies that lead to Pontiac's Uprising. Portrait and signature courtesy of King's Arms Press.

ans . . .they are constantly tormenting me for presents. . . ."[18]

Of course there were other issues that led to the eventual war as well. Nonetheless, the economic component of gifts cannot be disregarded or underestimated. In that context, in contrast to Dowd's position, presents *were* in fact "inherently valuable enough to warrant a war."[19]

Despite his request to Johnson for specific

guidelines on the regulation of trade, Amherst ignored the more important advice on presents from both Johnson and lower ranking British officers who saw the effects first hand at their outposts. The following two examples typify the advice and observations of these subordinates. Major William Walters, commander of Fort Niagara, noted to Johnson:

> You Will Know how necessary it is in the Summer to give the Indians some Smale [small] presents with a Little ammunition. . . . I mention this as You are sencible how necessary it is to give the Indians a Little Support. I have been at a great deal of trouble to Convince them of the good Intention that the English have

towards them. I Should be glad You Would be pleased to represent this affair to General Amherst that I May have it in my power to assist the Indians a Little. You Know they are a jealous people and Should we hold our hand intirely from them—they will Easily made believe We Intend them Some hurt.[20]

Ensign Thomas Hutchins, on return from mapping the Great Lakes in September 1762 summarized:

> They [the northern Ottawas and Chippewas] were disappointed in their expectation of my having presents for them; and as the French have always accustomed themselves, both in time of peace and during the late war, to make

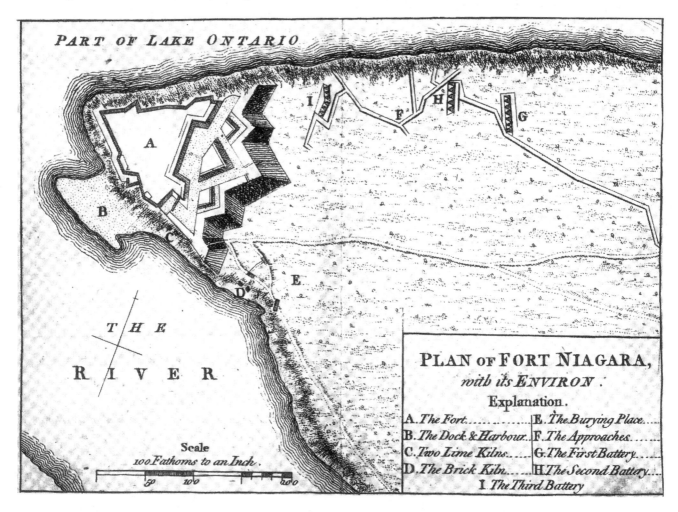

Plan of Fort Niagara with its Environs. From A Set Plans and Forts in America. Reduced from Actual Surveys. John Rocque, London, 1763. From the collection of Seymour I. Schwartz, M.D. Used with permission.

these people great presents three or four times a year and always allowed them a sufficient quantity of ammunition at the posts, they think it very strange that this custom should be so immediately broke off by the English, and the traders not allowed even to take so much ammunition with them as to enable those Indians to kill game sufficient for the support of their families.[21]

With respect to arms and ammunition, it is understandable that once Indians became accustomed to the white man's technology, it became a necessity to them. Ammunition was a particular problem because it was in short supply and the military and the traders needed it as well as the Indians. Captain Campbell at Detroit noted this in several letters to his superiors, first to Bouquet:

I am in. . .greatest want of Ammunition and the Traders here have but very little which I am afraid will have a very bad effect with the Indians; I would purchase it, at my own Expence if there was a possibility of Sending any from Fort Pitt this winter.[22]

In a second letter to Amherst the same day:

Before I had the honor of your Letter Disapproving of my giving Ammunition to the Indians, I forwarded a quantity by Sir William Johnson's particular decree to the other Posts and by that means could give but little to the garrisons at Miamis & Ouiatenon and have only one Barrell of powder Store here. I applied to Major Walters [at Niagara] for Ammunition but he informs me that Your Excellency disapproved of his sending the last ten Barrells of Powder So that I cannot expect anymore this Season.

The Indians Sold all their skins at Niagara for Rum, and are now in a Starving Condition for want of Ammunition, Which I'm affraid may drive them to Dispair. They apply to me daily and cannot be convinced I have no Ammunition for that purpose, As they were accustomed to be Supplyed by the Commanding Officer, and Unlikely the Traders have brought very little with them.[23]

And a third example later to Bouquet:

All the Indian Nations have gone to their Hunting, And by that means it will be quite here 'till spring. I hope the Genrl will change [h]is present way of thinking, with regard to Indian Affairs, As I am of Oppinion if they were Supplyed with Ammunition it would prevent their doing Mischief.[24]

Many other officers felt the same way; Colonel Bouquet commented:

Colonel Bouquet thinks it Necessary to be Represented to the General, that it has been Customary to give Powder, Lead, Vermilion, & Knives, to Indians going to War to the Southward; and that since those presents have been Suppressed, those Indians are become very Troublesome at Fort Pitt, & more so at the Out Posts, Stealing Horses, Cattle, or Committing other Disorders on the Communication which Obstruct the Trade, & Discourage the Country People, from bringing Provisions to the Fort; And the Colonel is of Opinion that those Disturbances could be prevented at a moderate Expence, if a Fixed Sum was Appropriated Yearly.[25]

To which Amherst replied:

It is to be hoped, from the Total Prohibition of Rum, that the Indians will become more Industrious, & be very well Able, by their Hunting, to provide for their Familys; As to Appropriating a particular Sum to be Laid out Yearly, in Presents to the Warriors, &ca, that I can by no means Agree to; Nor can I think it necessary to give them any Presents, by way of Bribes, for if they do not Behave properly they are to be Punished, & I Would Reward them whenever they Merit it: And Colonel Bouquet may, out of Charity to such as are in real Want, & Reduced by Age or Infirmities, Bestow what he thinks will be of most Service to them; the Expences Arising therefrom to be Allowed in the Deputy Agent's Accompts. . . .[26]

As if the commander in chief's philosophy regarding presents and ammunition was not enough cause for unrest among the Indians, the issue of rum was equally perplexing. Excessive consumption of alcohol can be damaging to all humans, and it has been long suspected that the

Brothers of the Forest, by Robert Griffing. In a remarkable display of intertribal unity, warriors from many different woodland tribes joined in Pontiac's Uprising. Courtesy of Robert Griffing and Paramount Press.

harmful effects on Indians and some other ethnic groups are even more severe. While eighteenth-century British officials would not have known about these studies, some modern research, although inconclusive, suggests a potential gene locale in Indian populations that might predispose them to alcoholism.[27]

The Indian culture was already more accepting of violence, and the use of alcohol might have increased these tendencies. At the same time, it often made them more prone to victimization by unscrupulous white men. Because of the effects of alcohol on their people, their chiefs often did not want them to have it. For one reason, it affected their trade as Captain Donald Campbell previously noted when he wrote that the Indians sold all their skins at Niagara for rum. The Indians themselves were well aware of how some traders took advantage of them while under the influence of rum. Complaints were common, as in this Onondaga chief's inquiry to Sir William Johnson:

Brother Gorah Warraghiagey [Johnson's Indian name]:

We the Six nations with surprise and concern behold the daily encroachments you are making upon our lands, contrary to your many promises made to us. Notwithstanding it was told to us by the General [Amherst] that they were only to be temporary posts for the protection of provisions, ammunitions, etc. and what is as bad as the before mentioned posts, when our hunters come out of the woods with furs, skins, meat and the like, there are always some of the people ready with liquor to intoxicate them and thereby deprive them of what they with labor and loss of time procured for the sustenance of their families. And what is worse, when they get our people quite drunk they plunder them of every thing they think worth taking, and on their making an inquiry when sober for what they were robbed of, our people are extremely ill treated and abused and obliged to go off without any satisfaction. We now desire to know from you Brother, whether those people at them posts have such orders [to evacuate and when they are to evacuate said posts.[28]

In yet another incident, Sir William Johnson admonished one George (Ury) Klock, a settler in the Mohawk Valley, for cheating the Indians out of land by getting them drunk. The affidavit of Klock's own brothers relates this unfortunate incident:

This Day appeared before me Sir William Johnson Bart. One of his Majesties Council of the province of New York, Capt. Jacob Klock of Conajoharee, in the county of Albany, who being duely Sworn on the holy Evangelists, Deposeth, and Sayeth that his Brother Jnjost Klock (who lives in his House, and was frequently called upon to be an Evidence to a Deed which George Klock their Brother prevailed upon the Indians to Execut) Declared to the Depont. That the Indians were Drunk at the time of signing said Deed-That the Depont. Often heard the Indians during this Winter Say, they would not part with, or Sell that Lands which Klock bought of [Philip] Livingston upon any Account.—Nevertheless the Depont. Understands, that since [that] time, several Indians by their getting Liquor from George Klock, and Receiving Promises of more, have been Induced to Sign said Deed. That said George Klock has been Tampering the whole Fall, & Winter, in Order to Prevail on them to Agree to Sign Said Deed, and that as he the Depont. Lives in the Neighbourhood of his Brother sd. George Klock, he has been frequently troubled, and Disturbed, day & night, and Obliged to get up at all Hours of the night to let in the Drunken Indians coming from sd.

G. Klock's House to the house of the Depont— And further the Depont. Sayth not—[29]

British officials were not insensitive to the negative consequences of rum and made efforts to protect both sides, although perhaps not as much as for humanitarian reasons as for the good of the fur trade. Amherst eventually issued an edict prohibiting the sale of rum to the Indians by anyone:

By order of His Excellency Sir Jeffery Amherst, Knight of the Bath, Major General & Commander in Chief of all His Majesty's Forces in North America

Whereas the use of Rum, and of all Strong Liquors is destructive to the Indians and attended with the most pernicious Consequences; All Indian Traders & others are expressly forbid to carry, sell, or give any Strong Liquor to the Indians, and the officers Commanding at the Several Posts in this Department are Strictly to adhere to this order, & not permit any of these pernicious liquors to pass on any account WhatSoever Given under my hand at Fort Pitt this 1st day of March 1762. . . .[30]

Bouquet's reply echoed the observations noted above by both Johnson and Campbell:

Since I am here, I have permitted no Strong Liquors to be Sold, given, or carried to the Indians, Your Orders thereupon Shall be Strictly obeid, and Sent to all the Posts in this Department. Niagara was Said to be the great Inlett, & Still some will be carried throughout these Woods, as the Traders engaged in that illicite Trade, know the Country, avoid the Posts, and assisted by the Indians, can not easily be discovered.[31]

Perhaps the best quote summing up Amherst's policy is his reply to Johnson:

I am very glad to find you are of the same opinion with me, in regard to the prohibition of Rum, and that in all your late passes, Spiritious Liquors have been forbid. . . . When the traders find this, they will of Course Carry more useful Commodities; and as Ammunition may be permitted to be sold to the Indians while they continue quiet, & that We have no reason to Suspect they have any Treacherous Designs towards us, I am hopefull they will be very well able to provide for their famlys, by Hunting, and that there can be no occasion for Distributing Presents at any of the Posts, since the Dependence thereon can only Serve to Render the Indians Slothfull & Indolent, and Burthen the Crown with a needless Expence.[32]

Another longstanding belief about the causes of the uprising was that many English officers and soldiers were arrogant toward the Indians and considered them to be an inferior race. Historians and authors have long highlighted Amherst's attitude toward the Indians, even labeling him a racist, which he probably was. Some historians have described Amherst's successor, General Thomas Gage, as more tolerant, however, he was as adamant as Amherst about "extripating" some tribes.[33]

Much has also been made of Amherst, Bouquet and Ecuyer's suggestion to use smallpox infected blankets, Bouquet's idea of using bloodhounds, and Gladwin's suggestion to consider the use of rum as means of subduing the Indians.[34]

One historian even suggests that Gladwin's alleged cruelty to the Indians—and one act in particular, the hanging of a female Panis slave convicted of stealing—actually incited Pontiac's siege at Detroit, which began the following day.[35]

Much of this alleged British cruelty was in reaction to the perceived atrocities the Indians committed prior to and during the conflict. It was seen as reason to justify Amherst's increasing anger, even to the extent of him calling for no prisoners to be taken. Judgement of these actions must be applied to both sides equally. The torture and deaths of Captain Charles Robertson, Sir Robert Davers, and Captain Donald Campbell at Detroit and Lieutenant Francis Gordon at Venango, the murders and cannibalistic acts the Indians committed at Michilimackinac, and the beheading of soldiers and the display of severed body parts on the Niagara Portage by the Senecas were all reprehensible in British eyes. The Delaware and Shawnee raids around Fort Pitt and the deliberate killing of innocent women and children on the Pennsylvania frontier were all are reasons why Amherst, Gladwin, Bouquet, and other British officers were so adamant about punishing the guilty perpetrators. Chief Wasson's attempt to justify the murder of Campbell (and for that matter, Pontiac's violation of truce etiquette by detaining Campbell in the first place) by saying that it was simply the standard of Indian culture is invalid. If this line of reasoning is considered, then it must equally be applied to both sides, and due consideration should also be given to whether or not the parties were operating within the accepted standards of their own societies.

Not all British officers were arrogant and mistreated the Indians. Captain Campbell's kindness to the Detroit Indians is well documented, despite his having to labor under tight restrictions, and those tribes liked and respected him. Although responsible for his murder, even Pontiac was reported to have been reluctant to give him up. In another example of empathy for the Indians, Major William Walters at Fort Niagara wrote:

I find by General Amherst's Letter; which I recd 27th March, that He is not willing [that] any thing should be given to the Indians. I Don't See how it is Possible to Avoid it. I have had, great, numbers of poor Indians at this post this past two winters, which I have Supported Chiefly with fish—Which cost no Expense. I have some times given them a pound or two of powder with a Little Ball in order to keep them Alive, Which I have Don at a very Easy rate— or Else Some of them Must have Starv'd. . .*therefore, in compassion, I cannot help giving them a Little Support.* [authors' emphasis][36]

Lieutenant Stair Campbell Carre, commanding at Fort Venango expressed similar kindness:

I received Your favour of 15th October by Custologa & am sorry that you have been troubled with a Complaint with so little reason; Since I came to this place, I always made it my particular Study to use all Indians who resorted here as well as possible, Nor do I recollect but one Instance of an Indian being in the least insulted;

The Intimidators, by Robert Griffing. Three Delaware warriors eye a British sentry at the gate to Fort Ligonier. Tension with the Indians began to build almost as soon as the British moved into their newly won territory west of the Appalachian Mountains. Courtesy of Robert Griffing and Paramount Press.

which was one Shanokin Daniel who received a Blow from a Soldier, but so far was *he* from not obtaining redress, (Conscious of his being partly in the wrong) he came several time to me with Mr. [Ensign Thomas] Hutchins & beg'd that the Soldier might be pardoned, which at least I consented to. . . .[37]

Also, despite the Wyandots initial concern over Fort Sandusky being built in 1761, commander Ensign Christopher Pauli mentioned, "there has been nodding else but civility Shoed to them," thus suggesting why the local chiefs apparently liked him, and quite possibly, it was the reason

why he was spared during the massacre of that garrison a year later.[38]

As one last example, Captain Gavin Cochrane, giving orders to Lieutenant James Dow, the commander at Fort Le Boeuf, directed him to "carefully avoid all Quarries with the Indians treating them civily."[39]

So it can be seen that, although there was often animosity between the British and the Indians, there were also numerous instances of respect and friendship.

Underlying all this was the Indian fear of uncontrolled English settlement and expansion on their lands. In another recent study, historian David Dixon provides an extensive look at the progression of this British acquisition of Indian land. Some brief comments and examples will illustrate these events.

One instance where Indians were duped out of their lands was the 1748 Ohio Company of Virginia grants, where the colony of Virginia received authority from the London Board of Trade to authorize land grants to trading partnerships. In the 1754 Albany Congress, the Iroquois Confederation, without authorization from the other tribes who had claims to the land (Delawares, Shawnees, and Mingoes among others), sold the same land between the Ohio and Susquehanna Rivers to both Pennsylvania and Connecticut. In the 1757 Treaty of Easton, Pennsylvania authorities, with the backing of the Board of Trade and Sir William Johnson, had to placate the Delawares by negating the pre-

vious land sales and reverting the rights back to those Indians who originally claimed ownership.[40]

During these years, British traders and settlers began to infiltrate the region, competing with the French, who had previously established trade among the Indians. Simultaneously, both the French and British governments attempted to secure the allegiance of the various tribes. This led to numerous isolated skirmishes, such as the 1752 attack on the Miami trading village at Pickawillany, Ohio, led by Charles Langlade.[41]

By 1760, the population of the British colonies was about 1.5 million people (including 400,000 slaves), but the wilderness areas of western New York, Pennsylvania, and Virginia were sparsely settled. The population of New York in 1756 was 96,765, with about 80,000 of that number living within eighty miles of New York City, while the 1760 population of Pennsylvania was approxi-

The Portage, by Robert Griffing. Travel through the forests of North America was often difficult. When waterways became impassable due to rapids or other obstructions, it was necessary to unload the boats or canoes and carry everything overland to navigable waters. Courtesy of Robert Griffing and Paramount Press.

mately 217,000. In contrast, French Quebec province had an estimated population of 65,000 in 1762, with most of that concentrated along the Saint Lawrence River.[42]

The Indians saw this infiltration as being officially condoned by the authorities, who had repeatedly assured them that it would not be permitted after the defeat of the French. Sir William Johnson promised it at the Detroit conference in 1761, Amherst assured them in 1760, and so did General Monckton at Fort Pitt the same year.

There are numerous examples of violations. The Johnson-Klock incident in New York has already been discussed. On the Niagara Portage, Amherst granted a company of merchants and current or retired military officers, including Major Walter Rutherfurd, John Duncan, John Bradstreet, and James Sterling warrants "to establish settlements on the Niagara carrying place & about there."[43]

Sterling and Duncan had built a huge house above the falls near Fort Schlosser for the use of the company. Johnson later accused them of intending "to monopolized the trade at the carrying place."[44]

This incensed the local Senecas. Johnson chastised Amherst, who later backed down when he received instructions from England prohibiting such transactions, claiming he had granted "only temporary permit until the King's pleasure was known, but without the least clause [cause] that could entitle them to an exclusive right of trade."[45]

Around Fort Pitt in 1760, Bouquet proposed the establishment of farm tracts as being "Articles Necessary for the Western Department" at several of the posts along the communication route to Philadelphia, including Bedford, Ligonier, Gist's Plantation (Mount Braddock, Fayette County, Pennsylvania), Fort Burd (Brownsville, Pennsylvania), and Fort Pitt "to raise oats, Indian Corn, Wheat, and Rye &a Power vested in the Commandg officer to grant such Lands."[46]

This was considered legitimate because it was intended for the subsistence of the garrisons and to support trade with the Indians. However, there

was a fine line in such arrangements because some of the tribes interpreted this as a means to permit further expansion and development on their lands. At times, Bouquet sent a mixed message, as when he later supported Indian complaints against settlers from encroaching on their lands. In a letter to Amherst, he addressed previous land treaty issues in what was a longstanding dispute with the governor of the colony:

> I have avoided troubling you by a minute account of all the triffling Events that occur daily here; in which number I must Class Mr. Fauquier's Letter to me, as I thought it intirely groundless, & expected that my Answer would have been fully satisfactory to him; As I know of no legal title People can have to Settle Indian Lands, but must be derived from the Powers lodged by the Crown in the Commander in chief, or the Governors of Provinces, I imagined to have obviated all Cavils by the Exceptions I made. . . . I had been repeatedly informed, that one Coll. [Thomas] Creasap, who is concerned in one of the Ohio Companies/the favourite Scheme of Virginia was proposing by way of Subscription to several familys, to remove from the frontiers of that Colony and Maryland, to form Settlements upon the Ohio. . . . In preventing in the district to me, a Scandalous breach of a recent Treaty [the Treaty of Easton of October 8–26, 1758, which included a guarantee that English settlement would not go beyond Pennsylvania's Allegheny Mountains], I can not at least be Charged with interested Views, or having exerted the little Power vest in me, to the Oppression of the Subject, or the Indian. . . . [Bouquet mentioned that Fauquier had offered him twenty-five thousand acres of those lands, but Bouquet turned it down.] [47]

Bouquet previously noted, "tho' the Governments of Virginia and Maryland did not accede to that treaty, I conceive that they are equally bound by it, and that no settlement will be permitted upon the Ohio till the Consent of the Indians can be procured."[48]

It is ironic that George Croghan negotiated at Easton on behalf of the Indian Department in the

Before the Siege by Robert Griffing shows Indians observing Fort Pitt shortly
before the outbreak of hostilities. Courtesy of Robert Griffing and Paramount Press.

absence of Sir William Johnson—especially because Croghan himself had obtained land grants around Fort Pitt from the Indians and established his home, Croghan Hall, which was later burned during the uprising.[49]

Bouquet was apparently also involved in some similar transactions, specifically Croghan's attempt to acquire "Warrents fer ye four Tracks [of land] Near [Fort] Bedford & that for ye bigg Spring. . . ."[50]

Even Sir William Johnson was not beyond such behavior on occasion, despite his efforts to balance his responsibilities to the crown and to the Indians. In the aforementioned George Klock scandal, although Johnson ruled in favor of the Indi-

ans, he privately admitted considering allowing other attempts to acquire the land from them, as revealed in one of his letters:

The Land which Ury [George] Klock is endeavouring to get at any rate from the Indians, adjoins that which the Indians gave me ye Deed for, and may be taken in, it is about 12 or 1400 Acres and can be sold as soon as pattented to a good price, indeed I never had any thoughts of Purchaseing it, finding the Ind[ian]s averse to Selling it, but they now could be prevailed on to dispose of it, rather than Ury Klock should get it. My Objection to his haveing it, was at the earnest desire of all the principal Indians, who was afraid Klock might by the unfair means he was using prevail on some of their lose Idle Young People (whome keeps constantly Drunk at his house) to Sign a Deed to him for it, notwithstanding the whole Castle of Conajohare have repeatedly forbid him tampering with their People about Land & Declared they would be no means dispose of any to him, for several reasons very sufficient, but too tedious now to mention. It may soon appear tho, before the Governour & Council, whom I expect will take proper steps to make an example of him for all his Villany.[51]

Later, even Gage got into the act by proposing a "Military Establishment." His letter to Bouquet meticulously outlined his plan:

My Chief Design in demanding a Tract of Land for the King, is in order to form a Military Establishment near Fort-Pitt; by granting the Land in Lotts of 100 or 150 Acres, on military Tenures; and on Such Conditions, as Shall be proper for the welfare & Security of such a Settlement; dependant only on The King, and his Generals. They Should have Courts of Justice of their own, & in every respect be a little Community by Themselves; of which the Commandant of the Fort should be the Governor. It is confidentially Said, that neither Virginia or Pensylvania can claim by their Charter up to the Ohio. As you have a perfect knowledge of the Country round fort-Pitt, I wish when you have leizure to think of Such a Project, that you would Sketch out the Spots proper to begin upon, and how to proceed till the whole Tract Should be Settled, in different Town Ships, taking in the Water upon the Right & left as much as possible, and always have in view Security and Defence. . . . A great many undigested thoughts have come into my head on this Subject, and I give them to you as they occurr.[52]

Other British officers had long-range plans for acquiring land grants in the colonies, among them Lieutenant Jehu Hay at Detroit, who wrote to Bouquet in March 1764, saying that he would "be glad to accept of the benefit of 2000 acres at present. . . ."[53]

Disagreements over trade and land acquisition were developing between the Cherokees and the southern colonies that were similar to those that led to the 1760 massacre of the British garrison at Fort Loudoun (Vonore, Tennessee).[54]

In many instances, the French view of settlement did not differ drastically from the British desire for complete ownership of the land, a fact that some historians overlook or excuse. The French system of *feudal seigniorty or seigneurie* required that, in return for the land grants, seigneurs (the persons given the grants) were to establish tenants as well as develop the land. The feudal seigniorty of eighteen square miles that the governor of New France Marquis de la Jonquiere granted in 1750 to his nephew Louis de Bonne, Sieur de Miselle, and Louis Le Gardeur, Sieur de Repentigny, two young army officers, was designed to protect French trading interests near Sault Sainte Marie on the Upper Great Lakes. The officers built Fort Repentigny for that purpose however, Repentigny, Miselle, and their heirs, not the Indians, were considered the landowners.[55]

It is clear that land encroachment was a major issue with the Indians. As one historian observes, the eastern tribes felt the expansion of the colonial population more because they were closest to it, while the more remote western tribes were slower to feel the impact.[56]

Finally, there is the question of what part French subterfuge played in the uprising. This has long been a controversial subject among historians. Parkman, Peckham, and others believed that the French were always a part of inciting the Indians to overthrow the British. However, a distinction needs to be made between military and governmental involvement compared to that of the French inhabitants. Dowd convincingly argues that it was the inhabitants and not the French military who were responsible. Obviously, the French government could not publically support the Indians after the Treaty of Paris. Yet, privately, some French officials such as the foreign minister were looking for "an opportune moment to strike back at the British."[57]

There is ample evidence to confirm the role of French inhabitants in aiding and abetting the Indians during the insurrection. For example, two

Frenchmen from Detroit, Jacques Godfroy and Mini Chene, took an active part in the seizure of Fort Ouiatenon on May 27, 1763.[58]

Frenchman also were present at the Navarre house when Captain Campbell and Lieutenant McDougall were held prisoner, and others regularly acted as informants to the Indians during the siege of Detroit. Both Major Gladwin and the merchant James Sterling describe this subterfuge, with the latter commenting, "The Indians are Supported & prompted on by the rascally French settlement we have around us; I know enough to hang a Dozen of Them, & I am sure that all the rest except three or four merit at last transportation, judge of the situation we were in when this affair commenced. . . ."[59]

There is clearly enough evidence to prove French encouragement and support for the uprising, but it came from the inhabitants and traders rather than the military and civil government.

In summary, it is fair to state that in simple terms, the revolt was a general uprising by the Indians against the British to preserve their culture and way of life. It was horrible and devastating, with a complicated array of human emotions occurring in a confusing and contradictory manner. Both sides had legitimate complaints, and both sides committed wrongs against the other. Perhaps Colonel Henry Bouquet's quote is as good as any for an assessment of the causes of the war: "by being too Saving of a few Presents to the Savages, which properly distributed would certainly have prevented it. . . ."[60]

The Conspiracy–Fort Michilimackinac 1763 by Robert Griffing depicts Chippewa and Sauk Indians discussing their plans for a surprise attack on the British garrison at Fort Michilimackinac. Courtesy of Robert Griffing and Paramount Press.

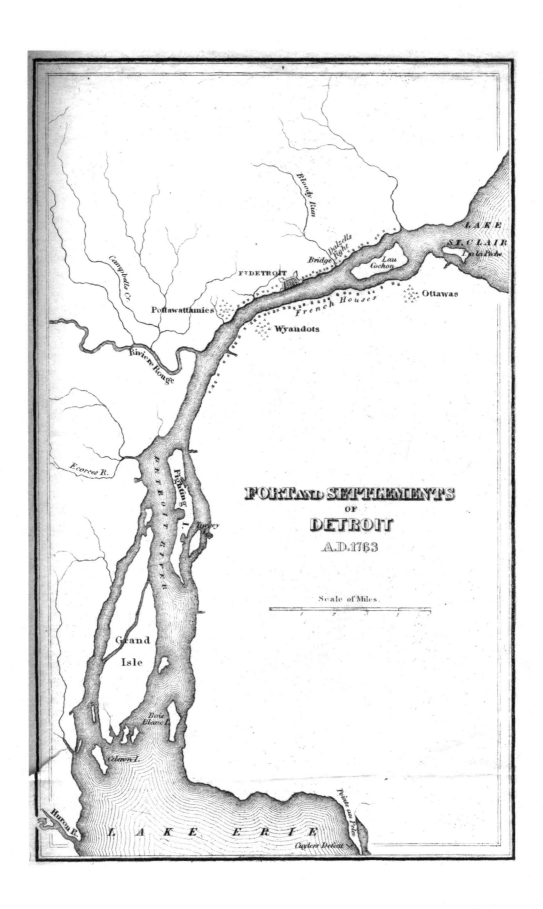

Chapter IV
The Whole World Is on Fire:
The War Begins in the West
1763

Lt. Jamet who fought with his sword against five for a long time (killing four)
but after receiving thirty-six wounds fell on their hands after which
they cutt off his Head and Killed six of their prisoners.
Lieutenant Jehu Hay

The Uprising Begins at Detroit

PONTIAC'S UPRISING did not complete-ly without warning. There were ominous signs beforehand. But as we have seen, the British large-ly ignored them. Major Gladwin learned that a Seneca war belt had been discovered at Fort Miami when post commander Ensign Robert Holmes reported that the chiefs told him:

> we were not to let this belt be known of till it arriv'd at Ouiattanen; and then we were to all Rise and put the English to death all about this place, and those at the other places.
>
> This Belt we receiv'd from the Shawanee Nation, & they receiv'd it from the Delawares, and they from the Senecas, who are very much enraged against the English. . . . We desire you to send this down to your General and George Croghan, and let them find out the man that was making this Mischief. For our parts we will be still and take no more notice of their Mis-chief neither will we be concern'd in it.[1]

It appears that this intelligence did not unduly alarm either Gladwin or Holmes. When Amherst received the belt, he forwarded it to Sir William Johnson without taking any specific action him-self:

I received a letter from Mr. Gladwin with accounts of the Indians having some bad designs. He sent me a bloody belt that Mr. Holmes sent him from the Miami's fort which the Indians had given up to him and declared it came from the Senecas. I sent it to Sir William Johnson to take such steps on the occasion as he might judge necessary.[2]

As Pontiac prepared for his first strike, he had about 460 warriors who he could count on. His own Ottawas were behind him for sure, as were the Potawatomies under Ninivois. The Wyandots on the other hand were still divided. Some were for Pontiac, under Takay, while those under Teata were generally against Pontiac's plan. On April 27, Pontiac called a large council on the Ecorse River, about ten miles southwest of Fort Detroit. There, he reiterated the message of the Delaware prophet Neolin, saying that the Indians should give up the ways and influences of the whites and go back to their old way of life. He modified Neolin's teach-ing enough to justify contact with the French, but the British were to be completely driven away.

On Sunday, May 1, Pontiac and forty to fifty warriors went to Detroit under the pretense of meeting with Major Gladwin. Most of the party performed a ceremonial dance in front of Captain Campbell's quarters, while the remaining few moved quietly about, making careful observations

Facing page. *Forts and Settlements of Detroit A.D. 1763,* drawn ca. 1870. Mapmaker unknown.
Tim J. Todish collection.

of the fort's defenses and the locations of the supply buildings. When the dancing was over, Pontiac said that he would return again in a few days with more of his followers to meet with Gladwin.

On May 2, an exploratory party left Fort Detroit in a bateau and a canoe. Captain Charles Robertson of the 77th (Montgomerie's) Highland Regiment commanded it, and it included two sailors, six soldiers, English adventurer Sir Robert Davers, civilian John Rutherfurd, and Davers' Indian slave. Robertson's mission was to take soundings of the Saint Clair River to see if it was deep enough to allow sailing ships to make the passage up to Fort Michilimackinac. Davers was just traveling, learning about the country's geography and the Indians that inhabited it. John Rutherfurd was a seventeen-year-old employee of trader James Sterling at Detroit, and Robertson had invited him to join the expedition.

The group had no inkling that there would be any Indian trouble; in fact they believed just the opposite. In his journal, Rutherfurd later wrote that they had "not the smallest degree dreading any interruption from the savages around us, who but a little before in full council had renewed their profession of friendship for the English and received from them presents to a considerable amount."[3]

On May 6, they delivered a few barrels of flour at La Pinnierre, where some Frenchmen were building a sawmill. These workers warned them most emphatically that the Indians planned to revolt against the English and they pleaded with them to return to Fort Detroit as quickly as they could. Rutherfurd reported that Captain Robertson doubted what the Frenchmen told them, and even if it was true, they did not believe that they would be attacked before nightfall. He felt that since it was still morning, they could go six miles farther to the mouth of the river, take their soundings, and still make it safely back to the fort that evening.

They proceeded north toward Lake Huron, and, when they reached the spot where the workers told them they would be ambushed (Port

Major Henry Gladwin, by John Hall, sometime after 1765. Courtesy the Detroit Institute of Arts, gift of Dexter M. Ferry Jr. Signature courtesy of the William L. Clements Library.

Huron, Michigan), they discovered the banks lined with three or four hundred Indians. Davers and his slave went ahead in a small canoe. They put into shore at the request of the Indians and smoked a pipe of peace until the bateau came up. As the bateau approached, Davers told them to row on past and not to let on that they suspected anything. They did so, trying to humor the Indians as much as they could. The Indians could walk along the shore faster than Robertson's men could row the bateau. The Indians kept showing them fish, maple sugar, and other goods to convince them to land, while asking for some bread and tobacco in return.

As the Indians moved along the shore, the men began to disappear, and soon only the women remained, "endeavoring to divert our attention by ridiculous stories and immodest gestures, that it was impossible to see what was going on behind them or what the men were about, who were then posting themselves behind a rising ground a little beyond us. As we came opposite that place the squaws, as it had been preconcerted, ran off as fast as they could."[4]

As soon as the women were clear, the warriors opened fire from about sixty yards away. Robertson was hit in the left side during the initial volley. He gave the order to sheer off, and, just as he did so, he was hit again, this time through the body. Rutherfurd took the helm and attempted to turn the boat around, but the Indians rushed on board and quickly overwhelmed them. When it was all over, Robertson, Davers, and the two sailors were dead, and the rest were taken prisoner. Robertson's body was eaten, and the skin from one of his arms was made into a tobacco pouch. Further details of Rutherfurd's amazing captivity will be related in Appendix E of this book.

On Thursday, May 5, Pontiac held a large council at the Potawatomi village about two miles south of the fort. He spoke passionately about the Indians' grievances against the British and argued that the time to strike was now. He told them that war belts had been sent to other tribes asking them to attack the forts in their areas. It was only right that they attack Fort Detroit first. His speech drew overwhelming support. The next step was to decide on a plan of attack. It was decided that in two days, on May 7, Pontiac and sixty trusted warriors would enter the fort and ask to meet with Gladwin. They would carry weapons hidden under their blankets, as would the Ottawas, men and women both, who would quietly spread themselves around the inside of the fort. At a given signal, the warriors would take up their weapons and attack the English, at the same time being careful not to harm any of the French habitants. The Wyandots and Potawatomies would surround the fort at a distance, so they could deal with the English who were outside the walls and also take up a station down river to cut off any

reenforcements that might be headed toward the fort.

Although the exact source is unknown, word of the treachery was leaked to Gladwin on the night of May 6. There are many stories about who the information came from. Robert Navarre, in his detailed journal, suggests that it was an Indian named Mahiganne who disapproved of Pontiac's actions. Another story claims that it was an old Indian woman named Catherine who gave the warning, while others attribute it to a sympathetic French inhabitant. One of the more convincing possibilities is that it came from a young French woman named Angelique Cuillerier, who was in love with and eventually married British trader James Sterling. Her father Antoine, half brother of the former French commandant Captain Bellestre, was a friend of Pontiac and was slated to be given command of the fort once the British were defeated. Gladwin himself never revealed where his information came from. On May 13, 1763, British trader and former Rogers' Rangers officer Caesar McCormick submitted a voucher to Gladwin that included £6.17.6 "To paid a Person for privet Intelligence."[5]

Of course it is not certain just what the intelligence was, but from the amount paid, it must have been substantial information, and may well have been paid to the person who first divulged Pontiac's scheme to Gladwin.

When Gladwin received the news about Pontiac's planned attack, he feverishly set about preparing his garrison to defend the fort. The exact number of men that he had at his disposal is not known. There were two under strength companies of the 60th Regiment and a twenty-two-man company of the Queen's American Rangers under Captain Joseph Hopkins. In addition, there were twenty or more British traders, some military veterans who could bear arms. Estimates of the garrison's total strength range from about 100 to about 170 men. Historian Howard Peckham places the number at about 120 soldiers and 20 or slightly more traders.[6]

The fort's ordnance consisted of two six-pound

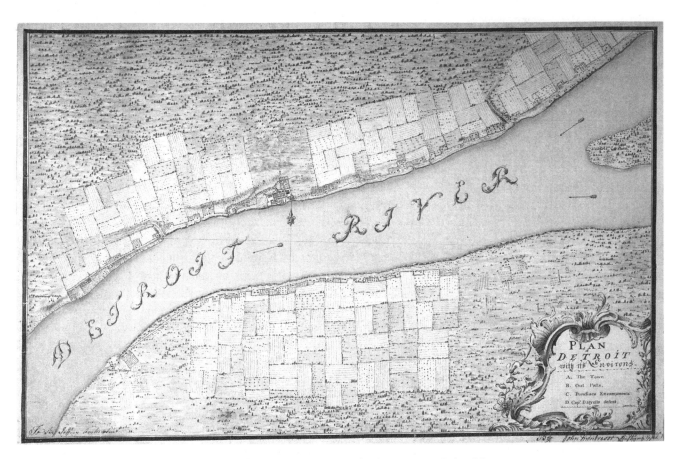

Plan of Detroit with its Environs, 1763, by Lieutenant John Montresor.
Courtesy of the William L. Clements Library.

cannons, one three pounder, and three mortars. Gladwin also had two ships, the six-gun schooner *Huron* and the larger sloop *Michigan.* One thing was certain—provisions were short, for no supplies had yet arrived that spring. Perhaps they had as little as two weeks' supply to feed the garrison and loyal inhabitants. Despite the obstacles, Gladwin was a loyal and dedicated soldier determined to do his duty .

On the morning of Saturday, May 7, none of the French inhabitants entered the fort, and in fact, many of the women and children who lived within the stockade had disappeared. This was a sure sign that trouble was brewing and that the French knew about it. At ten o'clock in the morning, about three hundred blanket-clad Indians entered the fort, moving past doubled sentries who stood fully

alert with fixed bayonets. Pontiac, ten minor chiefs, and a select delegation of warriors moved to Captain Campbell's quarters where the conference was to be held. The rest of the Indians milled about the fort in small groups, making careful note of the defenses and the location of the storehouses that would soon be plundered if everything went according to plan.

Only Gladwin and Campbell met Pontiac and his party, and even they had arms concealed in their pockets. The other officers were stationed about the fort with their men. All those who were not part of the guard were drawn up under arms in full view on the parade ground.

Shocked by this show of force, and obviously realizing that his plan had been discovered, Pontiac asked Gladwin why the other officers were not with him as usual and why the soldiers were all armed. Lieutenant Jehu Hay, who kept a diary that provides a firsthand look at many of the events of the siege, said that the Indians were so surprised that they "would scarcely sit down to council."[7]

Robert Rogers, in preparing a journal based on accounts of those who were present, wrote:

> Observing us thus prepared, their Chiefs came in a very condemned Manner, to Council, where they spoke a great deal of Nonsense to Major Gladwine and Capt. Campbell, protesting at the same Time the greatest Friendship imaginable to them, but expressing their Surprise at seeing all the Officers and Men under Arms. The Major then told them that he had certain Intelligence that some Indians were projecting Mischief, and on that Acct he was determined to have the Troops always under Arms upon such Occasions: That they being the oldest Nation, and the first that had come to Council, needed not to be astonished at that Precaution as he was resolved to do the same to all Nations.[8]

Pontiac then spoke of six chiefs who had died over the past winter and asked that the British give them some gifts to cover their loss. According to legend, during this speech, Pontiac held up a belt that was white on the top and green on the underside. If he turned the belt over with the green side up, it would be the signal to begin the attack. Seeing the preparations that had been made, Pontiac did not give the signal. Gladwin presented the Indians with six suits of clothing in memory of the deceased chiefs, as well as a little tobacco and bread. Frustrated and angry that the plan had been discovered, the Indians then filed out of the fort.

While Pontiac's plan for the quick capture of the largest post of the Upper Great Lakes had been temporarily thwarted, he was not about to risk losing the fervor of the moment, and he sent messengers to encourage the various nations to take part in the uprising. Similar to his plan for Detroit, each tribe was to devise a scheme in which to gain entry to the fort in their area and destroy or take garrison prisoner. The option was apparently left to the

discretion of that particular tribe. Most of the forts were merely small fortified trading posts and were taken in quick succession.

The Upper Posts Fall

Fort Sandusky (May 16)

The first strike outside of Detroit occurred at Fort Sandusky (Sandusky, Ohio). This was a logical target because it was on the vital communication link between Detroit and Fort Pitt. Sandusky's commandant, Ensign Christopher Pauli, had assisted Lieutenant Elias Meyer with the fort's construction in 1761. With Meyer's promotion and transfer to Quebec the following year, Pauli was left in charge of the fifteen-man garrison and the local traders.

Pontiac's allies quickly proceeded with their plan to take Fort Sandusky. The nearby Wyandots had been on good terms with Pauli. However, after being encouraged by Ottawas and Wyandots already involved in the attack on Detroit, the local Indians were convinced to join in the war. On the morning of May 16, a sentry notified Pauli that some Indians wished to speak with him. The officer had no cause for alarm, and a few of the Wyandots were admitted to the blockhouse. Shortly after the council began, Pauli was abruptly taken prisoner, and, to his horror, brought outside to see that all of the occupants of the fort had been murdered. Remarkably, the attack was conducted in the utmost silence. Lieutenant James MacDonald describes the incident in a letter to Colonel Bouquet:

> Upon the 22nd [May] we were told that Ensign Paulies who commanded at Sandusky was brought Prisoner by Ten Ottawas who reported, they had prevailed after a long consultation with the Wiandotts, who lived at Sandusky, to declare War against us, that some days ago they came early of a morning to the Block house there, and murthered every soul therein, consisting of Twenty seven Persons, Traders included, that Messrs Callender & Prenties [Prentice] formerly Captains in the Pennsylva-

nia Regiment were amongst that number, and that they had taken one hundred horses loaded with Indian Goods which with the plunder of the Garrison was agreed on to be given to the Wiandotts, before they condescended to join them. that all they wanted was the commanding officer.[9]

Having achieved their objectives of taking the commandant hostage and seizing the traders' goods, the Indians then burned the fort. Pauli was taken to the Wyandot camp near Detroit, and on July 4, he escaped to the safety of that fort.[10]

Fort Saint Joseph (May 25)

Sketch of Sandusky Bay by Captain Harry Gordon, August 1761. Courtesy of the LAC, Northcliffe Collections, Robert Monckton Papers, M. G. 18 M, Series 1, Volume XXXVII.

The Indians' next objective, Fort Saint Joseph, was west of Detroit at present-day Niles, Michigan. Although the atmosphere had been peaceful around the fort, relations between the British and the local Indians were tenuous. Louis Chevalier, a local French trader, had warned the post commander, Ensign Francis Schlosser, of a possible attack. However, Schlosser dismissed the matter with contempt, much like his counterpart at Fort Michilimackinac, Captain George Etherington, would do in the not too distant future.

On the morning of May 25, approximately one hundred Potawatomi Indians, the majority from Fort Detroit, came to the fort expressing their desire to visit with the commandant and "wish him good morning."[11]

At the same time, a Frenchman warned Schlosser that the Indians intended to make trouble. Now rightfully alarmed, Schlosser went to the barracks to assemble his men, but he found the building full of savages. He instructed a sergeant (possibly Sergeant Steiner) to order the men under arms, then he returned to his quarters to talk with the chiefs who had gathered there.[12] Suddenly, a cry was heard from the barracks, and Schlosser was immediately seized. The main body of Indi-

ans began a most horrifying slaughter, and in two short minutes all of the garrison except Schlosser and three other soldiers were killed.[13]

Louis Chevalier, who had initially tried to warn Schlosser of the impending attack, hid two of the civilian traders, T. A. Hamback and Richard Winston, in his house. In doing so, he exposed himself to great danger, but he saved them from almost certain death.[14]

Lieutenant Jehu Hay's journal entry for June 15, describes the attack as Schlosser related it to him:

> The account Mr. Schlosser gives of the way he was taken is that about seventeen Potawatomies came into his fort under pretense of holding a council, after they had engaged others to join them, to who they promised all the plunder. After they were in the fort, Washee, the Potawatomi chief, went into his [Schlosser's] room with three or four others, to whom he [Ens. Schlosser] had presented a belt. . .but before they made him an answer, a Frenchman came in and told him their design, upon which the cry was given in the fort and they seized him immediately. The young men that [had] agreed to join him [Washee] rushed into the fort, knocking down the sentinel, and

before the men could get to their arms put ten of them to death, which Washee tried to prevent in vain. The remaining three and himself they took prisoners. After this was done, all the chiefs of the St. Joseph Indians [the other Potawatomies had come from Detroit] came to Mr. Schlosser and told him that they knew nothing of the affair, that their young men crossed the river in the night unknown to them, and desired him to acquaint the commandant here that they were not concerned in the war, nor would be. . . .[15]

The fort was then looted, and Schlosser and the three soldiers were taken to Fort Detroit, where on June 14, Major Gladwin exchanged them for two Indian prisoners.

Fort Miami (May 27)

The commander of the fifteen-man garrison at Fort Miami (Fort Wayne, Indiana) was Ensign Robert Holmes, a former Lieutenant in Rogers' Rangers who had earned a solid record during the French and Indian War. On May 23, a Frenchman told him that he had heard cannon fire in the vicinity of Detroit, and Holmes began to ready his men for possible trouble. On May 25, Indians captured three members of the garrison. About this time, Pontiac's party, which was headed to Fort de Chartres, including the Frenchmen Jacques Godfroy and Mini Chene, arrived on the scene.

Ensign Holmes had taken an Indian mistress, and she consented to betray him. On May 27, before he knew that his three men had been taken prisoner or of the arrival of Pontiac's emissaries, his mistress came to him and asked if he would accompany her to treat a sick Indian woman. As he approached a cabin about three hundred yards from the fort, two shots rang out and Holmes fell dead. A sergeant in the fort heard the musket fire, and when he ran to investigate, the Indians seized him. The remaining eleven soldiers of the garrison shut themselves inside gates. Godfoy and Chene brought John Welch, a captured English trader, up to the fort. They ordered Welch to tell the soldiers that if they did not surrender they would all be killed. After a brief discussion, the garrison agreed to give up. Four of these soldiers were taken to Detroit to be shown to Pontiac, and the fate of the rest is unknown, although it has been assumed that they were taken prisoner to somewhere in the Illinois Country.

Lieutenant James MacDonald later wrote of the fort's capture:

Sunday the 5th of June we were acquainted that Fort Miamis was taken, that Ensign Holms who commanded them, had been informed (by two Frenchmen who arrived there the preceeding day) of Detroit attacked by the Indians, which he would hardly believe, but threatened to imprison the French for that Report. That an Indian woman had betrayed him out of the Fort by Pretending that another woman was very sick, and begged him to come to her Cabbin to let Blood of her, and when he had gone a little distance from the Fort was fired on and killed. the Serjeant hearing the report of the Fireing ran to see what it was, and was immediately taken Prisoner, the soldiers shut the Gates, and would have probably defended the Fort, if one Welch, a Trader, who had been taken prisoner, a few days before, had not advised them to open the Gates, adding that if they did not comply, the Indians would set fire to the Fort, and put them to Death, whereas if they opened the Gates they would be well treated whereupon the gates were opened and the soldiers grounded their arms.[16]

Captain Thomas Morris of the 17th Regiment also later wrote an account of the attack that he heard from one of the survivors. Holmes had been murdered after "a young squaw whom he kept having enticed him out of the garrison under a pretext of her mothers' wanting to be bled. They cut off his head, brought it to the fort, and threw it into the corporal's bed, and afterwards killed all of the garrison except five or six whom they reserved as victims to be sacrificed when they should lose a man in their wars with the English."[17]

Fort Ouiatenon (June 1)

Fort Ouiatenon was a small post on the

Wabash River at what is now West Lafayette, Indiana. Colleagues from the Miami and Detroit areas convinced the Weas and Kickapoos from the Fort Ouiatenon area to join in the rebellion. The post's commandant, Lieutenant Edward Jenkins, was seized when he went to meet the Indians in council outside the fort, and the entire twenty-man garrison of Royal Americans was ordered to surrender or be killed. They decided to give up, and due to their previously amicable relations with the local Indians and the influence of the French inhabitants, they were not harmed, nor was the fort destroyed. Lieutenant Jenkins, in his June 1, letter to Major Gladwin, describes how his post was captured:

> Sir: I have heared of your situation which gives me much pain, indeed we are not a great deal better, for this morning the Indians sent for me to speak with me, & immediately bound me when I got to their cabbin, & I soon found some of my soldiers in the same situation. They told me Detroit, Miamis and all these Posts were cutt off, and that it was a folly to make any resistance, therefor desired me to make the few soldiers I had in the Fort surrender, otherwise they would put all of us to death in case one man of theirs was killed. They were to have fallen on us all last night, but Monsieurs Maisonville & Lorrain, gave them Wampum not to kill us all, and when they told the Interpreter we were all to be killed & he knowing the Canadians of the Fort beged of them to make us Prisoners. They have put us into the French houses and both Indians and French use us very well. All these nations say they are very sorry, that they were obliged to do it by the other Nations. . . . I have nothing more to say but that I sincerely wish you a speedy succour, & that we may be able to revenge ourselves on them that deserve it. I remain with my sincerest wishes for your safety, &c., N.B. We expect to set off in a day or two for the Illinois."[18]

As noted, Jenkins and his men were eventually taken to Fort de Chartres, and then to Mobile, Alabama. There, he and his men were eventually transferred to the 22nd Regiment under Major Arthur Loftus. This was due to the reduction of the 1st Battalion of the Royal Americans under the terms of the recently implemented New Establishment.[19]

By this time, Indian control of the entire Upper Great Lakes area was almost complete, with the exception of Detroit, which was still under siege, and the forts to the north at Michilimackinac and La Baye.

Fort Michilimackinac (June 2)

News of the uprising had not yet reached the garrison at Fort Michilimackinac, nearly four hundred miles away by canoe north of Detroit. However, the local Chippewa knew of it through Pontiac's directives, and they eventually staged one of the most cleverly devised strategies to capture the British forts. Although it maintained the common element of surprise, their scheme was quite different from those previously employed.

Michilimackinac was the major fur-trading center on the Upper Great Lakes. As such, it had a larger garrison than the other posts, consisting of thirty-five to thirty-seven men and three officers. There were four British traders residing at the fort along with some three hundred French inhabitants and traders. The commandant, Captain George Etherington, was a veteran 60th officer who had served under Bouquet and Gladwin in the French and Indian War. The addition of Lieutenant John Jamet and his detachment of ten men from the small post at Sault Sainte Marie had reinforced the garrison. A disastrous fire in December 1762 had destroyed that fort and badly burned Jamet. The soldiers eventually made their way safely to Michilimackinac over fifty miles of ice and snow.

A few days prior, two of the French inhabitants, Laurent Du Charme and Lieutenant Charles Langlade, as well as Alexander Henry, the first English trader to the area, had warned Etherington of the Indian unrest. Regrettably, Etherington disregarded these warnings and threatened "to send the next person who should bring a story of the same kind a prisoner to Detroit."[20]

It was a sultry morning on June 2, when some-

Lieutenant Colonel George Etherington, about 1773, at the Island of Saint Vincent, West Indies. Attributed to John Trotter of Dublin, Ireland, ca. 1787. Courtesy of the Royal Green Jackets Museum, Winchester, England. Signature courtesy of the William L. Clements Library.

where between four and six hundred Indians, led by Chippewa chiefs Matchekewis and Minavavana (Le Grand Saulteur), gathered at the fort for a baggataway (lacrosse) contest against some visiting Sauks. Despite the previous warnings, Etherington did not place the garrison on alert. While the officers and soldiers watched the game outside the open gates of the fort, Indian women meandered next to the stockade. Unnoticed by the soldiers, they had concealed weapons beneath heavy, woolen blankets—inappropriate dress for the warm weather. As the game progressed, the Indi-

ans deliberately threw the ball near the gate of the fort and the players rushed inside, seemingly to retrieve it. Once inside, they took their weapons from the women and swiftly fell upon the unsuspecting British garrison. Alexander Henry, who survived by hiding in a house garret, witnessed the attack and later provided a vivid account of the event:

> I heard an Indian war cry and a noise of general confusion. . . .
>
> Going instantly to my window I saw a crowd of Indians within the fort furiously cutting down and scalping every Englishman they found. In particular I witnessed the fate of Lieutenant Jamet. . . .
>
> I had in the room which I was a fowling piece, loaded with swanshot. This I immediately seized and held it for a few minutes, waiting to hear the drum beat to arms. In this dreadful interval I saw several of my countrymen fall, and more than one struggling between the knees of an Indian who, holding him in this manner, scalped him while yet living.[21]

Another English trader, Henry Bostwick, also survived the attack and later recalled:

> I saw a soldier running towards the house for Shelter and the Indians after him, but as soon as he came near the Door, they [the French inhabitants] shut it against him which gave the Indians time to strike him with Hatchet; upon receiving the Blow he fell forward with so much force against the Door that he broke it open. . . .[22]

In the garret, Henry further related:

> Through an aperture which afforded me a view of the area of the fort I beheld, in shapes the foulest and most terrible, the ferocious triumphs of barbarian conquerors. The dead were scalped and mangled; the dying were writhing and shrieking under the unsatiated knife and tomahawk; and from the bodies of some, ripped open, their butchers were drinking the blood, scooped up in the hollow of joined hands and quaffed amid shouts of rage and victory. I was shaken not only with horror, but with fear.[23]

In all, twenty-one of the British garrison,

Chippewa warriors lead Captain George Etherington into captivity during the annual Fort Michilimackinac Pageant at reconstructed Fort Michilimackinac. Photo compliments of Todd E. Harburn.

including Lieutenant Jamet, and Warrant Tracy, a civilian trader, were killed, while none of the French inhabitants were molested.[24] As officer of the day, Jamet was apparently the only member of the garrison able to offer armed resistance. Despite a gallant attempt to defend his life, he was overpowered. According to Jehu Hay, Jamet "fought with his sword against five for a long time, but after receiving thirty-six wounds fell in their hands, after which they cut off his head. . . ."[25]

Captain Etherington and Lieutenant Leslie, both initially seized and carried into the woods, were later reunited with the surviving garrison members and the three traders, Henry Bostwick, Alexander Henry, and Ezekiel Solomon. Etherington later described the scene:

> [O]n the second instant the Chippewas who live in a plain near this fort, assembled to play ball, as they had done almost every day since their arrival. They play'd from morning till noon, then throwing their ball close to the gate and observing Lieut. Leslie and me a few paces out of it, they came behind us, seized, and carried us into the woods. In the meantime the rest rushed into the fort, where they found their squaws whom they had previously planted there, with their hatchets hid under their blankets, which they took and in an instant killed

Lieut. Gamet [Jamet] and fifteen rank and file, and a trader named Tracy; they wounded two and took the rest of the garrison prisoners, five of which they have since killed.[26]

The local Ottawas were incensed at the Chippewas for not including them in the plan to capture the fort, although, in somewhat of a paradox, they eventually assisted Etherington and his men during their captivity. The Ottawas had received a war belt from Pontiac encouraging them to join in the uprising, but had not yet reached a decision when the Chippewas struck. The Ottawas, under Chief Okinochumake, went to Michilimackinac, arriving on the evening of June 4. They immediately took all of the prisoners from the Chippewas. After a two-day conference, the Ottawas were given some of the plunder from the fort, and in return, they gave the Chippewas back four soldiers and one trader. Captain Etherington, Lieutenant Leslie, eleven soldiers, and two traders were taken to the nearby Ottawa village at L'Arbre Croche (Cross Village) some eighteen miles southwest of Michilimackinac on Lake Michigan. There, Etherington sent letters informing both Major Gladwin at Detroit and Lieutenant James Gorrell, commandant at Fort La Baye, of the situation. He also appointed Charles Langlade caretaker of the fort until British rule could be restored. His correspondence to Gladwin was sent via Father Pierre du Jaunay, the priest at Michilimackinac. Du Jaunay is also credited with intervening with the Indians to stop further bloodshed during the attack, "opening his house to serve as an asylum" thereby saving the lives of the remaining soldiers and traders but "greatly endangering his own."[27]

Leslie, Henry, and the others consulted Du Jaunay about possibly retaking the fort, however, the priest discouraged it due to the danger involved and extreme unliklihood of such a plan succeeding.[28]

Of Father du Jaunay, Etherington wrote, he "was very much obliged to. . .for the many good offices [he] has done us on this occasion." and praised the priest as "a very good man."[29]

Etherington's letters to Gorrell directed that

officer to come to his aid as soon as possible in the hopes of formulating an escape plan. In his letter of June 11, after relating the same details of the attack, he wrote:

> You'll therefore, on the receit of this which I send by a canoe of Ottawas, set out with all your garrison and what English traders you have with you, and come with the Indian who gives you this, who will conduct you safe to me. . .you are by no means to come to this post before you see me at the village twenty miles from this. . . . Tell the traders to bring what provisions they can with them, and be sure to bring all your ammunition; and recommend the care of the fort to the Indian chief. . . .[30]

A brief note is appropriate here. As has been mentioned, initially some of the Ottawas were upset with the Chippewas, Sauk, and Fox for not including them in the initial attack plan. During the negotiations, Gorrell noted:

> About eight or ten of the principal Indians that did the mischief, came to Capt. Etherington. . .[asking] if he would shake hands with them. Upon being refused, they said it was not on account of the Tawas [Ottawas] that they saved Capt. Etherington and the rest of his garrison, but on account of the Indians from La Bay with me [Gorrell], who came with their pipes full of tobacco for them to smoke; and ready to fire upon us, they would be obliged to lay down their arms on account of an old alliance between them. They said that though it was the Chippewas that struck, it was the Ottawas that began the war at Detroit, and instigated them to do the same. They said at the same time, that if the General [Amherst] would forgive and shake hands with them, they would never do the same again. . . .[31]

From Gorrell's account, it is confusing as to just which Indians he is talking about, however, it may have been some of the Sauk and Fox Indians who came to discuss being forgiven because they specifically stated, "it was the Chippewas that struck." This is of interest because some historians have noted that the Ottawas did not participate in the attack. Etherington even called them "our good friends" for protecting him and the sur-

vivors, despite the Ottawas initially treating them as prisoners.[32]

It is likely that their fear of eventual reprisal from the British influenced the Indians' behavior here. Although Etherington could make no promises, he said he would "speak in their favor" to Amherst, "but they must give up all their prisoners. . . ."[33]

After negotiating their release, Etherington left Michilimackinac in the care of Charles Langlade and Jacques Farli, one of the French traders. The latter was surprising because he was among the looters of British trade goods after the attack.[34]

The Ottawas then escorted the combined contingents under Etherington to Montreal, arriving there on August 13, "after a tedious passage of thirty-two days."[35]

Amherst was frank in his criticism of Etherington and Leslie for allowing the fort to be surprised. In his personal journal, he wrote:

> Capt. Etherington of the R.A. [Royal American] Regiment suffered himself to be surprised at Mickillimackinac on the 2nd of June when the Indians were playing at ball out of the Gate, and Captain and Lt. Lessley very stupidly and unlike officers walked out so as to permit the Indians who threw a ball toward the Fort, to intercept them, seized them and carried them into the woods, while many rushed into the Fort where they had planted the squaws with hatchets under their blankets; in an instant they had killed Lt. James [Jamet] and fifteen men and a trader, taking the rest prisoners, being fifteen more.[36]

The attack on Michilimackinac signified more than just the loss of another British fort. Being such a prominent post, its capture was a key victory for the Indians. This was important for their morale and unified their efforts as the uprising continued. It again demonstrated how the British underestimated the power and intelligence of the Indians. As a result, it was not only a costly lesson, but also a further indication that the revolt would not easily be stopped. Indeed, to both military and civilians, on the frontier and in the cities back east, it appeared as if the whole world was on fire.

Fort La Baye (June 21)

At Fort La Baye, Ensign Gorrell had a garrison of fifteen Royal Americans and several English traders. They had established a good relationship with the local Winnebagoes, Foxes, Sauks, and Menominees. Etherington's instructions to Gorrell ordered him to abandon Fort La Baye and join him at L'Arbre Croche as quickly as possible. Etherington's letter read in part:

> This place was taken by surprise on the fourth instant [actually June 2], by the Chippewas, at which time Lieut. Jamet and twenty more were killed, and all the rest taken prisoners; but our good friends the Ottawas have taken Lieut. Lesley, me, and eleven men out of their hands, and have promised to reinstate us again. You'll therefore, on receipt of this, which I send by a canoe of Ottawas, set out with all your garrison and what English traders you have with you, and come with the Indian who gives you this, who will conduct you safe to me. . .you are by no means to come to this post before you see me at the village twenty miles from this [L'Arbre Croche].[37]

As a result, upon receipt of Etherington's order, the fort was abandoned and entrusted to the Indians' care. Gorrel summoned them and "informed them, with a belt, of their brother Capt. Etherington's distress, (giving them large presents,) and asked their counsel and assistance; whereupon they called their whole town together, and all unanimously agreed to come along with me. . . ."[38]

On June 21, Gorrell's party set out with their Indian escort and safely arrived at L'Arbre Croche on the thirtieth. Upon their arrival, Gorrell told the Indians that his men would not give up their arms, and no attempt was made to force them to do so; in fact, surprisingly, the Indians treated the soldiers well. Over the next several days, the Ottawas and other friendly Indians met with the Chippewas and attempted to get them to agree to turn Fort Michilimackinac back over to Captain Etherington, but their efforts were unsuccessful. On July 18, escorted by the Ottawas, the combined contingents under Etherington left for Montreal, where they arrived on August 13, as previously noted.[39]

When news of the capture of Fort Michilimackinac reached General Amherst in New York, he was even more indignant toward the Indians, stating, "Michilimackinac, being a Post of the utmost consequence, must be Retaken, & Secured so as never to fall in the Hands of the Indians again. . . ."[40]

With Michilimackinac now lost, Amherst was determined that Forts Pitt and Detroit must be held at all costs. He sent his own aide, the brave and young Captain James Dalyell, to Albany to begin collecting reenforcements for a relief expedition for Detroit.

The Siege of Detroit Continues

While Pontiac's initial attempt to surprise the garrison of Fort Detroit had failed, attempts in other areas were successful. But, just because his plot was discovered did not mean that Pontiac was about to give up at Detroit.

L'Arbe Croche, site of the Ottawa Indian village where Captain Etherington and other survivors were taken after the attack on Fort Michilimackinac. Photo by Todd E. Harburn.

A view of Hog Island (Belle Isle) today. Former British sergeant James Fisher and his family lived on the south end of the island and were killed at the onset of the siege of Detroit. Photo by Todd E. Harburn.

After it became obvious that their plot had been discovered, the Ottawas went back to their village and met in council. Many of the young warriors criticized Pontiac for not giving the signal, but he explained that it was obvious that the British had learned of the plan and that an attack would certainly have resulted in Indian casualties. In the discussion that followed, the old Chippewa woman Catherine was accused of being the informer. Pontiac had her seized and took to her Gladwin, demanding to know if she was the "bad bird" that had set the English against the Ottawas. Gladwin denied it, but said that the word had come from an Indian. Whether this was true or not, it certainly fueled the suspicion that was growing within the Indians' ranks. Despite Gladwin's denial that Catherine was the informer, Pontiac had her flogged. Robert Rogers recorded that, "When they arrived at their Camp, Pondiac, their greatest Chief seized on the Prisoner and gave her three Strokes with a Stick on the Head, which laid her flat on the Ground, and the whole Nation assembled around her and called repeated Times kill her, kill her."[41]

The next day, May 8, Pontiac came to the fort with three chiefs and met with Gladwin, pledging peace and claiming that the incident the day before was all a misunderstanding. He offered Gladwin a peace calumet, which was accepted, and said that he would return on Monday with his young warriors to smoke the peace pipe and shake hands. Gladwin replied that the young warriors had no reason to visit him and that he would admit only Pontiac and his principle chiefs.

When Pontiac returned to his village, he invited the Potawatomies and Wyandots to come to play baggataway (lacrosse), thinking that the games would help to allay the British suspicions. That evening, after the game ended, he advised the visitors of his thwarted scheme and told them that he planned on leading his Ottawa warriors against the fort the next day.

On Monday morning, May 9, Gladwin continued strengthening his defenses, and British subjects living outside the stockade were given the opportunity to move inside the walls. At about eleven o'clock in the morning, the Indians crossed the river from the Ottawa town in sixty-five canoes. Pontiac and fifty warriors approached the gate of the fort. Gladwin sent his interpreters out to meet them with the message that only Pontiac and ten to fifteen of his leading men would be allowed to enter the fort. Pontiac replied that if all of his people could not enter the fort, "then none of them would enter it: that we might stay in our Fort, but he would keep the Country, adding that he would order a Party instantly to an Island where we had twenty-four Bullocks. . . ."[42]

Gladwin conceded somewhat and said that the Ottawas could enter, but only in small parties of a few at a time. His plan frustrated once again, Pontiac led all of his Ottawas back to their village.

Back at his camp, Pontiac took up a tomahawk and began chanting a war song. If he could not attack the English within the fort, then he would fall upon those on the outside. He moved his camp to the same side of the river as the fort, about two and a half miles upstream on the farm of Jean Baptiste Meloche. He ordered a party of warriors to attack a farm about one mile from the fort that a Mrs. Turnbull and her two sons owned. A short time later, these three settlers were killed and scalped, and the siege of Detroit had clearly begun.

Another party of Ottawas landed on Isle au Cochon (Hog Island, later, Belle Isle) intent on seizing the government cattle that were grazing there under the guard of two soldiers. A third soldier just happened to be visiting that day, and James Fisher, a retired sergeant, also lived on the island with his wife, four children, and a maid. Two soldiers, Fisher, his wife, and one child were killed outright. The remaining soldier, the servant, and the surviving three Fisher children were taken prisoner. A French workman was also killed, although apparently by mistake.

Other bands of Ottawa warriors began to fire on the fort from the shelter of nearby outbuildings and also on the schooner *Huron* and the sloop *Michigan*, which were anchored nearby. Pontiac also took steps to insure that the local French inhabitants did not assist or supply the garrison. He "cut off the communication from the fort to the inhabitants on each side so that we could not get the least thing brought into the fort. He told the inhabitants that the first of them that should bring us any provisions or anything that could be of any service to us, they would put that family to death."[43]

Later that afternoon, Chippewas from the Saginaw Valley brought word to Pontiac of the May 7, attack on Robertson's party, who had been taking soundings of the Saint Clair River. Pontiac sent word of this triumph to Gladwin through a French habitant.

Gladwin had one of his interpreters, Pierre La Butte, go to Pontiac to try to find out his plans. Several messages were sent back and forth, but nothing was accomplished. Both sides kept up a generally ineffective fire throughout the night. The garrison and traders were divided into groups and assigned rotating guard duties every six hours so that the Indians would not be able to surprise the fort during the night. To set the example, Gladwin and his officers stood watch the first night themselves. Despite all the confusion and uncertainty of the recent events at Detroit, the siege was nonetheless well underway.

On the morning of May 10, Pontiac held a council with Indian and French leaders at the home of his friend Antoine Cuillerier to plan future strategy. While many of the French were sympathetic to the Indians, they were reluctant to publicly display their support. It was decided to propose a truce while peace terms were discussed. Gladwin agreed, and early in the negotiations, Pontiac requested that Captain Campbell be sent out to negotiate for the garrison. Campbell, who had gained the trust of the Indians, was willing to be the negotiator. Gladwin was reluctant, especially when habitant Claude Jean Thomas Gouin warned of possible treachery. But Gladwin finally gave in, allowing, but not ordering, Campbell to undertake the dangerous mission. Lieutenant George McDougall volunteered to accompany Campbell. To insure Campbell's safety, Gladwin initially planned to detain the four chiefs that came to ask for him. The French habitants however, had talked Gladwin out of it, assuring him that the officers would be safe.

When the two officers met with Pontiac at the Cuillerier house, they were informed that the garrison would be given the same terms that the French had received—they had to give up the fort, their arms and stores, and have the Indians escort them to the British frontier settlements. Rather than let Campbell and McDougall take these terms to Gladwin, French habitants relayed the word, while the two officers were held in Indian custody—despite the promise "that Capt. Campbell and the other Officers that went with him, should return whenever they please."[44]

Initially, Pontiac told the officers that he was going to hold them for only two days, but even that promise was not honored.

Gladwin was furious over this breach of emissary protocol that even the Indians normally respected. He angrily replied that he would do nothing until his two officers were returned safely. Pontiac clearly understood that he was violating age-old tradition concerning the treatment of ambassadors, and, in fact, he even sent messengers to his Wyandot and Potawatomi supporters proudly notifying them of his actions.

The Potawatomies had just captured two couriers from Fort Saint Joseph with dispatches for Gladwin. Pontiac had them killed in spite of the agreed upon truce, which had not been formally terminated. Gladwin, in the meantime, took advantage of the lull to purchase all of the supplies that he could from the French habitants and had these supplies brought into the fort. That some of the French were willing to provide the garrison with sustenance is to their credit, as Pontiac had warned them that anyone assisting the English risked being put to death.

On May 11, Campbell was forced to write out the proposed terms of capitulation. This time, the garrison would be allowed to keep their arms, but everything else would be the same, and Pontiac stipulated that he should be allowed to keep a black boy belonging to one of the traders as his personal valet. Once again, Gladwin refused to even consider any negotiations until his officers were freed. During the day, Pontiac visited the habitants living around the fort and commanded them to give him supplies under the penalty of being plundered if they refused.

As the widespread attacks on the smaller British forts later played out, a number of the tribes claimed that they were forced to take part in the war against their will. There is evidence to support that in at least some cases, this could have been true. On the afternoon of May 11, it is known that Pontiac visited a small band of Christian Wyandots who had not yet taken part in the hostilities. Able to field only sixty warriors, under Pontiac's pressure, this band under Teata had no choice but to agree to join the uprising.

May 12, was Ascension Thursday, and the Christian Wyandots were granted permission to celebrate the feast before joining in the siege. The rest of the Indians held off their attack until the Christian Wyandots appeared, and once they did, the sniping at the fort resumed. One party took cover in some barns only about one hundred yards from the stockade. Firing hot shot (several spikes wrapped with iron wire and heated red hot) from a three pounder, the British were able to set the barns on fire, forcing the Indians to flee from their cover. The defenders had three men slightly wounded, while the Indians suffered three or four killed and about ten wounded. In the evening, Pontiac proposed a truce so that the dead could be buried, which Gladwin agreed to.

On the morning of May 13, a Frenchman brought word to the fort that the Indians had captured two traders who were approaching the fort, unaware of the siege. The capture netted the Indians rum, trade goods, and a critical seventeen barrels of gunpowder. The messenger informed Gladwin that the Indians were all drunk from the rum, so he immediately ordered Captain Hopkins to take a party of twenty-five volunteers and go by sloop to burn the Huron village and recapture the powder.[45] Luckily, unfavorable winds forced them to turn back, for it was later learned that the report was a ruse and a large party of Indians was waiting in ambush.

The Indians did not attack the fort on May 13, so detachments were sent out to burn the outbuildings that the Indians had been using as cover. Captain Hopkins was assigned to lead a party of forty men to burn one set of buildings, and when he returned, Lieutenant Hay and thirty men went out to destroy another group.

Pontiac met in council in his camp with the influential French habitants, where he urged them to become more active in the siege. Specifically, he wanted them to show him how to dig trenches for a European-style siege. Robert Navarre recorded in his journal that "The French were of no mind to do this, and anyway, most of them did not know how, and those who did know took good care not to say so, urging in their own defense that they did not know how to go about it."[46]

Pontiac also had Campbell write another letter to Gladwin, offering the same terms that he had earlier. This time he warned that if they British refused his offer, he would carry the fort by storm and put the occupants to death by torture. When a Frenchman delivered the message, Gladwin confidently replied that "since the King had sent him to command the Fort he would stay there till he died, and his [Pontiac's] threats or those of any other Indians did not disturb him any."[47]

While Gladwin did not believe that the Indians would risk an all out assault on the fort because of the heavy casualties they would suffer, he did understand that they could cause considerable damage with their fire arrows. He had ordered all available containers filled with water and placed about the fort. Pontiac did not immediately employ the use of fire however, probably because of the danger to the traders' stores, which he hoped to capture intact.

On the afternoon of the fourteenth, a delegation of the leading French inhabitants visited Pontiac. They explained that the war was ruining them because it had brought trade to a standstill. Pontiac replied that if they joined with him, and the British were driven away, trade would then again be possible. The Frenchmen replied that they could not do this because they had sworn loyalty to the British in 1760, and the council ended without anything being resolved. During the meeting, the firing on the fort continued, and the garrison fired back. One sergeant and one soldier were wounded.

The Indians made no overt attempts on the fort on May 15, so Gladwin again used the opportunity to burn the last building that was offering protection to the attackers. He also ordered embrasures cut into both sides of the gate on the west wall for the six-pound cannons, which had not yet been mounted effectively. One of these guns now commanded the road, and the other controlled the nearby fields and houses.

On May 16, Captain Hopkins, Lieutenant Hay, and ten men were ordered to take the sloop *Michigan* to fire on the Wyandot and Potawatomi vil-

Lieutenant Jehu Hay, ca. 1784, while serving as governor of Detroit. After a miniature in the G. H. Burroughs Collection, about 1922, M1597. Courtesy of the McCord Museum of Canadian History, Montreal.

lages. A favorable wind soon turned around, and they were forced to tack to make any headway. One time, as they were coming about, a sudden gust of wind ran the sloop aground only twenty feet from shore. To free themselves, they were forced to lower a boat and carry the anchor two hundred feet out into the river and then reel it in. This maneuver took them fifteen minutes, during which time they could have been easily overpowered had there been any Indians nearby.

On May 17, Pontiac again visited French habitants along the river to secure more food for his followers. Although they had no choice but to comply, there was a system to Pontiac's demands. Those living north and east of the fort would supply the Ottawas, those to the southwest would take care of the Potawatomies, and those living on the east side of the river would feed the Wyandots.

Concerned that the habitants, who were still allowed free access to the fort, were also carrying valuable intelligence to the garrison, the Indians established a guard of twenty warriors on the east and west sides of the fort to prevent this traffic.

Another large council of all loyal tribes was held on May 18, at which many French habitants and Campbell and McDougall were also present. Contradicting his earlier decision to make Antoine Cuillerier commandant of Detroit after it fell, Pontiac said that he was going to ask Major Pierre-Joseph Neyon de Villiers, the commander of Fort de Chartres, to send him an officer suitable for the position. It may be that what he was really trying to do was get an officer experienced in siege warfare sent to help him. Having a French officer present would also encourage the local habitants to be more supportive of his efforts. Pontiac went on to explain that his efforts were not for the Indians alone, that the British also had ill-used the French and both the Indians and the French would benefit from expulsion of the British. He emphasized that the warnings of the Delaware and Shawnee had come to pass. Now was the time for everyone to band together and drive the English back to the coast. A delegation of Indians and Frenchmen, who also carried war belts to encourage attacks on Forts Miami and Ouiatenon, delivered Pontiac's message. This is the same party that influenced Fort Miami to surrender, as has been previously discussed.

On May 21, the sloop *Michigan* was sent to the mouth of the river to meet and escort any supplies or reenforcements headed for the fort. One hundred and twenty more Chippewas from the Thames River in Canada, under Chief Sekahos, reinforced Pontiac, but, the next day's departure of a large force of Wyandots under Takay largely offset this. Pontiac's alliance was already beginning to show signs of weakness. In fact, some of his allies had already sent secret emissaries to Gladwin asking for peace, claiming that they had been forced into the war.

On May 22, and part of May 23, a heavy rain and high winds forced both sides to refrain from hostile activity. Two French blacksmiths were employed making "tomahawks, daggers, spears, and hooks" out of iron and steel from the warehouse.[48]

On the afternoon of the twenty-third, it was rumored that the Indians were going to attack with fire arrows, so ladders and containers of water were placed in strategic places around the fort.

In the days that followed, Pontiac led two attacks on the *Michigan*. Despite his superior numbers—about four hundred warriors in thirty canoes—the ship's crew was able to keep the Indians at bay. In another breach of the accepted rules of war, Pontiac brought Captain Campbell along, using him as a human shield and also forcing him to hail the ship. The defiant Campbell shouted that the Indians were forcing him to tell them to turn to the shore, but that the captain knew his orders and should sail the ship to safety.

Inside the fort, Gladwin was as worried about his provisions as Pontiac was on the outside. He appointed a committee of three men to inspect the houses of all of the French habitants in the fort and confiscate any surplus food, oil, tallow, and other necessary supplies, for which proper receipts were given. The seized supplies were then transferred to a common storehouse.

On May 24, at about eleven o'clock in the evening, the Indians began firing on the fort from Jacques Saint Martin's house near the flag bastion. They had prepared a large amount of combustible material to try to set fire to the stockade, but none of them dared approach close enough to attempt it. The British did little in reply to the Indians' fire until they heard one warrior speaking in a manner that caused them to believe that he was a leader. At that, they fired a four pounder loaded with solid and grapeshot toward that spot, after which they heard a death song, and the Indians' fire slackened considerably.

On May 25, a group of fifteen Frenchmen met with Pontiac to complain about how they were being forced to support his war effort. They strongly rebuked Pontiac for the way he had been treating the French habitants and ended by asking him if he thought the French king "will give you presents to cover up the wrong you have done to us? On the contrary, he will regard you as rebellious children and traitors, and instead of petting you he will make war upon you, and then you will have two nations upon you. . . ."[49]

Pontiac reminded them that he was not fighting for the Indians alone, but for the French as well. He agreed that they might have suffered some inconveniences, but that they were worth it because of the benefits the French too would enjoy when the British were defeated. He then made a subtle threat: "I know very well, also, that there are some among you, my brothers, who side with the English in making war upon us and that grieves me. As for them, I know them well and when our Great Father returns I shall name and point them out to him, and they will see whether they or we will be most satisfied with the result in the end."[50]

He concluded by saying, "I am French, and I want to die French, and I repeat that it is altogether yours interests and mine that I avenge."[51]

Pontiac then requested that the Indian women be allowed to plant corn in the habitants' fields, and they agreed. In fact, some of the French even plowed the fields for the Indians. Just how voluntary the French cooperation was is open to question. In his diary, Lieutenant Hay wrote that Pontiac "reigned at this time with most despotic sway over the French, making several of them plow land for him to put corn in the ground, and after they had done would kill their cattle."[52]

There were two limekilns near the river that the Indians were using for cover as they fired on anyone going to or from the water. Gladwin ordered construction of a portable bastion to be placed in a position to offer cover from this danger. Because there was no lumber in the fort, wooden walkways were taken up and used. The work was done on the fort's parade ground and was completed by five o'clock in the evening. The structure then had to be carried into location piece by piece. The habitants in the fort and many of the soldiers formed a line and passed the pieces out through an artillery embrasure in the river wall. Once everything was all bolted together, an attempt was made to raise it in to place, but it was unsuccessful because of a lack of manpower and because the Indians, seeing what was been done, opened up a steady fire on the workers. Another attempt was made at dawn the next day, and it was successful.

That same evening, the Indians received word that Fort Sandusky had been taken without a single Indian casualty.

Cuyler's Defeat (May 28)

On May 13, Lieutenant Abraham Cuyler of the Queen's Rangers left Fort Niagara with ninety-six men in ten bateaux, carrying 139 barrels of provisions for Detroit. At that point, the party was unaware of the uprising. At ten o'clock in the evening on May 28, they landed at Point Pelee, some twenty-five miles from the mouth of the Detroit River. As they began to set up their camp on the beach, hidden Indians watched them from the trees. A boy and a man were walking along the beach searching for firewood when suddenly the boy was grabbed and an Indian warrior tomahawked him. The man escaped and ran back to camp to give the alarm. Cuyler desperately tried to organize his defense as the Indians rushed them. The surprised soldiers tried to make for their bateaux and escape onto the lake. The Indians commandeered two boats and caught five of those the soldiers occupied. Cuyler and six men managed to escape in one bateau, after the Indians pursued them for a mile. The men met one other boat that had escaped, and together they made for Fort Sandusky. Arriving there the next day, they found the post burned. Out of his force of ninety-six men, only forty escaped, and five of those, included Cuyler, were wounded. Only nine barrels of provisions survived. Unable to continue on to Detroit, the party headed for Fort Presque Isle and eventually returned to Niagara.

The Indians put their prisoners and captured supplies in the bateaux and rowed for their camp near Detroit. The *Michigan* had sailed for Niagara, so they were not afraid of being challenged at the mouth of the Detroit River.

When he heard of the affair, General Amherst was critical of the way the soldiers had conducted themselves. In his journal entry for June 16, he wrote:

> He [Cuyler] disposed of his men in the best manner as he then could, but I fear they must have behaved as ill as possible, probably all fired on seeing the Indians, then on the appearance of some Indians threw away their arms after one shot and run to the lake. With this dastardly shameful behavior they got out with five boats. . . . The Greatest loss will always be where the worse behavior is, and they seem to have lost almost everything.[53]

Amherst's criticism may have been unnecessarily harsh, but the incident shows that the Indians still held a distinct advantage when they could surprise British troops while on the march.

The Siege Drags On

On May 28, Lieutenant Hay was ordered to take twenty men and destroy some breastworks that the Indians had made overnight to the southwest of the fort 125 yards from the gate. They had piled up timbers as tall as a man and supported them by stakes driven in the ground before and behind. What timbers Hay's men could not bring to the fort they burned, and they also cleared the area so that no one could approach within sixty-five yards without being seen.

Bad weather on May 29, allowed only limited activity by both sides. Two bateaux containing eighteen men and one woman were captured as they returned from a supply mission to Michilimackinac. Three successive victories—the fall of Fort Miami, Cuyler's defeat, and the capture of the Michilimackinac party—did much to raise the Indians' morale, and they held a three-day celebration with the rum that they had captured.

On May 30, several young French habitants asked to borrow a fishing seine that the fort used to supply fish for the garrison. It had not been used since the beginning of the siege, and the Frenchmen said if they could borrow it, they would share their catch. Two soldiers who knew how to use the seine went along, but before they could even put it in the water, the Indians started firing on them. They had correctly surmised that the garrison was going to benefit from the fishing and were not about to let that happen.

Also on the morning of the thirtieth, an Indian flotilla with the prisoners and captured supplies from Cuyler's defeat rowed past the fort in the captured bateaux. The beleaguered garrison at first thought that it was a relief force, but to their disappointment they soon saw the Indians in the boats with the captured soldiers. As they passed the fort, the soldiers in the first boat suddenly threw their two Indian captors overboard and made a break for the anchored schooner *Huron*. One soldier was also pulled out of the boat, and, after a struggle, one of the Indians tomahawked him. That Indian was in turn hit over the head with an oar and believed killed. The other three soldiers in the bateau managed to escape to the *Huron*, and they brought with them eight welcomed barrels of provisions, seven of pork and one of flour.

When these prisoners escaped, the Indians landed, bound the rest of their captives, and then marched them safely past the schooner. Once they arrived at Pontiac's camp, the prisoners were tortured and killed in a most cruel manner. Robert Navarre described what happened in his journal:

> [The Indians] made them strip naked, and other Indians then discharged their arrows into all parts of their bodies. Sometimes these poor unfortunates tried to pull back or lie down on the ground to avoid some arrow, but the Indians who were near made them get up by beating them with clubs and their fists. In order to satisfy these tigers thirsting for human blood, the poor victims had to keep standing till they fell dead in their tracks, and then those not engaged in killing fell upon the dead bodies and hacked them to pieces, cooked them, and feasted upon them. Some they treated with dif-

ferent cruelty, slashing them alive with gun-flints, stabbing them with spears, cutting off their hands and feet and letting them bathe in their own blood and die in agony; others were bound to stakes and burned by children in a slow fire.

There was no cruelty savagery could invent which these poor wretches did not suffer. . . . Even the Indian women took a hand, helping their husbands to glut themselves with the blood of these poor victims by likewise inflicting a thousand cruelties upon them. They vied with one another in seeing who could cause the greatest suffering; they slashed them with knife-cuts as we do when we want to lard beef; and some of the women mutilated them to the point of emasculation. . . . However, there were some whose lives were saved by being adopted to work as slaves in the camp of the savages and witness the tyrannical death of their countrymen. . . .[54]

The captured supplies included flour, bacon, and other provision, along with powder and lead, as well as liquor. The Indians got drunk on the liquor and fought among themselves, resulting in the deaths of at least two young warriors.

The liquor-fueled celebration continued on into May 31. Some warriors became so drunk that they took foolish chances in order to prove their bravery. Two of the young men recklessly charged the north gate as if they were going to take the fort all by themselves. The sentries shot them both. One received a musket ball through the head and two buckshots in the body but did not die immediately. He was brought into the fort and put on public display for as long as he lived; then he was buried in the corner of one of the bastions. The second one was shot twice through the body and crawled away before he died.

This same day, Wasson, chief of the Saginaw Chippewas, arrived with two hundred warriors. A council was held in Pontiac's camp, and it was decided to change the emphasis of the siege from attacking the fort to cutting it off so that no more supplies or reenforcements could reach it.

On June 1, two soldiers and a trader, who the Indians had adopted, escaped and came into the fort at about two o'clock in the morning, bringing the news of Wasson's arrival to the garrison.

In spite of the successes elsewhere, things had not been going well for the Indians at Detroit. Although the fort was still bottled up, under Gladwin's dogged leadership, the brave garrison showed no signs of giving up. What was needed was an all-out assault. With their overwhelming numbers, once they were over the walls, the Indians were certain to win. The problem was that this kind of fighting, where losses were inevitable, was against the Indian temperament. Pontiac commanded only so long as his followers believed in him, and they were under no obligation to follow orders that they disagreed with. That left Pontiac with the options of trying to starve the garrison out and trying to prevent reenforcements and additional supplies from reaching the fort.

On June 2, a soldier who was a prisoner of the Ottawas escaped and came into the fort totally naked. He carried a letter that had probably been found in the spoils from Culver's party, giving the details of the Treaty of Paris between France and England. Pontiac had given it to Captain Campbell to read to him through his interpreter. Campbell later helped the prisoner escape with the letter so that Gladwin would be aware of its contents. The news of the peace treaty was celebrated in the fort that evening with a band concert.

On June 4, news reached the Ottawa camp that Fort Miami had fallen and that Fort Pitt was under siege. On the fifth, two barges of supplies and several captured traders were brought into Pontiac's camp.

After several days of light activity, on June 7, the Indians fired on the fort from ten in the morning until seven at night. Because the nearby cover had been removed, they had to shoot from a considerable distance, and they caused little harm. Also on the seventh, word arrived of the capture of Fort Saint Joseph. Pontiac held another council, where plans for attacking the schooner *Huron* were discussed. A night attack using the recently captured barges was decided upon, but, for some reason, the plan was never carried out.

The Indians began firing on the fort again early on the eighth, but a light rain soon caused them to give up. That afternoon, the officers learned of an attack proposed for that night under cover of the rain. The garrison was put on alert, but nothing ever came of it.

Through the journal of Robert Navarre, a good picture of the makeup of Pontiac's force is possible for this period. He reports:

> Around evening of the same day it was learned through a Frenchman that the remainder of the band of Sekahos, chief of the Chippewas of the Thames River, had arrived during the preceding night, and that they numbered 45 men. With the coming of the last band the savages numbered 850, all actually in camp or around the lake, and all of different nations and under different chiefs; there were 250 Ottawas under Pontiac; 150 Potawatomies under Ninivois; 50 Hurons [Wyandots] governed by Takay; 250 Chippewas under Wassoon; 170 of the Chippewas under Sekahos; all of whom were under the authority of Pontiac, their over-chief.[55]

During this time, more chinks began to appear in the armor of Pontiac's alliance. Several groups of Indians quietly approached the fort to talk with Gladwin about peace, saying that they had only joined in the war because they were forced to. Ensign Francis Schlosser and two surviving soldiers from Fort Saint Joseph were also brought in and exchanged for Indian captives. Although there were no wholesale defections, these events did show that Pontiac's hold on his followers was beginning to weaken.

On June 11, a party of twenty men and an officer was sent out to burn one last house that the Indians could use for cover. After successfully completing that mission, the same party emptied and cleaned out the boats and bateaux by the river and made them ready in case they were needed.

On June 12, Lieutenant Hay reported, "Yesterday and today we buried five corpses that we took up in the river, two of whom we knew, but the rest were so mangled that it was impossible for anybody to have the least knowledge of them. . . ."[56]

These victims had been killed the day before and the crew of the sloop had brought them in.

On the June 14, the Indians asked trader Jacques Cavelier for some of his liquor. When he refused them, they became enraged and took all of his liquor as well as the rest of his trade goods and personal provisions.

On June 18, Father du Juanay arrived at Pontiac's village, bringing with him news of the capture of Fort Michilimackinac. The next day, he delivered a letter from Captain Etherington to Major Gladwin explaining the loss of the fort. Also on the eighteenth, Kinonchamek, son of Minavavana, arrived with some Chippewas, as did a number of Delawares and Shawnees. When these bands met in council with Pontiac on the June 19, they chastised him for killing prisoners after they were captured and for making things difficult for the French habitants around Detroit. This, they said, was unnecessary and went beyond the legitimate goals of their rebellion. Kinochamek stated:

> We have learned at home, my brothers, that you are waging war very differently from us. Like you, we have undertaken to chase the English out of our territory and we have succeeded. And we did it without glutting ourselves with their blood after we had taken them, as you have done; we surprised them while playing a game of lacrosse, at a time when they were unsuspecting. . . . We made prisoners of them and sent them unharmed to their Father in Montreal. The soldiers tried to defend their leaders; we killed them, but it was done in battle. We did not do any harm to the French, as you are doing; on the contrary we made them guardians and custodians of our captives.

Kinonchamek then said directly to Pontiac:

> But as for thee, thou hast taken prisoners upon the lake and the river, and after having brought them to thy camp thou hast killed them, and drunk their blood and eaten their flesh. . . . Moreover, in making war upon the English thou hast made war upon the French by killing their stock and devouring their provisions, and if they refuse anything, thou hast had thy followers pillage them.

Pontiac in the face of this speech was like a child surprised in some fault with no excuse to give, and he did not know what to say.[57]

After Kinonchamek finished, the chief of the Eries spoke for his people and for the Delawares, delivering a similar message. Pontiac offered nothing in his own defense, and the visitors left for their camps. On June 20, a cannon embrasure was cut into the north wall of the stockade to offer a defense against the Indians firing from that side. On June 21, word came that the sloop *Michigan* was returning from Niagara, and warriors were dispatched to try to intercept it. The Indians built makeshift earthworks on Turkey Island (Fighting Island), where the sloop had to pass. On the twenty-second, word came of the capture of Forts Presque Isle, Le Boeuf, and Venango, all to the east of Detroit. Kinonchamek and his party also departed for Michilimackinac.

On the evening of the twenty-third, the *Michigan* began its journey upriver, but as it neared Turkey Island the wind died, and it was forced to anchor. Soon after dark, the Indians quietly approached the sloop in canoes. A lookout saw them coming and called for the fifty-five soldiers secretly hidden below deck to quietly take up positions to receive them. When the Indians almost reached the ship, the signal for the troops to open fire was given. The night lit up with the flashes of muskets and cannon, and fourteen Indians were immediately killed, with as many more wounded. The survivors beat a hasty retreat and did not try again. The next morning, the sloop sailed back to Lake Erie to await a favorable wind for another attempt to reach the fort.

On Saturday, June 25, bad weather prevented either side from taking any hostile action.

Then on Sunday, June 26, at about four o'clock in the morning, Captain Hopkins and twenty-four men moved quietly out of the fort and surrounded a house about five hundred yards to the northeast, where they hoped to capture two Indians believed to be hiding there. When they searched the house, their prey was gone, but they did bring in two sows with their litters. Robert Navarre remarked,

"In some measure this capture was worth more than the prize they wished to make."[58]

That same Sunday, Pontiac attended Mass at the Wyandot mission. Afterward, he requisitioned three "chairs," (probably sedan chairs) from the French. He forced habitants to carry him and two followers along the shore as they requisitioned provisions from the locals. This time though, no doubt due to the chastisement of Kinonchamek, receipts were given for whatever was taken. Major Robert Rogers later recorded how Pontiac appropriated these supplies, and at the same time he admitted a certain admiration for his foe:

> In the late war of his, he appointed a commissary, and began to make money, or bills of credit, which he hath since punctually redeemed. His money was the figure of what he wanted in exchange for it, drawn upon bark, and the shape of an otter (his arms) drawn under it. Were proper measures taken, this Indian might be rendered very serviceable to the British trade and settlements in this country, more extensively so than any one that hath ever been in alliance with us on this continent.[59]

The commissary Pontiac appointed was Antoine Cuillerier.

The next day, June 27, Pontiac had Campbell write another letter to Gladwin. He advised him again to surrender, this time because Kinonchamek was going to return with eight hundred warriors. Gladwin again stated that he would not even consider any terms until Campbell and McDougall were freed. This time Pontiac answered that he could not do so because he held the two officers in high regard, and he could not let them return to the danger in fort, which he would soon capture.

Favorable winds finally returned on the twenty-eighth, and the *Michigan* was able to make it to the mouth of the River Rouge. Although becalmed there on the twenty-ninth, the sloop was not attacked, and on the thirtieth, it arrived safely at the fort. As it passed the Wyandot village, it fired a broadside of grapeshot, wounding several Indians. When it anchored at the fort, it brought not only reenforcements but also a welcomed 150 barrels of provisions and more ammunition.

Back in New York, at first, General Amherst had been unwilling to believe that the uprising was of major consequence, but by the middle of June, he was beginning to realize that he had a serious problem on his hands. On June 19, he wrote to Virginia governor William Hamilton, "I am taking Every Measure in my power to Assemble all the Force I can so as to be prepared for the Worst that can happen: the Motions of the Savages seem to be more General that I at first Imagined. . . ."[60]

Then, on June 29, he wrote to Colonel Bouquet, "I Wish to Hear of no Prisoners, should any of the Villains be met with in Arms: And Whoever of those who were Concerned in the Murder of Sir Robert Davers, Lieut: Robertson &ca; or were at the Attack of the Detachment going to the Detroit, and that may be hereafter taken, shall certainly be put to Death."[61]

He planned for Gladwin to play an important part in the retaking of the western posts. On July 2, Amherst wrote to Bouquet, "Major Gladwin is to have the Command of the Troops to be Employed in Retaking Possession of any of the Upper Posts that may have fallen into the Hands of the Indians, as well as for Securing that part of the Country for the future. . . ."[62]

During the early hours of July 2, Lieutenant McDougall and two captured traders managed to escape to the fort. They had wanted Captain Campbell to accompany them, but because he was overweight and nearsighted, he declined. He reportedly said, "he would have liked to follow them, but he was shortsighted and feared that in running from one danger he would rush headlong into another which might end his days before his time. He did not want to run any chances of dying till he had to."[63]

Pontiac called the French habitants together for a council on July 2. He criticized them for their indifference and told them now it was time for them to declare either for him or for the English. Along with his arguments in favor of supporting the Indian cause, Pontiac offered the following ultimatum: "I know very well you are going to say you do not side with them [the English], but your are siding with them when you report to them all that we do and say. For this reason there is only one way open today: either remain French as we are, or altogether English as they are. If you are French, accept this war-belt for yourselves, or your young men, and join us; if you are English we declare war upon you. . . ."[64]

One of the Frenchmen, possibly Navarre himself, although he does not claim credit in his journal, held up a copy of the terms of the capitulation of Montreal and reminded Pontiac that all of the Frenchmen were bound by it. If he could somehow find a way to release them from it, then and only then, they could consider joining him.

With his ultimatum, Pontiac offered a war belt, which led a number of French families to move inside the fort for fear that they would be forced to take up arms. One young man however, Zacharias Cicotte, accepted the belt and said that he would go and find other young men who felt as he did. It appears that there were a significant number of the young Frenchmen who were willing to openly support Pontiac, possibly as many as three hundred.[65]

The next morning, on the third, one of the young men who had joined Pontiac regretted his rashness and returned to his home. He brought Pontiac's war belt with him and presented it to his father. The father, who was a friend of Pontiac, took it to him and told him of the folly of enlisting the young Frenchmen in his cause. They would be the first to deny their loyalty and desert him if the war failed, and if it succeeded, then it would be the French who would get the credit and not the Indians. He asked Pontiac to take back the belt and to reconsider using the young habitants. Pontiac thanked his friend for his counsel and did take back the war belt. From then on, the Ottawas did not pressure the French to actively support the war, although the Chippewas and Potawatomies did on several occasions.

About this time, a plan was devised whereby

keys would be made to one of the gates to the fort and then used to unlock the gate on the night before a proposed attack. Although the plan was never enacted, three illicit keys were later recovered.

With his latest reenforcements, Gladwin had been able to post men in two detached blockhouses north of the fort. Four sentries were assigned to each station day and night. Then on July 4, he sent Lieutenant Hay and thirty men out to drive the Indians and some of their French allies from their breastworks northeast of the fort. When their opponents stood firm in the face of Hay's assault, Gladwin ordered Captain Hopkins out with forty more soldiers and some of the loyal French. They outflanked the Indians and drove them from the breastworks, killing two warriors in the process. A soldier who the Indians had once held captive scalped one of the dead, who happened to be the nephew of the Chippewa chief Wasson.

When Wasson heard of this, he went to Pontiac and angrily confronted him. As reported by inhabitant Pierre Labutte, Wasson told Pontiac, "he was the cause of all their ill luck, that he caused them to enter into the war and did nothing himself, that he was very brave in taking a loaf of bread or a beef from a Frenchman who made no resistance, but it was them who had all the men killed and wounded every day."[66]

Wasson demanded that Captain Campbell be turned over to him. Pontiac gave in to Wasson, and the captain was taken to the Chippewa camp. There he was stripped of his clothes, and Wasson killed him with a tomahawk, scalped him, and tore out and ate his heart. The mutilated body was eventually thrown into the river, and as it floated past the fort, it was recovered and given a Christian burial. Pontiac's detention of emissaries Campbell and McDougall had been a serious breach of protocol to begin with, and that he had now allowed the defenseless Campbell to be butchered while in his care was a blot on his honor from which he would never recover.. Wasson too must be held to blame, for he was well aware of Campbell's status—and the protocol in question

was not just a white tradition, but one that both races honored. Campbell was a talented soldier and an honorable man who had gained the respect of both races, and it is unfortunate that he met his end through such treachery.

In a twist of logic that is hard to understand, the Ottawas then demanded that the Wyandots give up Ensign Pauli from Sandusky for them to kill because the Chippewas had killed Campbell. Luckily, Pauli heard of Campbell's death and managed to escape to the fort before he could be handed over.

Inside the fort, Gladwin organized the loyal male French habitants into a militia company, which elected trader James Sterling as their captain. When Lieutenant Cuyler returned to Detroit aboard the *Michigan,* he brought with him a copy of the terms of the Treaty of Paris. Robert Navarre read them to the habitants that remained outside of the fort, making them all the more reluctant to offer any aid to the Indians.

On July 6, the *Michigan,* with Captain Hopkins and Ensign Pauli on board, was ordered to fire on Pontiac's camp. Light winds made for slow sailing, and the Indians had time to move their women and children to safety. But still, considerable damage was done to the camp. To prevent future occurrences, Pontiac moved the village to a new, less vulnerable location about five miles from the fort.

About this time, Pontiac suffered the loss of two significant groups of followers. One contingent of Potawatomies came to speak with Gladwin, saying that they had heard of the peace treaty between England and France and were now going to return to their village. They offered to exchange two English prisoners for a chief that Gladwin held. Gladwin said that despite their recent hostile actions, he would release the chief and recommend them to General Amherst if they brought in all of the prisoners that they still held. He also gave them a belt of wampum to carry to their fellow Potawatomies around Saint Joseph, encouraging them to make peace as well.

When the Potawatomies returned the next day

before leaving to get the rest of their prisoners, some of the Wyandots who also wanted to make peace accompanied them. Gladwin offered them the same conditions—that they release all of their prisoners and cease all hostile actions against the English. On July 9, they returned with Ensign Christie from Fort Presque Isle and eight other captives, including a woman and a child. They were told that they also must return all trade goods that had been plundered before peace would be granted to them, and this they also promised to do.

On the night of July 9, using fire rafts, the Indians undertook an ambitious scheme to burn the two British ships. Four captured bateaux were lashed together and filled with combustible materials. They were set on fire and set to drift downstream with the current and into the ships. Alert sentries saw the fire rafts approaching however, and the ships were maneuvered so that the rafts harmlessly passed them by.

After learning about the defection of the Wyandots, Pontiac and fifteen warriors went to their camp on the morning of the tenth. Although he threatened them for making peace with the English, he was in no position to really do anything about it. A few were persuaded to remain with Pontiac, but the majority under Teata was still committed to peace.

Realizing that he needed another victory to bolster the confidence of his followers, Pontiac decided to try again to burn the two ships on the river. This time, two fire rafts were made up, and the second would be released only after the first forced the ships to take evasive action. About midnight on the eleventh, the first raft was launched. Aboard the *Michigan*, Captain Hopkins had a cannon fired at the first raft when it was released. The shot so terrified the Indians who were holding the second raft that they let go of it before it was set on fire. The British hooked it as it passed by and pulled it ashore. Pontiac's second attempt to burn the British ships had also failed. Lieutenant Hay speculated that this effort "was not entirely the invention and work of Indians. . . ."[67]

The next day, the *Huron* was sent to Niagara for more supplies and a request for fifty more men.

The Potawatomies came to the fort on July 12, with their prisoners—three traders and seven soldiers. Just as Gladwin was about to release their chief, one of the traders, Chapman Abraham, said that the Potawatomies were still holding a number of prisoners. Gladwin accused them of breaking his trust by not bringing in all of their captives. Just then, Lieutenant McDougall recognized an Ottawa in the group, and Gladwin ordered him seized as a spy and locked up under heavy guard. The Potawatomies left the fort at this point, unhappy that their treachery had been exposed.

The next night, the thirteenth, in order to avenge their treatment in the previous day's negotiations, the Potawatomies attacked the sentinels outside the fort. One of the French militiamen was seriously wounded in the attack, and he died the next evening. He was quickly buried in the Saint Anne parish cemetery to keep his death a secret, but in a short time the Indians received word of it. The slain militiaman was Jacques Cavelier, the same person whose supplies the Indians had recently looted.

On July 18, as a sign of the garrison's growing confidence in their ability to hold out, the water gate was ordered left open from 9:00 a.m. until 6:00 p.m., to be guarded by two sentinels. About nine o'clock that evening, some Indians traded musket fire with the sloop and then verbally insulted the men on board. One of those on board the sloop had been held prisoner for a time and spoke Chippewa fairly well, so he was able to return their insults in kind.

Still not giving up on fire rafts, Pontiac had two barns taken down for lumber. His efforts were reported to the garrison however, and on July 20, Gladwin had five-inch-thick oak planking added to two bateaux, raising their gunwales to the height of a man to protect their crews. He installed a swivel gun in each. When finished, these boats were tested in the river in front of the fort, and they performed very well. On the twenty-first, Gladwin "ordered four grappling-hooks to be rigged, two for each boat, one of each pair supplied with an iron chain fifteen feet long, the other hook made of steel or cast iron and attached to ten fathoms of cable. The two boats thus equipped were to go meet the fire-raft and cast their grappling hooks with the chains upon it, while the other hooks or half anchors were to be dropped; in this way the course of the raft would be arrested and the sloop saved. . . ."[68]

On July 24, the modified bateaux and one barge were sent upriver to check on the construction of the new fire rafts. The Indians, thinking that the approaching boats could be easily taken, came out twenty strong in two canoes to meet them. The English let the Indians get well within range of their guns and then gave them a volley from their muskets and the swivel guns. This caused the Indians to beat a hasty retreat, but they continued to fire from the shore. One soldier was slightly wounded when a ball passed through his hat and tore away a lock of his hair. Although the soldiers did not find the new rafts, the Indians gave up further construction of them because they knew that the armed bateaux would intercept them.

On the twenty-fifth and twenty-sixth, a large council was held where the entire strategy of the war was apparently discussed among the Ottawas, Chippewas, Wyandots, Eries, and Delawares. Pontiac was able to instill a renewed enthusiasm in his followers, even the Potawatomies and most of the Wyandots. It was fortunate, because at about the same time, his delegation to Fort de Chartres returned with news that was less than encouraging. Major de Villiers advised the French habitants to take no part in the uprising and sent word to Pontiac that he could send no aid because of the rumored peace treaty between France and Great Britain. He had sent

envoys to New Orleans to determine if it was true, and if not, then he would offer what support he could. Of course the truth was already known at Detroit.

On the night of July 28, a heavy fog hovered over the Detroit River near the fort. About half past four in the morning, the sound of musket and cannon fire was heard from the direction of the Wyandot village. Captain Hopkins and a dozen volunteers quietly boarded a bateau and went out to check on the activity. For a while, all was silent again, but then, out of the early morning fog, a line of bateaux filled with British soldiers appeared. It was Captain James Dalyell and his command of 260 men—a force larger than the fort's current garrison. Accompanying Dalyell was Robert Rogers, the famous Ranger.

The Battle of Bloody Run

James Dalyell was a well-connected and ambitious young officer. First commissioned a lieutenant in the 60th (Royal American) Regiment in 1756, he was one of the promising young officers Colonel Thomas Gage selected for the newly raised 80th Regiment of Light Armed Foot, which was intended to eventually replace the expensive and sometimes unruly American Rangers. In December 1757, he was awarded a captain's billet in the 80th. After a string of British victories, the defeat of New France was inevitable, and many officers were facing reduction to half pay. In September 1760, Dalyell, no doubt with the help of influential friends and relatives, was able to secure a captain's position in the prestigious and secure 1st Regiment of Foot. It should be noted that under the preferment system of the British army at the time, the progress of Dalyell's career was not unusual, and he had proven on numerous occa-

Facing page. Captain James Dalyell, by Cosmo Alexander. This is the only known portrait of Dalyell, and it is the first time it has been published in a historical publication. Courtesy of the Honorable Tam and Mrs. Kathleen Dalyell, the House of Binns, Linlithgow, Scotland.

Overleaf. *Ambush at Bloody Run*, July 31, 1763, by Gary Zaboly. Captain James Dalyell and Major Robert Rogers direct British troops just after the ambush at the bridge over Parent's Creek. Courtesy of Todd E. Harburn and Gary Zaboly.

sions that on his own merits, he was a brave, dedicated, and talented soldier.

Robert Rogers, in spite of his many contributions during the French and Indian War, was one of the officers who lost his commission when his unit was disbanded. He had served in the Cherokee War as captain of a South Carolina Independent Company, but had arrived too late to take part in any of the action. With Amherst's assistance, he traded his South Carolina commission for one as captain of a New York Independent Company so that he could be closer to his new wife. It was at Amherst's personal request that Rogers joined the Detroit relief expedition. Although he had once been Dalyell's superior, he now would be serving under him, but he was willing to do so "in Obedience to the Calls of my Country."[69]

Having met Pontiac on his 1760 expedition, with his typical bravado, Rogers sent him a gift upon his return to Detroit:

> In 1763, when I went to throw provisions into the garrison at Detroit, I sent this Indian a bottle of brandy by a Frenchman. His counsellors advised him not to taste it, insinuating that it was poisoned, and sent with a design to kill him; but Ponteack, with a nobleness of mind, laughed at their suspicions, saying it was not in my power to kill him. . . .[70]

For the relief expedition, Robert recruited his brother James as his lieutenant and several bateaumen and New York Provincials to serve as Rangers, about forty men in all.[71]

This unit is different than the Queen's American Rangers under Captain Hopkins and can be considered a revival of the famous French and Indian War *Rogers' Rangers*. Once they reached Fort Detroit, Rogers' former lieutenant, Caesar McCormack, and several other traders placed themselves under his command. In addition to Rogers' men, Dalyell's force consisted of several companies of the 55th and 60th Regiments. At Fort Niagara he added an additional eighty men from the 80th Light Infantry Regiment, bringing his total to about 260 men.

Along the route, they stopped at the ruins of Forts Presque Isle and Sandusky. From the ruins of Fort Sandusky, they marched three miles inland to the deserted Wyandot village of Junundat, hoping to catch the inhabitants by surprise. Rogers led the advance guard into the town and found it deserted. They gathered up the provisions and furs that were left behind, and then they burned the town and the surrounding cornfields.

As the party approached Detroit, they had to be more concerned than ever about an Indian ambush. Even with the fog that concealed their advance up the Detroit River, they were spotted; sixteen men were wounded and musket fire killed one before they safely reached Detroit.[72]

When he reached the fort, Dalyell immediately pressed Gladwin for the opportunity to strike a decisive offensive blow against the Indians. Amherst had written Sir William Johnson that he hoped that the garrison could now "pursue such Offensive Operations as will Revenge the Death of poor Captain Campbell & the Rest of Our Unhappy Countrymen."[73]

Shortly after the resulting battle, the *Gentleman's Magazine* reported that Dalyell "insisted with the commandant that they might be easily surprised in their camp, totally routed, and driven out of the settlement. . . ."[74]

Many writers have speculated on Dalyell's motives—his headstrongness, his contempt for the Indians' fighting skills, his desire to please Amherst and further his own career, all coupled with a fear that with the new reinforcements Pontiac would give up the siege and slip away without punishment. No doubt there is some truth to all of these theories, but there are also other factors to consider. Dalyell was an experienced officer who had considerable combat experience. As an officer of the 80th, he had been in the thick of the Battle of Fort Anne in 1758 with Rogers and his Rangers. To say that he had no appreciation for the abilities of his Indian adversaries is unrealistic. As an aggressive officer, he no doubt wanted to use the new reenforcements to their greatest advantage, and a surprise attack on Pontiac's own village certainly would have given the English a psychological edge. Even Gladwin had been confident enough to mount a few offensive operations recently, so the concept was not that far out of line.

On the other hand, being new to the siege, he should have paid more heed to Gladwin's experienced counsel. Not only was word of the plan sure to be carried to Pontiac by sympathetic French habitants, but high ground across the river gave a clear view of the interior of the fort, and any preparations for such an attack could easily be observed.

The Indians had already thought of the possibility of such an attack, and, in fact, they had tried to encourage it. On July 30, the Wyandots had burned items that they no longer wanted, loaded the rest of their camp into canoes, and paddled down the river out of sight. They were trying to make the defenders believe that they were departing for good, but once out of sight, the warriors moved back into positions around their old encampment, hoping to ambush any party sent to burn the remains of the village. After waiting patiently for two days, they unhappily moved back into their village.

Scene of the Battle of Bloody Run, near the Players Club on Woodward Avenue in modern Detroit. Photo by Todd E. Harburn.

In the end, Gladwin reluctantly gave his consent for Dalyell's mission. He was allotted 247 officers and men, over half of them from the 55th Regiment. The remainder included a partial company of the Queen's American Rangers, some of Rogers'

newly raised Rangers, and elements of the 60th and 80th Regiments, as well as an officer of the Royal Artillery.

At half past two in the morning, on the brightly moonlit night of July 31, the force silently filed out of the water gate of Fort Detroit.[75]

Because of the weather, which was described as sultry, the soldiers were stripped down to their waistcoats, and all were armed with muskets, bayonets, and swords. Captain Robert Gray of the 55th was second in command and Captain James Grant of the 80th was third. Lieutenant George McDougall was adjutant, and Lieutenants Edward Abbott of the Royal Artillery and Diedrich Brehm of the 60th followed alongside in the two armed bateaux. Lieutenant Archibald Brown of the 55th was in command of the twenty-five-man advance guard, while Dalyell and Gray led the main body. Captain Grant was in charge of the rear guard. Strangely, Robert Rogers, the most experienced Indian fighter in the group, was with the main body instead of with the advance guard. Two brave and loyal French habitants, Jacques Duperon Baby and Jacques St. Martin, acted as guides. About a mile and a half from the fort, the party was formed into platoons. If they were attacked from the front, they were to return fire using a technique known as street firing. The front rank would fire a volley and then retire to the rear and reload. The second rank would do the same, then the third, and so on, so that the column would keep up an almost continual fire to the front.

Two miles from the fort, the column approached a narrow wooden bridge across Parent's Creek, near Baptiste Meloche's farm (modern Elmwood Cemetery). As Gladwin had feared, Pontiac had been informed of the attack and chose this spot to wait in ambush. He had deployed his approximately 400 warriors into two main bodies. The largest, about 250 strong, he sent well to the rear, ready to cut off the British retreat. The rest secreted themselves around Meloche's house and fences and behind a ridge just across the bridge. A bright moon illuminated the road as the wary column advanced.

The Battle of Bloody Run, July 31, 1763, by Gary Zaboly. Major Robert Rogers and Rangers in action at the Jacques Campau House. Courtesy of Robert J. Rogers and Gary Zaboly.

As the first men of Brown's advance guard reached the middle of the bridge, the noise and flash of dozens of Indian muskets broke the nighttime stillness. Several men dropped, and Brown was wounded in the thigh. The main body responded quickly, advancing across the creek and driving the Indians from the nearby ridge. Dalyell too received a wound in his thigh, but it did not take him out of the action.

Just as they heard the firing to the front, Grant's rear guard took a heavy volley from their left flank. Grant quickly faced his men toward the unseen threat and fired a volley of his own, caus-

ing the Indians to fall back, with the British following in pursuit. When he heard the firing behind him, Dalyell realized that the enemy was trying to cut him off, and immediately he sent orders to Grant to secure the houses and fence lines along the road to keep the path of retreat open.

At the first fire, Rogers and a party of Rangers took possession of the Jacques Campau house and were able to protect the column's exposed flank from that position. Rogers reported that his men "kept up a very brisk fire through the Windows of the House, which were very large; but I fortified them with Beaver Skins as there were many in the House, and also the Chamber, beating the Boards off the Roof, and making a Breast-Work of them with Skins."[76]

Firing on the main body continued with great intensity. Dalyell filled Brehm's bateau with as many wounded as he could and sent it back to the fort. He then went to the rear and conferred with Captain Grant, who urged him to either press on or retreat, for staying in place would only give the Indians more time to surround them. Dalyell decided to retreat and returned to the main body to give the orders. Initially, the withdrawal was conducted in good order, with Rogers and the Rangers giving effective covering fire from the Campau house. Grant was ordered to fall back to an orchard and nearby house to provide additional cover.

The Indians still held one strong position along the road, using a pile of firewood and the basement of a house under construction for cover. From here they were able to delay the retreat for a full hour. Finally, a headlong charge dislodged them. While rushing to aid a sergeant of the 55th who was wounded in the charge, the brave Dalyell was fatally shot.[77]

Captain Gray was also seriously wounded in the charge, but the Indians were forced to flee. Several of the wounded were placed in Abbott's bateau, which was sent back to the fort for more ammunition as the retreat continued.

With Dalyell's death, Lieutenant McDougall notified Captain Grant that Captain Gray was also badly hurt, and he, Grant, was now in command. Lieutenant James Blain brought word that Rogers' party was now cut off and under attack from all sides. Grant ordered Lieutenant Brehm to move up with his

bateau and lay down a heavy fire so that Rogers' men could make their escape. He also sent Ensign Pauli back to the excavated basement with twenty men to keep the road open for them. With this assistance, Rogers was able to bring his men to safety after holding his position for about two hours with the loss of only two men. The rest of the withdrawal went smoothly, with small groups covering each other then withdrawing in succession until the survivors had safely reached the fort. By eight o'clock in the morning, it was all over.

Dalyell, who Lieutenant Hay said had "behaved with all the bravery in the world," was dead.[78] In addition, one sergeant, and eighteen men had been killed. Captain Grant and two other officers were wounded, along with thirty-nine men. Three of these later died of their wounds. An unknown number were also taken prisoner. In all, the losses amounted to about twenty-five percent of the original force. The exact number of Indian losses is not known, but they were relatively light. Jehu Hay said they had five killed and eleven wounded. In a letter to Horatio Gates, Lieutenant James MacDonald said he believed there were

A surviving section of Parents Creek in Elmwood Cemetery, Detroit.
After the battle it became known as "Bloody Run."
Photo by Todd E. Harburn.

seven killed and a dozen wounded. The Chippewa Peewash said that six Indians had been lost.[79]

The Indians recovered Dalyell's body. They cut out his heart and rubbed it on their prisoners' faces. They also cut off his head and mounted it on a pole. The next day, Jacques Campau took what was left of the body to the fort for burial. It was reported that after his victory, Pontiac held a feast at which he served the flesh of some of the dead soldiers as meat. When he heard of Dalyell's death, General Amherst wrote in his journal that he lamented "the loss of a worthy man and most excellent officer."[80]

After the battle, the water of Parent's Creek ran red with the blood of the fallen soldiers, and ever since, it has been known as Bloody Run. Until it was cut down in 1886, a huge tree along the line of march, measured at sixteen feet in circumference by historian Benjamin Lossing in 1860, still bore bullet scars from that fateful day. Today, the modern metropolis of Detroit has obliterated virtually all traces of the desperate fight.

Chapter V
The Uprising Spreads East: The Siege of Fort Pitt and the Pennsylvania Posts
Summer 1763

To crush the little opposition they may dare to offer along the Road. . . .
Colonel Henry Bouquet

The Siege of Fort Pitt Begins

It is now time to turn our attention to the Indian activities at Fort Pitt and at the other eastern posts caught in the uprising. At Fort Pitt, Captain Simon Ecuyer of the 60th Regiment, a former Swiss officer and friend of Colonel Bouquet, was in command of the largest and most expensive of the western posts. From late December 1762, Ecuyer was aware of the mounting Indian unrest, getting regular reports from Pittsburgh-based Indian Department deputies George Croghan and Alexander McKee, as well as from various traders.[1]

In early December, Croghan held a conference with the Ohio Country Seneca, Delaware, and Shawnee tribes, during which they declared their noninvolvement in the proposed 1761 uprising. The Indian agent reported:

[I] had an opertunity of Sakeing with Several preseple Warrers of the Sinicas Dallaways & Shaunas all wh[ich] Made No Scruple of Confesing ye belt Menshon[e]d in Mr Mckees Intilagence & Say thet its ye Belt Given to the Waweaughtannas [Ouiatenons or Wea Indians] by ye french offiser att ye Elinoies: they Say they Never Intended to make Warr on ye English, Butt Say its full time for them to prepair to Defend themsleves & thire Cuntry from us who they are Convens[e]d Designe to make Warr on them. They Say if we Did Nott Intend that we Wold Nott prohibitt ye Sale of as much powder

& Lead as wold Suply them to hunt with nor Refuse thire Warrers powder & Lead & other Nesesarys to Carey on ye Warr against ye Southren Indians thire Natural Enemys [i.e. the Cherokees] . . . .

Itt is Cartian that ye Dallaways have Received a Belt from ye Indians on Susquehanna [Senecas] & Sence that has ordred all thire Warrers to Stay Near there Towns to hunt this Winter and apeers More Sulky then usul to the Treaders Resideing Amungst them Its Lucky that those Indians & ye Indians over ye Lackes are Nott upon good Terms with Each other att present how ever if any of them Should brake with us itt must End in a Gineral Indian Warr with us . . . .[2]

Another Shawnee chief (most likely Red Hawk) confirmed the same information to Ecuyer. The chief came to Fort Pitt almost two months later in January 1763 and assured the British commandant that he was "very sorry to tell you that all the Indian Nations are very Jealous of the English. . . ." and that those reasons were "the true Cause of all this Jealousy."[3]

Although the different tribes would eventually unite in the uprising, that jealously would be among the reasons for their failure in the long term. Croghan was prophetic, and his fears were realized as the uprising rapidly spread east among the Ohio Country tribes and New York and Pennsylvania Senecas. Mckee had reported these same sentiments. He had gone to the Delaware and

Shawnee villages between January and April to assure the tribes that the treaty only ceded to the British the lands that the French had actually possessed. He also continued to press the Indians to return the remainder of their white captives. This was a very difficult task for a multitude of reasons, especially because the prisoners were widely dis-tributed even to the far western Great Lakes. In addition, a substantial number had been assimilat-ed into the native culture and had no desire to return.

The Indians continued to express their com-plaints to McKee, as they had Croghan, Bouquet, and Ecuyer. They were concerned with the contin-

Fort Pitt Under Siege, by Robert Griffing. Indian warriors survey the fort and its British garrison from the north side of the Allegheny River during the siege. Courtesy of Robert Griffing and Paramount Press.

ued influx of settlers into their lands, as well as differences over trade and supplies. Mckee related these issues upon his return, and they were further addressed in a series of conferences held at Fort Pitt later that month.[4]

The situation around Pittsburgh was tense, just as it had been around Detroit. It was clear that if war with the British broke out, regardless of who was responsible, other tribes would follow—which is exactly what occurred once Pontiac took the initiative.

Captain Ecuyer's attention had been temporarily diverted when another devastating flood hit Fort Pitt in March. While damage was not as severe as it had been the year before, the repairs only added to the existing stress.[5]

Despite the damage to the fort and concern over the cost of repairs, Ecuyer still had to tend to the usual garrison business and Indian affairs. Toward the later part of May, while still unaware of Pontiac's siege of Detroit, some of the merchants at Pitt began to notice peculiar behavior among the local Indians. On May 29, Ecuyer related that Mckee had informed him that the Mingoes and Delawares had traded a quantity of furs for as much powder and lead as they could get. Later, it was discovered that their nearby towns were abandoned, that they had stolen rum and several horses from the way station at nearby Bushy Run, and that they robbed a trader on the road. On that very same day, Ecuyer received news that the same Indians that the Delaware Wolfe led had attacked civilians. Similar to Pontiac's actions at Detroit, the Indians began attacking civilians at their homes in the outlying regions around Fort Pitt. Ecuyer further noted:

> As I was going to close my letter 3 men arrived from [William] Clapham's [Sr.] with the unfortunate news, that yesterday at 3 o'clock in the afternoon, the Indians killed Clapham, and pillaged and massacred everything in his house [one of Clapham's men, a woman, his wife, and one child]; these 3 men were at work and escaped through the woods. I sent them at once with arms to warn our people at Bushy Run. . . . I tremble for our small posts; as for this one, I shall answer for it. If any persons are to come here, they must have an escort, for the situation is serious.[6]

Trader William Trent, formerly an officer in the Virginia regiment, also noted the above incident and added, "the women that were killed at Colonel Clapham's were treated in such a brutal manner that decency forbids the mentioning." [7] Trent was soon after made commander of the militia at Fort Pitt and received high praise from Ecuyer for his assistance and advice during the siege. Like Lieutenant Jehu Hey at Detroit, Trent kept a journal throughout the siege of Fort Pitt, which corroborates Ecuyer's and other accounts during those weeks, often providing additional detail.

The following day, Ecuyer reported further attacks:

> Yesterday evening the Indians massacred the two men we had at the saw mill; they took both scalps and left a war club or tomahawk, which means I think, a declaration of war. At the same time they stole four of the King's horses. . . being at Tuscavaiva [Tuscarawas, a Delaware village near present-day Boliver, Ohio]. . . . Beaver [also known as Tamaqua, a Delaware chief; Shingas, another Delaware chief was also present] had warned Thos. Cohoun [Calhoon], a trader to depart immediately with all the white men that he could take, fourteen in all. . .but when they reached Beaver Creek they were attacked, and he alone arrived here with much difficulty. He thinks the whole party was killed, for he heard 7 or 8 death crie. . . .[Actually two men in his party survived and arrived safely at Fort Pitt].
>
> I think the uprising is general. . . . I think according to reports that I am surrounded by Indians. I am neglecting nothing to give them a good reception, and I believe we shall be attacked tomorrow morning. With the help of God I am passably ready. Everyone works and I am not sleeping; but I am afraid that my Express will be stopped.
>
> I have formed two militia companies, which amount to 80 or 90 men. I have had the oxen and cows brought near in case of need. In short I have neglected nothing, and will spare neither care nor trouble. I would wish that I were capable of doing more in the service of the King, whom I have the honor of serving. Whatever happens I shall do all in my power. Excuse haste as they say.[8]

The Delaware chiefs had sent false information with Calhoon that Detroit had been taken and that they did not plan to join the uprising, pledging their friendship to the British. However, this was suspect, as they had not permitted Calhoon's party to bring any of their arms, saying that the three Indians who were sent to guide them to Fort Pitt were sufficient. During the journey, Calhoon was informed that Detroit had not completely fallen but was besieged.

The siege of Fort Pitt had begun and the situation was indeed serious. The Delawares, Mingoes and Shawnee were the first area tribes to accept belts from Pontiac and join the insurrection. The surrounding area was infiltrated with Indians for about a mile, and travel to the outlying settlements was blocked or hindered. Although Ecuyer sent couriers to warn the posts at Venango, Le Boeuf, and Presque Isle, they were either forced back or killed. Ecuyer managed to have his letters of May 29, and May 30, sent out to Bouquet, which reached him in Philadelphia by June 5. During the preceding four days, Ecuyer and his garrison, along with the inhabitants, continued preparations for the defense of the post, which he described in detail:

> My garrison consists of 250 men in all, as many regulars as militia, all very determined to conquer or die. . . . Here is a summary of our work; I have demolished the lower town and brought the wood into the fort. I have had the upper town burned. Everybody is in the fort where I have had two ovens and a forge built. I have surrounded our bastions with barrels full of earth, made good platforms and embrasures for our cannons. I have a good entrenchment on the mined bastion, and on the two curtains left and right of it; all around the ramparts my men are covered by strong planks fastened by stakes with an opening between two for rifle fire without being exposed in any way. . . . I have likewise made batteries at the neck of the bastions which connect with the barracks. I have had all the powder of the merchants stored in the King's magazine. I have also prepared everything in case of fire, my bastions are all provided with casks full of water, as well as the interior of the fort. The women are appointed for this service, every one must be called upon for work in this life. The rascals are burning the surrounding houses, they have burned the saw mill. . . . I have

made Trent Major commanding the militia in our companies, giving the best to the Grenadiers. Since they are mixed with our men, we can draw better parties from them. Three companies serve 24 hours, and at two o'clock in the morning the whole garrison is at its post or place of alarm, so that I believe we are guarded against any surprise. . . . [9]

Word of the attack on Fort Pitt quickly spread east among the settlements. This resulted in panic, causing the settlers to abandon their homes and personal effects and flee to the nearest forts, either Fort Ligonier or Fort Bedford. Small intermediate posts at Stoney Creek, Juniata Crossings, and Fort Burd were abandoned, with the latter's garrison transferred to Fort Cumberland in nearby Maryland.[10]

The Eastern Dependent Posts Fall

Fort Ligonier (June 2)

Two other abandoned posts, Forts Lyttleton and Loudoun, were temporarily regarrisoned later in July. Fort Ligonier, about fifty miles east of Fort Pitt (Ligonier, Pennsylvania) had received warning from the Byerlys and other families who had reached there safely. The commandant was Lieutenant Archibald Blane, whose garrison numbered only eight Royal Americans. Ligonier, like most of the other Pennsylvania forts, was in severely neglected condition. It was a vital post, as the last major stop before Fort Pitt. After establishing a

Reconstructed Fort Ligonier. Photo by Tim J. Todish.

perimeter around Fort Pitt, the Indians wasted no time attacking Ligonier and harassing the outlying areas. Lieutenant Blane described the action:

> By the two Expresses from Capt Ecuyer, which I hope you have received, you would be informed of the proceedings of the Indians, therefore, shall only inform you, of what relates to my Garrison, which Thursday last [June 2], was attacked by a body of Indians, about five in the Morning but as they only fired upon us from the skirts of the Woods, I contented myself with giving them three Chears, without spending a single shot upon them, but as they still continued their poping, upon the side next the Town, about five P.M. I sent the Serjt of the Royal americans with a proper detachment to Fire the Houses, which (I believe) effectutaly disapointed them in their plan, for soon after they all disapeared; nor has any shewn themselves since; All the Inhabitants from Bushy run to Stony Creek are safe here. . . I am so hurried with my <u>medly</u> that I hope you'll excuse the uncorrectness of my Letter. . . .[11]

For the next several weeks, like Fort Pitt, Ligonier would be under siege. Blane organized a militia from among the civilians and had structural repairs made to the stockade. The Indians heavily guarded the main road, but Blane was able to get couriers in and out and even received a small group of reinforcements from Fort Bedford. In late June, Ligonier was attacked again, which Blane recounted:

> In my former Letters I acquainted you of the first effort the Indians made upon us, and of the disapointment they met, Upon the 21st they made a second attempt, in a very Serious manner for near two Hours, but with the like success as the first, they began with attempting to cut off the retreat of a Small party of 15 Men,

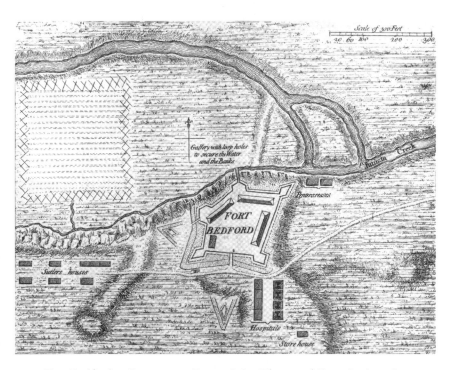

Fort Bedford at Raystown. From *A Set Plans and Forts in America. Reduced from Actual Surveys.* John Rocque, London, 1763. The collection of Seymour I. Schwartz, M.D. Used with permission.

who from their impatience to come at four Indians, which shewed themselves, in a great measure forced me to let them out.

The Enimy (I think above 100) lay in Ambush by the Side of the Creek, about 400 Yards from the Fort, and just as the Party was returning, pretty near where they lay, they rushed out, when they undoubtedly must have succeeded, had it not been for a deep Morrass which interveened, It was imediatly after, they began their Attack, and tho' I dare say they fired upwards of 1000 Shot no body received any damage so far my good fortune in Dangers still attends me. . . .

The 21st at Night and the next Morning they killed 13 of the Inhabitants' Cow, Burned a House the flames of which we could see from the Fort & another the 26th.[12]

Fort Bedford (June 3)

Fort Bedford at Raystown (Bedford, Pennsylvania), some fifty miles farther east, was never openly attacked as Ligonier was. The commandant was Captain Louis Ourry. Although a substantially larger fort than the others along the Pittsburgh–Philadelphia road, Bedford still had a small garrison consisting of only twelve Royal Americans. Bedford received the largest number of displaced families, most of whom wanted to flee farther east to Carlisle, although the officer "Convinceed them that there was greater Danger in Flight than in Standing their Ground,"[13] as the marauding Indian bands would have easily overtaken them. Out of the initial confusion, Ourry was able to organize the defenses at his post. Like his fellow officers Ecuyer and Blane, he organized a militia from the refugees, whom he also praised for their assistance. The fort had been allowed to deteriorate in recent years much like Ligonier and other Pennsylvania forts. Ourry sent a letter to Bouquet on June 3, describing the immediate situation:

> I have also the Satisfaction to find myself well Supported by the generality of the Country People. But, I assure you, the Panic amongst them was so great and, unluckily, too much encouraged by those who had not resolution enough to wait for further intelligence, that it has been with the greatest Difficulty, & utmost exertion of my Weak Oratory, that I could persuade the Wavering to remain, but, having once convinced the most reasonable of the Folly of Flying from a Fort tenable, & well provided, before an Enemy, which, for ought they knew, would overtake them before Night; and removed the grand Difficulty, of those that fled from their Plantations, vizt the want of Subsistance, & Lodging for their Wives & Children: the whole, except a very few, determined chearfully to Assist me in the Deffence of this Barrier
>
> No less than 93 Families are now come here for refuge. I expect Ten more before Night. My Militia Returns amount already to 155 Men, in two Companies, under the Captains [John] Proctor & [Christopher] Lems. My Regulars are increased by Expresses &c: to 3 Corporals & 9 Private, no Despicable Garrison!
>
> We have patched up two Spirit Stirring Drums and our Parrade makes no Small appearance Morning & Evening.[14]

Throughout June and July, Ourry kept Bouquet and Amherst informed of the events as they developed at Bedford and the surrounding area by couriers, who also performed scouting duties. By July 2, this had become increasingly difficult due to wandering bands of Indians attacking anyone caught in the open. Ourry was able to accomplish this by using small parties of experienced woodsmen, even devising a clever disguise in which "the Signal of our Indian Scouts is a piece of our Regimental white Lace, round the head of one of the party, & on seeing friends they all display a yard or two of it in their hands.[15]

The uprising was expanding across the Pennsylvania frontier and into neighboring Virginia, Maryland, and New York, similar to what was happening in the Great Lakes. British authorities soon would be forced to acknowledge how general and serious it had become.

George Croghan was in Philadelphia in early June, and after learning of the hostilities he quickly returned to Fort Pitt. Along the way, he raised twenty-five volunteers at Shippensburg to garrison Fort Lyttleton, another small and decaying fort. Croghan arrived at Fort Bedford on June 14, and assisted in interrogating recently captured Indian prisoners.

During this time, Bouquet and Amherst were planning a major relief effort for Fort Pitt. Political and logistical issues, as well as other events, hampered their plans. Perhaps the most devastating was the loss of the British forts at Venango, Le Boeuf, and Presque Isle along the vital Lake Erie communication route. The Delawares, Mingoes, and Shawnees besieging Fort Pitt pressed the Senecas under Chief Kiasutha to join the uprising and cut off the British posts to the north. The Senecas of Pennsylvania and western New York had long resented the British, a mutual feeling that both Amherst and Bouquet shared. Amherst attributed the hostilities to nothing "but the Rash Attempts of that Turbulent Tribe the Senecas, who Richly Deserve a Severe Chastizment from our Hands, for their Treacherous Behavior on many Occasions."[16]

Ironically, the same day Amherst penned the above, the Senecas at Niagara were "informed this day by a Senecas Chachim [most likely Kiasutha] to quit this place, as they have rec[eive]d a belt from the Indians about Pittsborough, to take up the Bloody Hatchet, and that all the Surrounding Indians in them parts are absoutely determined thereupon. . . . They likewise have sent with the Belt three Scalps that they took in or about Pittsburg. . . ."[17]

Both groups of Senecas would soon join the uprising.

Fort Le Boeuf (June 18)

Ensign George Price, commander at Fort Le Boeuf, had a garrison of thirteen Royal Americans and one woman. He later wrote to Bouquet about the fall of his post:

> The 18th Instant I was attacked and the Indians, taking possession of the lower store fired my House [Fort Le Boeuf] with their Arrows, so that I was obliged to Retreat out of it in the Night which I did unseen & brought in with me Seven Men; Six are still in the Woods but I hope will get in safe some where. We arriv'd at Venango the 20th at One at Night and found the block House burn'd to the Ground. I am a little fatigued but in good health as is most of those that came with me. . . .[18]

Trent, in his journal, further related Price's account of the attack and his courageous attempt to defend the post:

> The 25th. . . . About 5 o'clock in the afternoon, two soldiers belonging to the garrison of Le Boeuf came in and informed us that Ensign Price would be here the next morning. . . .
>
> The 26th, Six o'clock in the morning Ensign Price, with five men came in from Le Boeuf and gave the following account of his miraculous escape from that place. . . . Early in the morning of the 18th instant five Indians came to his post and asked for some tobacco and provisions, which he gave them. Soon after they went off, about thirty men came down the road leading to Presqu' Isle, laid their arms a short distance off, and came and asked liberty to come in and

said they were going to war against the Cherokees, would stay with him that night and that they proposed to pass by Fort Pitt in order to speak with Mr. Croghan; Mr. Price suspecting their design had all his people under arms and would not suffer them to go in, upon this the Indians took up their arms and got to the back of an out store, where they picked out the stones it was underpinned with and got into it, then they began to roll out the barrels of provisions and shoot, fired arrows into the top of the block house which was put out several times, this continued till some time in the night, when Mr. Price, finding it impossible to defend the place any longer or prevent it being consumed, took advantage of the night, got all his people out at a window and made off without being observed, but unfortunately left six of his men and a woman who he supposes fell into the hands of the enemy, sometime after he left the block house, the Indians began to fire upon it, when he came to Venango he found it in ashes, kept the road all the way here and saw the bones of several people who had been killed while going to Vanning: they were Six Nation Indians [Senecas] who attacked him. . . .[19]

The following day, the surviving members of Price's garrison came stumbling in to Fort Pitt:

> Six o'clock in the afternoon four men and one woman of the garrison of Le Boeuf came in, who, it was feared, had fallen into the hands of the enemy; they say they left the other two men of that garrison about thirty miles off, not being able to come along. The other soldier from Presqu' Isle, [Benjamin Gray] who, it was thought, was captured, came in with these people and confirms the account already received respecting that garrison. These soldiers say, soon after they left the fort they heard two guns and the death halloo.[20]

Fort Venango (June 16, or June 17)

Fort Venango was the first British fort lost to the Indians as the hostilities spread along the communication road north from Fort Pitt to Lake Erie, occurring on either June 16, or June 17. Lieutenant Francis Gordon (of Captain Harry Gordon's Com-

Officer, Grenadier Company, 60th or Royal American Regiment of Foot. The grenadiers were stationed mainly at Fort Pitt, although some also served at Forts Detroit and Sandusky. Courtesy of Major General Giles H. Mills, CB, OBE. The Royal Green Jackets Museum, Winchester, England.

pany) commanded the small post of fifteen or sixteen men. Similar in construction to Sandusky, Presque Isle, and Le Boeuf, Venango was essentially a blockhouse surrounded by a small stock-

ade. Because there were no survivors, the only contemporary account of its demise, aside from the scene Price observed, is is the one Mohawk Indian chief Thomas described to Sir William Johnson later the next month:

> Thomas, a Canajoharie Chief, confirmed the account of the taking of Vanango, which was done by a party of Chenussios [Genesee Senecas] residing in the neighborhood thereof, and that after putting the garrison to the sword, they made the officer write the reasons which induced them to act as they had done, which were: first, the scarcity and dearness of powder for these two years past, being obliged to pay 2 deerskins for a gill of powder; and so in proportion, for other articles, and that they complained they were ill treated and never redressed. Secondly, that the many posts which the English kept possession of induced them to believe they intended to posses all their country, for all which they were determined to destroy them. After writing this, **they put the officer to death**, [emphasis by Johnson] and sent the paper with a party of warriors then going to Fort Pitt, in order to do mischief on the communication, where they proposed to drop it, that it might be found by the English.[21]

Fort Presque Isle (June 20)

The attacking force quickly moved on to Fort Presque Isle. The garrison there consisted of twenty-nine men along with one woman and some traders. It was larger than the others along the communication route—the better to protect the link between the major posts at Pitt, Niagara, and Detroit. In command was Ensign John Christie, whom Amherst initially praised for his resolution "in being prepared for the Defence of his Post."[22]

The young officer, however, would quickly lose favor with his superiors. A force of about 200 Wyandot, Chippewas, and Ottawas from Detroit joined the Senecas and Delawares. They attacked on the morning of June 20, from the heights overlooking the fort. Christie later described the action to Gladwin during a court of inquiry at Detroit after the Indians released him on July 9:

I am sorry to have to acquaint you of my misfortune. On the 20th June at day break I was
surrounded at my Post at Presqu'Isle by about
Two hundred Indians a Quarter of an hour
after they began to Fire on the Block house and
Continued all that day very smartly. Likewise
Fire Arrows were threwn into the Roof of the
Blockhouse and Basteions I received my greatest hurt from the Two Hills and one assending
from the Lake and the other from the Bottom,
they having made holes in the night to secure
themselves. Notwithstanding two or three did
their endeavour to get in the Trench were killed
which made them Cease fireing some hours at
which they was employed in digging of Passes
threw the Earth In Order to get at the bottom of
the house. 21st They Commenced fireing as hot
as ever and also with Fire Arrows which set the
house a Second time on fire the same day the
Barrels of Water I had provided Was spent in
Extinguishing said Fires, and found it impossible to get at a Well which was sunk on the
Parade therefore was Obliged to sink one in the
house by hard Labour whilst we were digging
to get at the well we were again set on fire but
got it extingushed by throwing of some shin-
gles from the Roof. At the same time they had
approached as far as the Commanding Officers
Room on the parade they set it on fire and
Communicated it to the Faishens [Fascines]
round the Fort we Continued our Fireing till
midnight when one of them whom spoak
French informed me it was in vain to pretend to
hold out for they could now set fire to the
house when they pleased if I would not Surrender we may Expect no Quarters finding
they had made their approaches aforesaid That
they Could set me on fire above and below. My
Men being Fatagued to the greatest Extreamity
and not being able to Extingushing such fireing
and resist their Numbers I asked them in English if there was any amongst them which
understood that Language an English Man
then Called up to me that if I Ceased my fireing
he would speak with me he told me they were
of the Urin [Huron or Wyandot] Nation that
had been Compelled to take up Arms by the
Ottawas ag[ains]t Detroit that there was part of
other Nations with him that they Only wanted
the house and that they would have now soon

Wyandot (or Huron) Indian Warrior, by Dirk
Gringhuis. Courtesy of Mackinac State Historic Parks.

that I might have libberty to go with my Garrison where I pleased. I desired them to leave of their fireing and I would give them an answer in the morning earily. After Considering my Cituation and of the Impossibility of holding out any longer I sent out two Solders as if to Treat with them that they may find out their Disposition & how they had made their Approaches and to give me a Signall if they found what I imagined to be true finding it to be so, and the vessels Hover[in]g between the two points all the while I was engaged could give me no Assistance I came out with my People they then took us Prisoners myselfe and four Soldiers & a Woman was brought to the Wiandote Town [at Fort Detroit] the rest of my Garrison was taken by the other Nations; I was Delivered up to Detroit with One Soldier and a Woman the other two they killed at their Town the night I arrived there I was delivered up to Fort Detroit the 9th Instant.[23]

When the Indians broke their promises and took Christie and the others prisoner, the aforementioned soldier Benjamin Gray (of Capt. Cochrane's Company) and two others fled into the woods. They later made their way safely to Fort Pitt, luckily joining up with the survivors from Le Boeuf along the way. Gray related to Captain Ecuyer that he was sure the attacking force at Presque Isle was "of four nations, that is, Ottawas, Chippewas, Wyandots, and Senecas. . . ."[24]

Christie later confirmed this at his court of inquiry, where he elaborated on further details of the attack.[25]

During a court of inquiry at Detroit three days earlier, Lieutenant Cuyler of the Queen's Rangers, who had been on board the schooner *Huron* en route from Niagara to Detroit, said he witnessed the attack out in Lake Erie and "That he was not able to give them any assistance having nothing but a small Boat to land men in which would not carry above ten at a time, and being two miles from the shore. . . ."[26]

Following the loss of Presque Isle, both Bouquet and Amherst were furious with Christie. They condemned his actions in extremely harsh language in correspondence with fellow officers.

Bouquet wrote to Ecuyer:

You can imagine how I look upon the shameful conduct of Christie who dishonors the corps by an infamous capitulation with savages who have never kept one, and delivers up to them a post of the greatest importance. . . . I do not know the reason for the loss of Venango, hence I shall say nothing about it. As regards to Ensign Price's conduct [at Le Boeuf], it will be examined and he will be acquitted or condemned on the principles of duty and honor, and on the circumstances. . . .[27]

On the same day he further commented to Ourry:

Humanity makes me hope that Christie is dead, as his scandalous Capitulation for a Post of that consequence, & so impregnable to Savages, deserves the most severe Punishment: The Same of that Action will be a lasting Blot upon the Corps he belonged to. I hope that the Conduct of those who remain will be worthy of Men of Honour, who now how to meet Death with Firmness, if their duty & the Service of their Country require it; and who would scorn to disgrace themselves by the least Appearance of a dishonorable Act.[28]

Amherst was just as critical. In his personal journals, he wrote:

It is amazing that an officer could put so much faith in the promises of the Indians as to capitulate with them, when there are so many recent instances of their never failing to massacre the people whom they can persuade to put themselves in their power. The officer, and garrison would have had a much better chance for their lives if they had defended themselves to the last, and if not relieved, they had confided to a retreat thro' the woods or got off in a boat in the night. . . .[29]

He further added in a letter to Bouquet on the same date:

A Fixed Resolution should be taken by Every Commanding Officer, whose Post is Attacked by Savages, Never to Trust to their Promises, but to Defend his Post to the last Extremity. . . . We have so many Recent Instances of their Breach of Faith, in this Particular, that I am Surprized any Officer in his Senses, would Enter into Terms with such Barbarians.[30]

The commander in chief was even more graphic to General Gage:

> There is too much certainty that Presque Isle is destroyed, incredible as it is that Any consideration should induce Ensign Christie to capitulate with the Devils, his brains Must have been turned, and they have beat them out, Indian like, with every excruciating torment which they could contrieve to exercise upon him. . . .[31]

It is fair to suggest that both Bouquet and Amherst were being too harsh in their assessments of Christie's actions. It was easy for them to express such opinions while sitting in relative comfort and safety—Bouquet with a large force at Carlisle en route to Pittsburgh and Amherst in New York City. It was also more reasonable to expect the larger posts at Detroit and Pittsburgh, with more troops and resources, to hold out. Applying these same standards to the smaller posts was unfair. It can be reasonably argued that it was the better part of valor for Christie to surrender in the hope of fighting again in the future—particularly because the Englishman assured him with promises of good treatment. Bouquet and Amherst's frustration over the loss of these posts is understandable, but it is undeniable that the officers at the smaller posts faced extremely difficult situations, and whatever decisions they made were under very dangerous circumstances.

Fort Pitt Continues to Hold Out

Amherst and Bouquet Plan for the Relief of Fort Pitt

On June 6, Amherst issued orders for the relief expedition to Fort Pitt. He instructed Major Allan Campbell of the 42nd Regiment "to take Command of Three Companies of Light Infantry of the 17th, 42nd, & 77th Regiments for a particular Service."[32]

The companies encamped at Staten Island near Watson's Ferry and awaited further orders. Within a week, Amherst received news about Pontiac's attack on Detroit, and although he did not believe the rumors that the post was entirely cut off, he reluctantly acknowledged that the "Affair of the Indians, appears to be more General than I had Apprehended. . . . " He "ordered the two Companies of Light Infantry of the 42nd and 77th. . .to march towards Philadelphia, and the Company of the 17th to embark for Albany and proceed to Fort Stanwix."[33]

Amherst was concerned about getting relief to Fort Pitt, and he was also very concerned about the effectiveness of these Highland units. They were reduced in numbers and in poor health due to the ravages of malaria during the recent Havana campaign. He wrote to Bouquet "that they are so reduced as to make but a very small number of Men, the Whole remains of the Nine Companys of the 77th not Exceeding Eighty Men."[34]

Amherst also ordered a detachment of the Royal Artillery to join the expedition.[35] At this time, Amherst had still not heard any definite news that "the Indians have been able to do Mischief at the Detroit or the upper Posts. . . ."[36]

However, as reports continued to reach him over the next several days, he ordered the remaining troops that he had held at Staten Island to proceed on to join Bouquet:

> To effect this most essential Service, I intend to collect agreeable to what I wrote you in my Last, all the Force I can at Presqu' Isle & Niagara, that I may push them forward as occasion may require. I have there fore ordered the remains of the 42nd & 77th Regts., the first consisting of 214 men including officers, & the Latter of 133 men officers Included, which will march this morning or early tomorrow morning under the command of Major Campbell of the 42nd. . . .[37]

It is important to note the political disagreement among the Pennsylvania colonial assembly, which caused additional stress on the military administrators attempting to deal with the insurrection. Both Bouquet and Amherst were in regular correspondence with Pennsylvania governor James Hamilton, urging the colonial assembly to

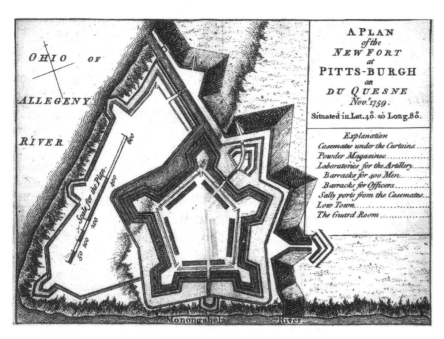

A Plan of the New Fort at Pitts-burgh or DuQuesne. From *A Set Plans and Forts in America. Reduced from Actual Surveys.* John Rocque, London, 1763. From the collection of Seymour I. Schwartz, M.D. Used with permission.

authorize additional Provincial troops for the relief expedition. However, there was considerable disagreement among the assembly members on this issue. Many regarded it as the responsibility of the crown, and there was already a dispute regarding compensation for the Pennsylvania troops that had served in the French and Indian War. When they authorized seven hundred men on July 6, they would not allow them to serve under British officers, including Bouquet, much to his and Amherst's dismay. This was eventually reversed in another vote, but by that time, Fort Pitt had been relieved, and the immediate need for the troops had passed. This incident is another example of the friction between the British military and the colonial governments, a problem that ultimately was one of the causes of the American Revolution.[38]

Once Bouquet received his orders from Amherst, he began making the arrangements for the expedition. Due to a shortage of supplies at Philadelphia ("no powder" as one specific example), the colonel was forced to obtain provisions such as flour, carriages, and ammunition from traders and merchants along the way.[39] Three hundred pack horses, complete with saddles, halters, bells, ropes, etc. were eventually contracted from Robert Callender at Carlisle.[40]

In addition, thirty-two wagons, drivers, and a supply of flour were obtained from (Matthias) Slough and (Joseph) Simon in Lancaster.[41]

The two Light Infantry Companies of the 42nd and 77th Regiments arrived in Philadelphia on June 18, under the command of Captain James Robertson of the 77th Regiment. Bouquet quickly sent them on to Carlisle.[42]

On June 24, Bouquet himself departed with a contingent of Royal Americans to rendevous with the Light Infantry Companies, and all parties arrived at Carlisle on June 28.[43]

That same day, Captain John Stewart (Stuart), with the additional 42nd Company left Philadelphia for Lancaster and Carlisle. The remaining companies of the 42nd and 77th Regiments consisting of 273 men (not counting officers, sergeants, and drummers) under Major Allan Campbell arrived at Ashton, just outside Philadelphia on July 1.[44] As these reserve contingents proceeded to their rendezvous, Bouquet expressed to the commander in chief, "The reenforcement have ordered this way, so considerable by the additional number of officers, will fully enable me to crush the little opposition they may dare to offer along the Road. . . ."[45]

On July 7, Amherst wrote to Bouquet about the fall of Presque Isle, Le Boeuf, and Venango saying, "the Loss. . .gives me great Concern: But it must make no Alteration in my Plan. . . . And I would have you Follow the same Directions I have already given You for Sending Troops forward to Presqu'Isle. . . ."[46] Bouquet was then to continue

Colonel Henry Bouquet, of the 60th or Royal American Regiment. Collection of Lieutenant Colonel Ian McCulloch. Used with permission.

his march to relieve Fort Pitt and the posts along the way from Carlisle, while Amherst was determined to continue efforts to coordinate the relief of Gladwin at Detroit. The general had sent Captain Dalyell for that purpose, and his expedition was already en route.

Once at Carlisle, where he secured the above noted provisions, Bouquet sent Lieutenant Donald Campbell of the 77th Regiment and Lieutenant J. McIntosh of the 42nd Regiment (either James or John; the exact identity is not known) with an advanced contingent consisting of "Two Serjeants,

Two Corporals, and thirty private, of the Two Companies. . . ."[47] onto Fort Bedford, as he was concerned about relieving that post as quickly as possible rather than waiting until the rest of the expedition arrived. Campbell and his thirty men reached Fort Bedford safely on July 9, and Captain James Robertson and the Light Infantry Company arrived two days later, "although much fatigued."[48]

Indian activity near Fort Bedford began to subside due to Bouquet's approaching army and other reinforcements, such as the volunteers at Fort Littleton. Still, the relief columns had to exercise caution, and Ourry's disguised Indian scouts assisted them. Bouquet noted that, although "A general Panick has seized this extensive Country. . . . There appears to be few Savages yet on these Frontiers, but every Tree is become an Indian for the terrified Inhabitant."[49]

The terror Bouquet described was not surprising. Throughout June and July, the Indians continued their pattern of plundering, burning farms, attacking settlers who had chanced returning to their homesteads, and, at times, even those who ventured out from the relative safety of the besieged forts. One incident Captain Ourry noted provides a glimpse of the terror these civilians and their families experienced:

> Yesterday morning soon after Sunrise, a Party of about 20 Indians fired upon Col Croghan's Haymakers in his meadow, & killed & Scalped three men. On the first fire I sent a Party to the Assistance of the Mowers, they were 14 with Arms, & had Sentries without them in the Woods, but on the first Shot the whole run, which gave the Savages the opportunity to Tomahawk & Scalp those they could Catch. Two were brought in alive but died immediately, the third was dead being Shot thro' the body. I buried them all three in the Evening. . . .[50]

As Bouquet's expedition progressed, the siege at Fort Pitt continued. The Indians periodically engaged in sorties to harass the garrison, appear-

Facing page. *Warriors* by Robert Griffing. Scottish Highland soldiers, like the member of the 77th (Montgomerie's) Highland Regiment, shown here, played an important part in the Pontiac Uprising. Because of their fierce courage in battle, the Indians developed a special respect for them. Courtesy of Robert Griffing and Paramount Press.

ing at various locations, including along both rivers and particularly on Grant's Hill (where British forces under Major James Grant had been defeated in the ill-fated 1758 attack against then Fort Duquesne). Captain Ecuyer made every effort to insure that the post was ready for any attack and that soldiers and civilians alike did their part. Fatigue and irritability appeared from time to time, but Ecuyer maintained strict military discipline. Excerpts from his letters and orderly book provide an interesting look at the daily routine and the skirmishes that took place. It also offers a sense of the atmosphere that existed among the inhabitants. His letter of June 26, describes one of the engagements with the Indians:

> [E]xcepting some slight alarms from time to time, until the afternoon of the 2nd, when the savages showed themselves and descended into the plain, driving into the woods a part of our horses, and killing some cattle, after which they attacked the fort from all sides excepting from the other side of the Monongehela, but at a great distance. I had, however, a militia killed and another wounded. I dispersed them a little later with a howitzer and two cannon shots, which assuredly were not without effect. We fired but three guns against these Indians, of whom one was killed. . . . On the night of the 23d and 24th they prowled around the fort to reconnoitre, and after midnight the Delawares asked to speak to Mr. McKee. . . . The returns of the month: the three deaths are three of my men killed. I have besides that a regular wounded, two militia killed and two wounded. The garrison consists of 338 men all counted, 104 women, 106 children. . . .[51]

Throughout the siege, Ecuyer kept up a regular night guard in the five bastions of the fort, usually consisting of about six officers and anywhere from sixty to 112 rank and file.[52]

During June and July, the Indians held several conferences with Ecuyer and McKee. Each time, the Indians professed their friendship, stating that it was the Ottawas and other western tribes who were responsible for the violence. The Delaware and Shawnee chiefs repeated their grievances and asked the British to leave Fort Pitt and return home. Ecuyer thanked them for their friendship, although he obviously was not duped; he related on one occasion that he did "not believe such vagabonds."[53] Ecuyer made it clear that he would defend his post to the end and chastised the Indians for having "attacked without provacation, murdered & plundered our Warriors and Traders, took off our Horses & Cattles, and at the Same time you tell us, your Hearts are good towards your Brothers the English." He further warned with some bravado that if "any one [Indian] should apear near the Fort, or fire upon my Warriors, I shall not only return the fire but shall throw shells about and fire Canons at them with hundred and twenty balls in each, therefore Keep off I don't want to hurt you!"[54]

In all likelihood, the Indians had no intention of allowing the British to leave the fort peacefully, nor would Ecuyer have any reason to believe their promises.

It was at one of these conferences, on June 26, that Ecuyer and Trent gave the Indians blankets and handkerchiefs from the fort's smallpox hospital as presents, hoping to infect them with the disease. The special hospital had been established under the drawbridge entrance of the fort to prevent the "Spreading of that distemper " when it had broken out in the garrison earlier in the month.[55]

It was also during this time that both the infamous letter exchange between Bouquet and Amherst about infecting the Indians with smallpox and Bouquet's suggestion about "Hunting them down by dogs" took place. Amherst's oft-quoted suggestion for use of the dreaded smallpox was written on July 7, inquiring, "Could it not be contrived to Send the Small Pox among those Disaffected Tribes of Indians? We must, on this occasion, Use Every Strategem in our power to Reduce them. . . ." and three days later suggesting to Bouquet that "You will Do well to try to Innoculate the Indians, by means of Blankets, as well as to Try Every other Method, that can Serve to Extirpate this Execrable Race. —I should be very glad your Scheme for Hunting them down by Dogs could take Effect; but England is at too great a Distance to think of that at present."[56] Historians have discussed this proposed germ warfare at length, and some recent analyses suggest that it did not have the anticipated effect.

Some historians sympathetic to the Indian side overlook the fact that the Indians attempted similar tactics themselves when they poisoned the well at Fort Ligonier in 1761. [57]

Meanwhile, Captain Ourry's apprehension was, to a large degree, mitigated on July 11, when the relief detachment under Captain Robertson arrived at Bedford. Campbell's men had reached Fort Ligonier two days earlier on the ninth, and Campbell relieved Blane as commandant due to his seniority. Despite desertions, sickness, and other difficulties, Bouquet's main column reached Fort Loudoun by July 19, and then pushed on to Bedford, arriving on July 25. While at Loudoun, Bouquet sent instructions for Robertson to take a party down to Fort Cumberland, Maryland, to obtain "thirty or more Horses loaded with One hundred and Fifty Weight of Muskett Balls Each. . . ."[58]

The expedition halted at Fort Bedford for a much needed two-day rest. There, Bouquet left one officer and thirty men, who were unable to march farther, to reinforce the garrison. Slowly, the expedition was making its way to Fort Pitt. However, once Bedford and Ligonier were relieved, the siege at Pitt intensified, as the Indians withdrew back there in hopes of taking it before the relief column arrived. Provisions were running dangerously low, and, with the hot weather, there was concern that the resolve of the garrison and inhabitants might waver. Sightings of larger numbers of Indians milling around added to the unrest.

Captain Trent describes a July 28 assault on Fort Pitt by about four hundred Delaware, Shawnee, Mingo, Huron, and Ottawa Indians:

> July 28th, In the morning the Indians were seen crossing the river by Shanopins' Town on horseback or swimming. Half an hour after, about 2 0'clock, they fired on our people in the garden, who I had desired not to stay as I was positive they were coming down, but they paid

no regard to it, they go in with only one man wounded in the knee. Soon after they began firing the fort and continued it the whole day and night. Captain Ecuyer was wounded in the leg with an arrow, a Corporal and one of the men, mortally.

> July 29th, Continued firing on the fort, the whole day, from the Ohio bank, they kept up a very smart fire, this day and yesterday a number of shells were thrown to disperse them, but they only sifted places, this day and yesterday about 1,500 small arms fired on them from the fort. Wounded this day: Marcus Huling's leg broken, Sergeant Hermon shot through the lungs, a grenadier shot through the leg, fired three round shots from a six pounder, as they were passing the river in canoes; obliged them once to throw themselves into the river, one of them said to be cut in two by one of the shot. These two days killed several of them from the fort, one of them wounded and drowned in the river, attempting to swim over and five more seen carried out of the canoe on the farther side of the Ohio, supposed to be wounded. The roofs of he Governor's House and the Barracks much hurt by the enemy's fire. In the night they shot several arrows at the fort, some with fire, mostly fell short.[59]

Ecuyer also provides a look at the constant state of alert and stress that his garrison and the inhabitants were under:

> The officers commanding at bastions are desired not to allow on any account the men to raise fixed shades against the parapet in the night time, as it would not only very much prevent the men from doing their duty in case of attack, but also stop the passage from sending orders back and forwards when required.[60]

Trent briefly outlines the action during the next four to five days, which involved both sides firing random shots and the troops throwing some grenades into the ditch at the Indians. By August

Overleaf:
One Mile to Bushy Run Station, a painting by Robert Griffing, shows the first day of fighting on August 5, 1763. Courtesy of Robert Griffing and Paramount Press.

4, he noted that things were quiet, as most of the Indians had withdrawn to attack the relief expedition that they knew was coming. Surprisingly, Ecuyer still was able to send correspondence to Bouquet. He summarized the events of the last several days, telling of the council with the Indians and of the five-day attack, commenting that he "did not permit any one to fire until they saw the object, and as soon as they showed their noses they were picked off like flies, for I have good marksmen."[61]

Despite the harsh conditions, in the same dispatch the commandant praised his troops for their bravery, high spirits, and willingness to continue the fight. He maintained his sense of humor, particularly regarding his own injury adding, "Only two arrows came into the fort, one of which had the insolence to caress my left leg."[62]

Thus, Ecuyer, and his beleaguered garrison continued to hold out. The relief of Fort Pitt was soon to be, although not without one last major effort by the Indians. After the intense five-day siege and then the sudden departure of the Indians, a sense of dread permeated the garrison that the relief column would not reach them in time. After another six grueling days of waiting, at dawn on August 10, three couriers from Bouquet arrived informing the anxious garrison of the stunning victory near Bushy Run Station.

The Battle of Bushy Run

Many excellent descriptions and analyses of the Battle of Bushy Run, which more correctly should be called the Battle of Edge Hill, have been written over the years, but perhaps Bouquet's own eyewitness account is still the most vivid. His August 5, and August 6, letters to Amherst describe the intense action—the first from the camp at Edge Hill, twenty-six miles from Fort Pitt:

The Second Instant [August 2] the Troops and Convoy arrived at Ligonier where I could obtain no Intelligence of the Enemy, The Expresses sent Since the begining of July, have been either killed, or obliged to return, all the Passes being occupied by the Enemy. In this uncertainty I determined to leave all the Waggons with the Powder, and a quantity of Stores and Provisions at Ligonier, and on the 4th proceeded with the Troops & about 340 Horses loaded with Flour.

I intended to have halted to Day at Busy Run/ a mile beyond this camp/ and after having refreshed the Men and Horses, to have marched in the night over Turtle Creek, a very dangerous Defile of Several Miles, commanded by high and craggy Hills; But at one o'Clock this afternoon, after a March of 17 miles, the savages suddenly attacked our advanced guard, which was immediately supported by the two Light Infantry Companies of the 42nd Regiment, who drove the Enemy from their Ambuscade, & pursued them a good Way. The savages returned to the attack and the Fire being obstinate on our Front and extending along our Flanks, we made a general Charge with the whole Line to dislodge the savages from the Heights, in which attempt we succeeded, without obtaining by it any decisive advantage, for as soon as they were driven from one Post, they appeared on another, till by continual Reinforcements, they were at last able to surround us, & attacked the Convoy lefft in our Rear: This obliged us to march back to protect it; The Action then became general, and though we were attacked on every Side, and the Savages exerted themselves with uncommon Resolution, they were constantly repulsed with Loss. We also Suffered considerably, Capt Lieut [John] Graham, and Lieut. James McIntosh of the 42nd are killed, & Capt. Graham wounded. Of the R.A.R. [Royal American Regiment] Lieut. [James] Dow who acted as A.D.Q.M.G. [Acting Deputy Quartermaster General] is shot through the body. Of the 77th Lieut. Donald Campbell, and Mr. Peebles, a Volunteer, are wounded.

Our Loss in Men including Rangers and Drivers exceeds Sixty killed or wounded.

The action has lasted from one o'Clock till Night, and we expect to begin again at Daybreak.

Whatever our Fate may be, I thought it necessary to give your Excellency this early Information, that you may, at all Events, take such measures as you will think proper with the Provinces for their own Safety, and the Effectual relief of Fort Pitt, as in case of another Engagement, I fear insurmontable difficulties in protecting & transporting our Provisions; being already So much weakened by the Losses of this Day in Men, and Horses, besides the additional Necessity of carrying the wounded, whose situation is truly deplorable.

I cannot sufficiently acknowledge the constant assistance I have received from Major Campbell during this long action, nor Express my admiration of the cool and steady behaviour of the Troops, who did not fire a Shot without orders, and drove the Enemy from their Posts with fixed Bayonets: The Conduct of the officers is much above my Praises.[63]

It is clear from Bouquet's first dispatch that his outlook was not optimistic, yet with his usual determination, he was willing to accept whatever they encountered.

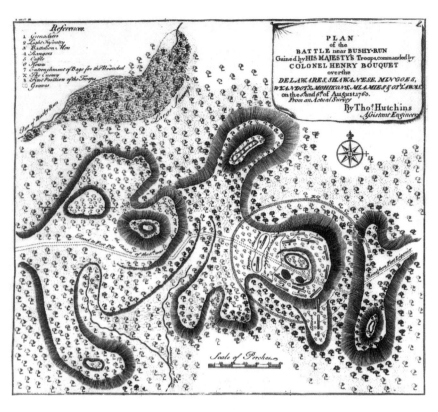

Plan of the Battle near Bushy Run. Assistant Engineer Lieutenant Thomas Hutchins, a participant in the battle, drew this diagram. From William Smith, *An Historical Account of the Expedition against the Ohio Indians, in the Year MDCCLXIV*. From the collection of Seymour I. Schwartz, M.D. Used with permission.

The next day, after several hours of fierce fighting, due to his tactical ingenuity in employing a feigned retreat, the British troops emerged the victors over a substantially larger Indian force in what many historians consider the greatest military victory ever in frontier warfare. Bouquet's description of the second day's engagement details the intense action:

I had the honour to inform you Excellency in my Letter of yesterday of our first Engagement with the Savages.

We took Post last night on the Hill where our Convoy halted when the Front was attacked/a comodious Piece of ground, & just spacious enough for our Purpose/There we encircled the whole & covered our wounded with the Flour Bags.

In the morning the Savages surrounded our Camp, at the distance of about 500 yards, & by shouting and yelping quite round that extensive Circumference thought to have terrified us with their numbers: They attacked us early, and under Favour of an incessant Fire, made Several bold Efforts to penetrate our Camp, and tho' they failed in the attempt, our Situation was not the less perplexing, having experienced that brisk attacks had little Effect upon an Enemy who always gave way when pressed, and appeared again immediately: Our Troops were besides extremely fatigued with the long march, and as long Action of the preceding Day, and distressed to the last Degree by a total want of water, much more intolerable than the Enemy's Fire.

Tied to our Convoy we could not lose Sight of it without exposing it & our wounded to fall a Prey to the Savages, who pressed upon us on

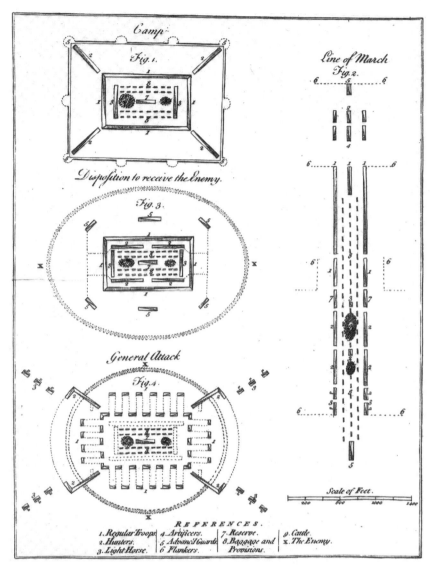

The Battle of Bushy Run, by Thomas Jefferys, showing four plans: 1) Camp, 2) Line of March, 3) Disposition to receive the Enemy, and 4) General Attack. From William Smith, *An Historical Account of the Expedition against the Ohio Indians, in the Year MDCCLXIV.* From the collection of Seymour I. Schwartz, M.D. Used with permission.

or to Stand their ground when attacked. With this View two Companies of Light Infantry were ordered within the Circle, & the Troops on their right and lefft opened their Files and filled up the Space; that it might Seem they were intended to cover the Retreat. The third Light Infantry Company, and the Grenadiers of the 42nd were ordered to Support the two first Companies. This manoeuvre Succeeded to our Wish, for the few Troops who took Possession of the ground lately occupied by the two Light Infantry Companies, being brought in nearer to the Center of the Circle, The Barbarians mistaking these motions for a Retreat hurried headlong on, and advancing upon us with the most daring intrepidity galled us excessively with their heavy Fire; but at the very moment that certain of Success, they thought themselves Master of the Camp, Major Campbell at the head of the two first Companies sallied out, from a Part of the Hill they could not observe, and fell upon their right Flank. They resolutely returned the Fire, but could not Stand the irresistible Shock of our men, who rushing in among them, killed many of them, and put the rest to Flight. The Orders Sent to the other two Companies were delivered So timely by Captain Basset, & executed with such celerity and spirit that the routed Savages, who happened to run that moment before their Front, received their full Fire, when uncovered by the Trees. The four Companies did not give them time to load a Second time, nor even to look behind them, but pursued them till they were totally dispersed. The lefft of the Savages, which had not been attacked, were kept in awe by the Remains of our Troops posted on the Brow of the Hill for that Purpose; nor durst

every Side, and to move it was impracticable, having lost many Horses, and most of the Drivers, Stupified by Fear, hid themselves in the Bushes, or were incapable of hearing or obeying any Orders.

The Savages growing every moment more audacious it was thought proper Still to increase their Confidence; by that means, if possible, to intice them to come close upon us, they attempt to support, or assist their Right, but being witness to their Defeat, followed their Example and fled.

Our brave men disdained so much to touch the dead Body of a vanquished Enemy that scarce a Scalp was taken, except by the Rangers & Pack Horse Drivers.

The Woods being now cleared and the Pursuit over, the four Companies took Possession of a Hill in our Front, and as soon as Litters could be made for the wounded, and the Flour and every thing destroyed, which for want of Horses could not be carried, we marched without molestation to this Camp. After the Severe Correction we had given the Savages a few hours before, it was natural to Suppose we Should enjoy Some Rest; but we had hardly fixed our Camp when they fired upon us again: This was very provoking! However the Light Infantry dispersed them before they could receive Orders for that Purpose. I hope we Shall be no more disturbed, for if we have another Action, we Shall hardly be able to carry our wounded.

The behaviour of the Troops on this Occasion Speaks for itself So Strongly, that for me to attempt their Eulogium would but detract from their merit.[64]

It is interesting that Robert Kirkwood, a Highland soldier who fought in the battle, later wrote about an occasionally seen departure from standard British dress policy. Kirkwood noted, "it was agreed, that the remaining part of the 42nd regiment should strip to their waistcoats" for more comfort maneuverability during the battle.[65]

Also noteworthy is Bouquet's unabashed praise for his troops, which he also later related to Lieutenant James McDonald in a letter stating, "The Highlanders are the bravest men I ever saw."[66]

Bouquet's casualty return lists a total of fifty killed, sixty wounded, and five missing.[67] Twenty Indian dead were reported recovered from the field, but in all probability there were many more, given the accounts of the battle as well as the fact that it was Indian custom to carry off as many of their dead and wounded as possible.[68]

Some final comments about how a few historians have downplayed the significance of Bouquet's victory are necessary here. We (the authors) do not feel that this revisionist assessment is valid. While minor Indian resistance continued for the next year, and beyond, the bands involved were acting independently. In reality, the backbone of the revolt was broken at Bushy Run, and the Indians never again mounted a unified front under Pontiac or anyone else the way they had in 1763.

Aside from the personal acclaim it would bring Bouquet from the British government and the colonial assemblies, his victory clearly remains as the one event that stopped the momentum of the uprising. Moreover, it is significant for his ingenuity of turning the Indians' own tactics against them, i.e. the *feigned retreat*, a strategy the Indians themselves often used in warfare. He lured the enemy in as close as possible, having some of his force seem to break and run, only to have other detachments hidden in reserve. Then he ambushed the confidently advancing enemy from a flank position.

Finally, the bravery and courage of both sides, justifiably noted by Bouquet, cannot be overlooked. His tribute to his own soldiers is noted above, but he also acknowledged his adversaries for their "greatest bravery and resolution" displayed during the two-day engagement.[69]

In the end, both the Indians and the British were just doing their jobs for the cause they believed in.

Following the battle, Bouquet's troops made their way to Fort Pitt, moving cautiously because of the danger of lurking Indians and the difficulties of transporting their wounded. When he received Bouquet's couriers as previously noted, Ecuyer sent a detachment under the command of Captain Ralph Phillips to meet them.[70]

The relief force successfully arrived at Fort Pitt at about two o'clock that same afternoon to the great relief of Ecuyer and all of the garrison and inhabitants, whom Bouquet praised for having "acted with Spirit against the Enemy, and in the repairs of the Fort."[71]

Bushy Run Battlefield Monument on the site of Bouquet's camp. Photo by Todd E. Harburn.

Fort Pitt was secure, "as nothing more can be done to this Post for the present," Bouquet noted. He sent Major Allan Campbell with four hundred soldiers to Ligonier to "bring up the Remains of our Convoy" and from there to send the "The Women, Children, and useless People [including wounded]. . .to Fort Bedford under the escort of thirty militia men and Captain Barret with his Rangers and volunteers."[72]

Campbell returned to Pitt by August 22, with the remaining provisions (much of the flour had to be destroyed to make room for transport of the wounded), and then left for Ligonier and Bedford with the remaining inhabitants, wagons, and packhorses. Bouquet ordered Campbell to leave reenforcements at Ligonier, where Lieutenant Blane was to remain in command. The unserviceable wagons and packhorses were to be sent on to Fort Loudoun. Captain Lieutenant Thomas Basset

(an engineer who apparently was in poor health) was to escort the caravan on to Fort Bedford, where he was to leave the remaining inhabitants and wounded before traveling to New York with dispatches for General Amherst. Basset arrived there on August 26, and informed the general of Bouquet's victory, for which Amherst related his "highest satisfaction [in] Confirming my hopes of your having Reached Fort Pitt, & Routed the Savages who had Attacked Your Little Army."[73]

While the Battle of Bushy Run was a devastating blow to the war on the eastern front, the British were well aware that the uprising was not yet totally eradicated. Bouquet remained cautious, expressing concern that "the Enemy will keep Spies upon the Road to obtain Intelligence of our intentions, and give themselves time to provide for the Safety of their families when their own Towns will be threatened."[74]

Captain Ourry at Fort Bedford expressed initial euphoria to Bouquet over the Bushy Run victory: "I believe you have given the Savages such a Dose as has effectually cured them of the Itch of meddling with us, for they have not appeared on this Communication Since, that I know of."[75]

However, there were still some small bands of Delawares on the Pennsylvania frontier that would harass the settlements for the remainder the fall, and Ourry acknowledged that "Col [Adam] Stephen had arrived here [at Bedford] with 98 vollunteers. . . . Some of his Parties have been very Successfull in Virginia & Maryland, in overtaking & routing Several Gangs of Savages. . . ."[76]

Although the Indians would not further assault the posts on the Fort Pitt–Philadelphia communication route, nonetheless, the garrisons still had to be maintained to deter this potential threat and also to provide a staging area for the eventual offensive campaigns against the remaining hostile tribes in the Ohio Country and at Detroit. This would become a more difficult challenge to the British than initially thought for several reasons. General Amherst was now reluctantly implementing the troop reductions called for in the postwar establishment. The Senecas along the Niagara Portage continued attacks over the next three months. Finally, the delay in organizing the campaign due to the reluctance of the Pennsylvania government to authorize necessary troops, particularly trained woodsmen, played a part. Bouquet expressed his concern, writing, "Had the Provinces assisted us, this would have been the favourable moment to have crushed the Barbarians a service we cannot Effect with our Forces alone."[77]

By early September, Bouquet had a further concern. He noted, "The Mingoes, Delawares, and Shawanese are now collecting their men at Muskingham, and the Heads of Sioto; as it is very probably that they will attempt to cut off the Communication to this Post, Our Parties must be Strong, to avoid a Check."[78]

It also became apparent that Bouquet did not have troops to spare to send to Presque Isle to join the Detroit relief expedition, as Amherst wished. Thus, even though Bouquet thwarted the main thrust of the uprising on the Pennsylvania frontier, there still remained the problem of the western and Great Lakes tribes. Many Indians were not ready to "bury the hatchet" just yet—other than in some unfortunate British soldier or civilian's head.

Chapter VI
The Platoons:
"The Unknown Campaign"
and the Battle of Buffalo Creek
Fall 1763

[A] meritorious Act, for the Good of Mankind.
General Jeffery Amherst

The Formation of the Platoons

WHILE BOUQUET'S DECISIVE VICTORY over the Indians at the Battle of Bushy Run temporarily stabilized the eastern front of the uprising, the war in the west, and particularly the siege of Detroit, still needed to be lifted. Although, at the time of Bushy Run, Amherst had not yet heard of Dalyell's rout at Detroit, he was aware of Cuyler's defeat at Point Pelee.[1]

He knew that additional troops had to be sent to Detroit, that the Niagara Portage had to be defended, and that the more important smaller posts had to be reestablished, particularly Presque Isle and Michilimackinac. It will be recalled that in late June, Amherst had ordered additional troops from the 42nd and 77th Regiments to Pittsburgh, after having sent their Light Infantry Companies there two weeks earlier. He also had sent the Light Infantry Company of the 17th Regiment to Niagara. At the same time, he formed the last remnants of the 42nd and 77th Regiments into a composite unit that was to proceed to Albany. There, they were to relieve a portion of the 55th Regiment that had been ordered on to Oswego.[2]

He intended that from Niagara, these troops would go to Presque Isle to join the 42nd and 77th troops from Fort Pitt. That plan never materialized, however, as the 42nd and 77th became mired at Fort Pitt at the end of the siege, and Bouquet was not able to send them on.

Amherst was determined to reestablish Fort Presque Isle and eventually send further relief to Detroit in hopes of putting an end to the uprising once and for all. Niagara was the key to this plan because control of the critical portage was essential for communication with the western posts. To accomplish this, because of the shortage of troops, Amherst was forced to adopt a different approach using specially organized units. He alluded to this on July 7, when he wrote, "We must Do the Best we can with the Numbers We have."[3]

This new and generally unrecognized plan of Amherst's concentrated many of the available troops into what were called "the Platoons." Remnants from several regiments, some of which were scheduled to be disbanded, were utilized. Men from the 15th, 17th, 22nd, 42nd, 55th, 60th, 77th, and 80th Regiments and the New York Independent Companies were organized into seven composite Platoons, each under the command of an officer. Simply put, their objective was to act offen-

Facing page. Private, 55th Regiment of Foot, by Gary Zaboly. This painting shows adaptations made to the conventional British infantry uniform and equipment during the French and Indian War. The units serving on the frontier during Pontiac's Uprising probably also practiced many of these changes. Courtesy of Tim J. Todish and Gary Zaboly.

sively on their way to Niagara, using what would now be called search and destroy tactics among the Seneca settlements in western New York to "Chastize" that tribe "who have so Treacherously engaged in the present Mischief."[4]

Once at Niagara, the Platoons were to advance to reinforce Gladwin and Dalyell, possibly rendezvousing with the latter before both forces arrived at Detroit. It appears that the Platoons were organized as three independent units of about twenty-three soldiers each. One Platoon was under Lieutenant Thomas Gamble of the 15th Regiment.[5] The second was under Lieutenant James Johnson, formerly of Gorham's Rangers, and the third was under Lieutenant Patrick Sinclair of the 15th Regiment.[6]

Four other Platoons of six officers and twenty-two men each were to be under the overall command of Captain Valentine Gardner of the 55th Regiment—one under Lieutenant Redmund Magra of the 22nd Regiment and the others under three half-pay lieutenants from the recently disbanded New York Independent Companies. They were Lieutenants John Paynter, John Stoughton and Erick Sutherland, with Sutherland appointed as acting paymaster of the Platoons.[7]

About this time, Amherst ordered an additional force from Albany that was not a part of the Platoons to proceed to Niagara. This was the previously mentioned detachment the of 42nd and 77th Highland Regiments, commanded by Captain William Erving and Lieutenant Thomas Mante. Both Erving and Mante came from the 77th Regiment, and Mante later wrote one of the first histories of the Seven Years' War and the Pontiac Uprising.[8]

Erving's detachment was to proceed to Presque Isle, where they were to meet the detachment of the 42nd Regiment from Fort Pitt. However, due to the manpower shortage, Amherst was forced to draw from Erving's force to complete Gardner's Platoons. Captain Gardner's orders stipulated:

Sir:

    As I find you want Seventeen Men to Com-

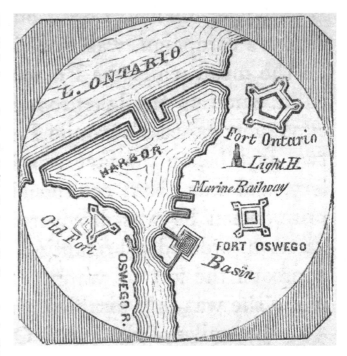

Fort Ontario, one of three forts at Oswego, was an important logistical post on Lake Ontario and was where Pontiac and the western Indians made the final peace agreement in 1766. From Benson Lossing's *Field Book of the American Revolution*. Tim J. Todish collection.

pleat the Detachment ordered to proceed under your Command I herewith Enclose your Order to Captain Erving to. . .furnish you with that Number, from the Men of the 42nd & 77th now at Albany: which men you will Incorporate with your Detachment, providing them with Arms & Necessarys in the Same Manner as the Others: If there should be any who Desire to keep their own Arms they may do it; and when they joyn Major Gladwin or Captain Dalyell, you will Acquaint them that you have such men with you, that when the Service will permit, they may be Ordered to joyn their Respective corps.[9]

Evidence shows that the Platoons were to be independent detachments, all ordered to join together at Niagara. They were ordered to attack the Senecas, meet any resistance along the way, and, essentially, take no prisoners.

Lieutenants Gamble and Sinclair received instructions similar to Gardner's "for proceeding with a Platoon under his Command to Joyn Major Gladwin, to Act offensively against the Savages" on August 15, 1763, at New York. Specifically his instructions read:

> The Platoon under your Command being Completed to Twenty two Men Including a Serjeant & Corporal; You will Embark with them in the sloop which Lt. Colonel [James] Robertson has provided for your Reception, & proceed Directly to Albany; Where on your arrival you will be Supplyed with Sundry Articles from Colonel Bradstreet as mention in the Orders herewith.
>
> Major Gorham will Order you Muskets compleat for your Men, Likewise Eighteen Rounds of Ammunition, & Ball to Compleat your Men to Sixty Rounds. He will also deliver to you for your men Every thing in the same manner as to the others who went under Captain Lt. Gardiner.
>
> You will not permit the Men to go on shore at Albany, 'till you have provided them with every thing for their March and when you have Equipt them fit for Light infrantry duties you will then [illegible] Obvserving the following directions:
>
> It is my Intention that your Platoon should be Altogether Independent of those gone under the Command of Captain Lt. Gardiner; And that it is to be soley under your Command 'till you Joyn Captain Dalyell or Major Gladwin. And that no Opportunity may be Lost of punishing the Indians, against whom you are to Act offensively; I would have you, according to the Information you may Receive at Fort Stanwix, or any of the other Posts, Employ your men in an Offensive manner, Remaining for that purpose at any of the Posts, 'till you shall Judge it Necessary to proceed. —As the six Nations have hither to behaved as Friends the Senecas Excepted; they are to be Regarded & Treated accordingly; so that it is not likely that you will be retarded on your march should you come in the way of any of the Settlements belonging to the Senecas, who have so Treacherously Engaged in the present Mischief, You will as far as your Force will permit you, Destroy their Hutts and Plantations, putting to Death everyone of that nation that may fall in

your Hands; the Same is to be Observed in Regard to any others, a meritorious Act, for the Good of Mankind.

> It will be unnecessary after what has so recently happened, to Caution you against Trusting to the Indians in any manner whatsoever. On your Arrival at Niagara, You will Employ your Platoon in Active service against the Indians in that Neighbourhood, should there be any probability of Coming up with them, for Which you will get Information of Major Wilkins, But if matters are Quiet there, You will take the first Opportunity, of which the Commanding Officer will Acquaint you, of proceeding Either in the Vessell, or Boats, to Joyn Major Gladwin, or Captain Dalyell, at the Detroit, or wherever they may be: And which ever of them you Joyn first, you will shew him these Orders, & follow & Obey such further Directions as you may Receive from him. . . .

At the end of these orders, Amherst repeated his promise of:

> a Reward of One Hundred Pounds to the Man who shall Kill <u>Pontiac</u>, the Chief of the <u>Ottawas</u>, a Cowardly Villain, but who was the first Instigator the Mischiefs.[10]

It is clear from these orders that Amherst intended the Platoons to be independent units that could move and strike targets more quickly than if they were to travel as one large party. They were temporary creations drawn from a mixture of the men available from several units to meet the pressing needs that the Indian uprising brought about.

Amherst's instructions to Gamble also provide an important view of the clothing these special troops wore, for when they arrived at Albany, "Colonel Bradstreet on shewing him these Orders will furnish you with Twenty Three pair of <u>Leggins</u>; Twenty Three <u>Powder Horns</u>, Twenty Three <u>Blankets</u>; & Twenty Three <u>Flannel Waiscoasts without Sleeves</u>, for your Platoon, out of the stores there, of the same Kind that were Delivered to Captain Lieut. Gardinier's Detachment, for which you will give a proper Receipt."[11]

The additional men from the 42nd and 77th Regiments at Albany were eventually to be drafted into the 42nd Regiment during the planned

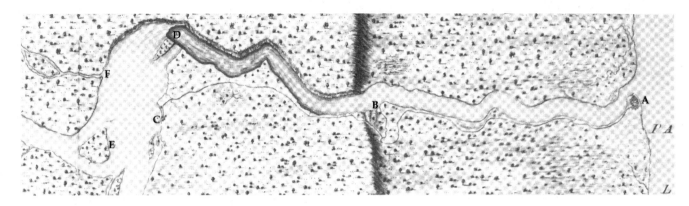

This 1765 map of the all-important Niagara Portage is by William Brasier. It is a copy of one made in 1760 by engineer George Demler. Legend: A: Fort Niagara; B: the Lower Landing and site of the tram railway; C: Fort Schlosser; D: Niagara Falls; E: Navy Island; F: the Chippewa River. The portage trail is the solid line following the east lower side of the Niagara River between Fort Schlosser and Fort Niagara. Courtesy of the William L. Clements Library.

troop reductions. This is made clear in several letters between Amherst and Bouquet during September. On September 7, Amherst directed to Bouquet a "Return of the Men of the 42nd and 77th, already gone by the way of Albany, & of those that are now Ordered from thence [to Niagara] under the Command of Captain Erving, that you may Reckon them as part of the 42nd Regiment, when you Complete that Corps to the New Establishment . . . .[12] Amherst had assumed that these men, some of whom were temporarily assigned the the Platoons, had already reached Niagara. However, the return shows that only Gardner's contingent had actually left Albany by that date.[13]

There is no record of Bouquet sending additional 42nd troops in August or September. After the relief of Fort Pitt, he kept small contingents of the 42nd and 77th there along with a detachment of the 60th, while sending the majority of the 42nd and 77th back to Fort Ligonier with Major Allan Campbell.[14]

It is known from subsequent correspondence between Amherst and Bouquet that it became "Impracticable to Send forward the 42nd to Presqu'Isle. . . ." although Amherst directed that "it will be Necessary that One or two Officers of that Corps, who are to Stand on the New Establishment should Immediately proceed Either by Route from Pittsburgh or come this way to Pres-

qu'Isle to take command of the 40 men gone from Albany as mentioned in my Last as Captain Erving and Lieut: Mont [Mante] must Return to joyn the 77th who are Ordered home to be reduced. The Men of the 42nd & 77th will either remain at Presqu'Isle or Niagara as Circumstances may require & and are to be reckoned as belonging to the 42nd Regiment, in the Formation of the Corps according to the New Establishment."[15]

Even once the Platoons were assembled, the task of getting them to Niagara was not an easy one. Unfortunately, they met with similar obstacles and disasters as the Cuyler and Dalyell expeditions. One problem was logistics—not having enough supplies—and another was mismanagement. The Platoons were also hit with sickness, desertions, an ambush, and a devastating encounter with a storm on Lake Erie. As these problems developed, it became clear that it would be impossible to reestablish Presque Isle and reinforce Detroit before winter set in, so most of the Platoons were ordered to remain at Niagara, while some were sent back to New York and eventually disbanded.

Bad luck had followed them from the start. As the Platoons were en route to Niagara, Wilkins made another attempt to send relief to Detroit, which also met with disaster. The schooner *Huron* and the sloop *Michigan* left Detroit for Niagara, carrying the wounded from Bloody Run and the recently escaped Indian captive John Rutherfurd. On August 26, Wilkins sent the ships back to Detroit loaded with provisions. Misfortune struck two days later when a storm on Lake Erie wrecked the *Michigan* at Catfish Creek (Eighteen Mile Creek, New York). As Amherst described the situation:

> The Sloop in which Captain [Edward] Hope, with a Detachment of the 17th Regiment, & Lieut. [John] Montresor Sailed from Niagara about the Middle of Last Month, was Unfortunately Drove on a Bank, between that & Presqu'Isle on the 28th August; And I Fear She will be Lost; All the People were Saved; Lieut. Montresor took <u>post</u> ashore, & Sent Advice to Major Wilkins, who Ordered Captain Cochrane, with Boats, & Men, to their Relief: & I Conclude they will have proceeded directly to Presqu'Isle, from whence I would chuse the Indians should be gone. . . .[16]

Amherst's conclusions were wrong however. Montresor skillfully designed and supervised the construction of a temporary fortification on a bluff seventy feet above the water. One hundred reinforcements arrived from Niagara on September 2. On the following day, the Indians attacked the post, getting within fifty yards, but were valiantly held off during a three-hour battle, with the British suffering only three soldiers killed. The *Michigan* was deemed a complete loss and was dismantled for salvage lumber and materials. The party left for Niagara on September 18. The *Huron* had managed to make it to Detroit and back and eventually took Hope, Montresor, and their detachment on to Detroit with at least some provisions.[17]

During this time, Gardner's contingent of the Platoons was on its way to Fort Niagara, where they arrived on September 4. However, instead of being allowed to pursue the Senecas as Amherst ordered, post commander Major Wilkins employed them in routine garrison, escort, and road repair duties. Gardner showed his dissatisfaction in his report to the general:

> I believe it is my duty to inform you that I arrived at Niagara the 4th Inst in the evening

with the four Plattoons under my command. Agreeable to your orders I ply'd to Major Wilkins for Boats to proceed to Detroit, but was refused for reason which I assum the Maj has Informe'd your Excellency off—Since my arrival the Plattoons have been emply'd by orders of Major Wilkins, in repairing the roads between this, and little Niagara, in Escorting Boats and Provision over the nine miles. And Major Duncan & I had found the least probability of success in a visit to the Seneca's I woud have waited on them with the Plattoons, for I beg you will rest assured that nothing in life wou'd give me greater satisfaction then an opportunity of executing your orders and intentions to the utmost of your wishes which I hope before long to have.

> I hope before this, you have receiv'd from Major Duncan the Descriptions of the Seven men that Deserted from me on my way from Albany to Ontario. Major Wilkins has ordered Lieutenant Gailheast to do duty in the 80th Regt, a great loss to the Plattoons be deprived of so good an Officer as One hundred and one Private. I recollect nothing else that it is my duty to inform you off. . . .[18]

The Battle of Devil's Hole

While the Platoons were tending to these duties, another setback hit the British along the Niagara Portage, further delaying the relief of Presque Isle and Detroit. The Devil's Hole Massacre was the costliest defeat of the war in terms of men killed. After delivering supplies to Fort Schlosser for the schooner *Huron*, on September 14, a convoy was returning to Fort Niagara over the portage road when somewhere between three hundred and five hundred Chenussio [Genesse] Senecas attack it. They struck where the road passed above Devil's Hole, about three miles from Fort Schlosser. It was named for a deep crevice that the Indians thought a demon inhabited. At this point along the Niagara River, eighty feet down the rocky cliffs, there is also a dangerous whirlpool. John Stedman, the master of the portage, Provincial Captain Thomas Johnson, a sergeant, and about twenty-five men of the 80th Regiment escorted the empty convoy of twelve wagons, sixteen oxen, and twenty horses. When the Indians sprung their violent surprise attack from the dense forest near the road, some of the frightened horses carried wagons and drivers over the cliff to their deaths in the gorge below. Some soldiers also jumped over the cliff in a frantic effort to escape, while others fought desperately to the end. Incredibly, three persons survived—a drummer boy who leapt off the cliff, a driver who hid in the forest, and Stedman, who escaped and rode back to the safety of Fort Schlosser.[19]

The onslaught was far from finished. Hearing the firing, two companies of the 80th Regiment under Lieutenants George Campbell and William Frazier encamped about a mile away near the Lower Landing (Lewiston), rushed to the scene only to be ambushed themselves. The reinforcements fought valiantly but were wiped out to a man. The Indians scalped them and took their clothing, arms, and ammunition. Sir William Johnson later described the desperate and horrifying action as told to him by Indian participants:

> The reinforcements were attacked about midway on the carrying place, and being hard put to, gave way, on which the Indians filed off to the right and made a wing so as to cut them from the Fort. . . . The party, imagining themselves surrounded, and being hard pushed by the heavy fire from the Indians in the woods, they jumped down the precipice, by which most of them were killed, those who survived the fall, ran along shore as far as they could,

Above. The site of Fort Schlosser at the north end of the Niagara Portage. Photo by Todd E. Harburn.
Middle. Looking down to the Niagara River from the site of the Battle of Devil's Hole. Many British soldiers either jumped or were forced over the side. Photo by Tim J. Todish.
Below. The bluffs at the site of the Battle of Devil's Hole, as seen from the Niagara River. Photo by Tim J. Todish. The authors wish to acknowledge the late "Captain" Ron Meesig, retired U.S. Postal Inspector and Niagara charter fishing boat captain, who took us up the river in his boat so that we could view these historic sites from the water.

when prevented by rocks, they took to the river and were by the rapidity thereof destroyed." Another Indian related that some of the soldiers who jumped over the precipice "in falling stuck fast in the forks of trees, from whence they were taken down yet alive by the Indians and scalped.[20]

Captain George Etherington (who was on his way to Niagara after surviving the attack on Michilimackinac) provided further details:

[J]ust as you imagin'd I overtook the 46th Regiment before they got to this place [Niagara] which was on the twelvth instant—the next day an express arriv'd from the little landing telling us that the Waggons with an Escort of a Serjt. And Twenty four Men of the 80th Regiment were cutt of betwixt that Post and the upper landing, and that Leut. Campbell & Frazer with two Companys of the 80th were gone to the Waggons, upon which Major Wilkens with all the 60th Regiment were here sett out to support Mr. Campbell, but on our arrival at the little landing wee were inform'd by two of the Men that came in Wound that the two Compys were intirly cutt of and the Indians were very numberous some say'd five hundred and some say'd four. Major Wilkins stayd at the little landing till the arrival of a reinforcement from the 46th should arrive but before they came it was night, and it was then thought too late to preceed. Accordingly we all came back to the Fort that night and sett off next morning very early when we came up to the graves we found Leut Cambell and Sixteen Men on the road all stript and scalpt and thirty two more in the same situation which the Enemy had thrown down the Rocks which with what men we found dead afterwards we can make out [seventy] six men kild and eight or nine wounded the Names of the officers are as follows. Capt. Johnson & Leut [Abraham] Dayton of the [New] yorkers, Leuts. Campbell and Frazier of the [80th] light Infantry and Leut [John] Rosco of the Artillery. They have kild all the Bullocks and horses except a very few, an which were not in the Teems and those can't be found—by every thing that we can learn this is done by the Senecas please Excuse the inexactness of this scrawl and believe me.[21]

John Rutherfurd had escaped his captors at Detroit and was bound for Niagara on the *Michigan* when it sank. He noted that on their return to Fort Niagara, they "marched over the carrying place at the Falls of Niagara just three days after the Indians had defeated our troops, and saw there about eight dead bodies, unburied, scalped, and sadly mangled."[22]

Following the Devil's Hole disaster, the British had to reformulate their plans for the relief of Detroit. Major Wilkins was slow to respond, and not much was done in the next month. Particularly questionable is why the Platoons were not used to pursue the Senecas as they had been formed to do. With the arrival of the 46th Regiment, Lieutenant Colonel William Browning succeeded Wilkins in command. Further plans for Detroit or Presque Isle were delayed because Browning was still awaiting the arrival of Captain Erving's detachment. On his arrival, he was to "take the first opportunity of proceeding with the men under your command to Presqu'Isle where in all probability the 42nd Regt. May be."[23] Amherst would soon learn that this was not to be.

During this time, the Platoons with Captain Gardner were encamped at the Lower Landing, where they remained awaiting further orders. A return ten days after the Devil's Hole Massacre records "4 Platoons, Captain Gardiner: 1 Capt. 5 Lieuts. 1 Surg. 7 Serjts. 97 Pvts. Fit for Duty. 2 Pvts. Sick at Hospital. 2 Pvts. At Fort Stanwix" encamped at the landing, although this had been reduced to "45 Pvts Fit for Duty" by October 12, apparently due to sickness.[24]

After Erving's detachment arrived at Schenectady, he had to ask Colonel Bradstreet for boats to transport them to Oswego because they were unable to march overland. During the journey, some of Erving's men suffered from sickness, including himself and Lieutenant Mante. They had to send the party on ahead under a sergeant of the 42nd Regiment. Upon arrival at Oswego, the commander, Major Alexander Duncan, reported that he sent Sergeant Simpson and the party on to Niagara to receive further orders from Lieutenant Colonel Browning.

The Indians still were harassing the region, killing a soldier and some oxen near Fort Schlosser. Browning noted, "Eleven of them [Oxen] were again kild by the Indians at his [Wilkins] Camp at Little Niagara, & one man Scalpd."[25]

The Battle of Buffalo Creek

The week after Erving's detachment arrived at Niagara, Wilkins' relief force, which included the Platoons, was finally ready to embark for Detroit. The plan to rebuild Presque Isle was scrapped, as it was too late in the season. The devastating blows that would end the Platoon experiment came in two incidents that followed—a battle and a storm. While the battles of Bloody Run and Bushy Run are well known, the Battle of Buffalo Creek is relatively obscure.

Major Wilkins left the Lower Landing on October 19, with "the 80th, with Some Platoons & artill'y people with the 60th Reg in all about 670 with Provisions & Stores. . . ."[26]

At the east end of Lake Erie near Buffalo Creek (in modern Buffalo), a band of eighty to ninety Indians suddenly ambushed them from the bluffs on the east side of the Niagara River. In the ensuing battle, contingents of the Platoons, gallantly led by Captain Gardner, pursued the Indians in a hard fought battle, eventually scattering them, although not without British casualties. A report in the *New York Mercury* recounted the intense action:

> Last Monday, Capt. Gardiner, of the 55th and Lieut Stoughton, came to Town from Albany. They belonged to a Detachment of 600 men, under the Command of Major Wilkins, destined for Detroit, from Niagara; but on the 19th of October at the East End of Lake Erie, 160 of our People, being in their Boats, were fired upon from the Beech by about 80 Indians, which killed and wounded 13 Men, (and among them Lieut. Johnson, late of Gorham's killed) in the two sternmost Boats, the Remainder of the Detachment being a-head about Half a Mile. Capt. Gardiner, who was in the Boats adjoining, immediately ordered the Men (50) under his Command ashore, and took Posses-

Site of the Battle of Buffalo Creek along the Niagara River. Photo by Todd E. Harburn.

sion of the Ground from which the Enemy had firyed, and as soon as he ordered our People landing, he, with Lieut Stoughton, and 23 Men, pursued the Indians, and in a few Minutes a smart Skirmish ensued, which lasted near an Hour, and in which 3 Men were killed on the Spot, and Capt. Gardiner, with Lieut Stoughton, and 10 others, very badly wounded. During the Skirmish, the Troops that did not follow the Indians, formed on the Bank and coverd the Boats.[27]

Major Wilkins provided some additional details of the intense action:

> [A]t our setting out from the east end of Lake Erie, the Enemy attack'd our rear boats belonging to the platoons, Capt. Gardinier of the platoons immediately drove the Savages into the cover where they made a stand & kill'd 3 men & wounded the Capt & Lieut Stoghton & 6 men, I immediately went with the 26th and 60th Reg. (Nearest at hand) to their assistance, & found the Enemy posted in thick cover on the other side of an impassable swamp, shots was exchanged for some time while hearing nothing off the Enemy I waited with a company of the 60th til the whole embark'd & pushed off by companies, many savages appeard on the shore when we was about 2 miles off. I saw the improbability of getting at them on any terms so went on for Detroit. At the beginning of this affair, Lt. Johnson & another boat of the platoons go into & was carried down the Rapids to fort Schlosser & I find that the Lieut arrived at this place & soon died of his wounds rec'd in his boat, I cannot at present get an exact

Site of the Battle of Buffalo Creek, showing the bluffs where the Indians commenced their attack and where the Platoons under Captain Valentine Gardner launched their counterattack. Photo by Todd E. Harburn.

> return of his men kill'd & wounded in the two boats, the Schooner lay near anchor, I thought it most prudent to order all the wounded on board but by some neglect some of them went on in the boats and are now here in a fair way of recovery. . . .[28]

After the battle, Wilkins and the larger part of the relief force headed on to Detroit, while Captain Joshua Loring, the naval commander, took the wounded and some survivors back to Niagara. Lieutenant Colonel Browning noted their return a few days later:

> On the 28th Instant, Capt. Loring, Capt Gardiner, Lieut. Houghton, one Serg of the 47th and two men of Lt. Houghton's Platoon arrivd here, Capt Loring extremely ill, Capt Gardiner and Lt. Houghton much wounded with the Serg and two men, they after the affair of the 20th at the rapids, proceeded in the Schooner and Look'd into Presquie'Isles, the weather too boisterous and Contrary to Enter the harbour, or to proceed, but obligd to make the first Anchorages. . . . Some of the wounded went forward in the boats but Can not Learn their number. . . .[29]

In another letter to Gage the same day, Browning reported that he had "Sent none of the 80th away as I found there were no hospitals, I indeed Sent, the Sick of the 55th to their Regt and Some Provincials and Sick of the Platoons (Sent Down here). . .as they were naked and without Subsis-

tance, Lying in the utmost misery and distress, no Probability of their ever being of the Least Service and their times (as I was Informed) nearly expir'd, were breeding Sickness in the Fort, and Eating Provisions." He also assumed that Major Wilkins "was making his passage in good time although this weather, sometimes very unfavourable."[30]

The End of the Platoons and the Wilkins Expedition

Despite the crowded conditions and scarcity of food, Browning expected that "Majr Wilkin's and most of his people" would spend the winter at Niagara when they returned from Detroit.[31]

Browning's assessment of the "very unfavourable" weather on the Great Lakes at that time of year was all too prophetic. Wilkins and his expedition would never reach Detroit. About midnight on November 7, a disastrous storm struck the detachment on Lake Erie. General Gage later described the destruction:

> I am sorry to acquaint you with the Misfortune which befell that Gentleman's [Wilkins] Detachment on Lake Erie, on their way to Succour the Detroit. They embarked in the Night of the 7th Novr, a violent Storm arose about 12 o'Clock in which they lost Lt. [John] Davidson of the Artillery, Lt. Painter [Paynter] of the Platoon & Doctor [Joseph] Williams [surgeon] of the 80th Regiment with four Serjeants and Sixty three Rank & File, a great many Boats, Provision, one Six Pounder, and almost all their Ammunition. This obliged Them to return again to Niagara. Major Wilkins is on his way hither with a Number of men of your Battn. . . .[32]

Thus, Mother Nature, rather than the Indians, put an inauspicious end to the Platoons. The men were paid for their services through November 30, and were discharged in December and January as their enlistments expired. It was a disappointing ending to what could have been a great effort in putting down the final flames of the rebellion by a specially organized force.

The Indians continued to "persevere in infesting the Carrying Place." Browning reported several incidents to Amherst, including one at the Lower Landing where a party of a "Sergt & ten men sent to bring in wood were attacked with seven killed, one man escaping, another was overtaken by three Indians, very near the fort and his head cutt off. . . ."[33]

Despite these sporadic incidents, the level of hostile activity waned as winter approached. At Detroit, Major Gladwin wrote that he "had the mortification to hear, by an express from Major Wilkins"of the misfortune that had befallen the storm-wrecked troops attempting to relieve his post. Having long requested permission to return home to England, he realized that he would now have to endure another hard winter at Detroit and was resolved in the fact that he would have "to maintain my post till a relief arrives in spring."[34]

In reality, he would not be relieved until August of 1764.

The year 1763 was rapidly coming to a close. The major Indian outbreaks had been put down, although rather than winning a complete victory, the British had largely forced a stalemate. Even with the number of British forts taken, by the fall, Pontiac's uprising was rapidly losing steam. Indians, who by nature were not inclined to engage in lengthy military operations, had shown remarkable resiliency over the summer. Still, the two strongest British posts, Fort Detroit and Fort Pitt, held out. Although the Indians suffered a significant defeat at Bushy Run, they had enjoyed some success in the battles during the fall. For the British, Detroit still had not been relieved. There remained the task of finalizing the peace with the Ohio and eastern Indians, as well as taking possession of the Illinois Country posts the French had ceded.

The Proclamation of 1763

As the fall progressed and the Indian resolve weakened, the British government was also reassessing its position. The uprising, which had been costly both financially and in terms of lives, had taken some of the luster off the recent victory over the French. Even before the outbreak of hostilities, the home government was looking for ways to deal effectively, and in their minds at least, fairly, with the Indians. They also realized that during the course of the war with France, the colonies had gained significant political and economic power and freedom, and they were looking for ways to bring this in check.

With these aims in mind, on October 7, King George III issued the Royal Proclamation of 1763. The Proclamation had four main provisions:
1. It would limit and control settlement.
2. It would regulate the Indian trade.
3. It would protect the Indians from unscrupulous traders.
4. Purchase of Indian lands was permitted only with the approval of the Indian superintendents.

Another important effect of the act was that it recognized the Indians as distinct nations under the king's sovereignty. The provisions of the Proclamation of 1763 would not only affect the policies of the British and colonial governments, but also those of the future United States of America.

In simple terms, the Proclamation meant that British settlement and hunting was prohibited beyond the crest of the Appalachian Mountains. The Indian trade in these areas would be strictly regulated. These restrictions did not sit well with a lot of the colonists. Many had fought against the French and felt that these lands were theirs by right of conquest. Settlers already living in the prohibited territory were expected to move back behind the line. Land speculators, including George Washington and Thomas Jefferson, who envisioned the opportunity to make large profits as the lands were developed, now saw those plans stymied. Overall, the colonists highly resented Britain's attempts to restrict what they saw as their potential for growth. Many on both sides saw the settlement line as only temporary, inevitably moving westward over time. They were right.

Planning for 1764

With the failure of the Platoons, and the lateness of the season, nothing further could be done other than to secure the western garrisons for the winter. At Detroit, Pontiac had already "Sued for peace in a Submissive manner" to Gladwin.[35]

Nonetheless, the chief refused to believe a letter from Major de Villiers, the French commandant at Fort de Chartres, offering no support for his continued resistance, and telling him to make peace with the British. Pontiac would ignore his promise to Gladwin and continue his efforts to secure allies for the renewal of hostilities in the spring.[36]

In Pontiac's mind, the Indians were only giving up for the winter, as they needed to journey to their winter hunting grounds and care for their families.

Amherst's and Bouquet's plan for the Ohio campaigns, which they had begun working on back in August and early September after Bushy Run, had to be put on hold until the next year. Colonel Adam Stephen had made arrangements for upward of one thousand militia volunteers from Virginia, Pennsylvania, and Maryland. However, the plan met with resistance and delay again from the colonial legislatures, particularly Pennsylvania. They were reluctant both to spend money for the troops and have them serve beyond their own borders.[37]

This was exasperating to both Bouquet and Amherst, as they felt it was the colonies' responsibility to help support the British government in protecting their interests on the frontier. Lord George Montague Dunk, 2nd Earl of Halifax, recent president of the Board of Trade and lord lieutenant of Ireland, empowered Amherst to "call upon the colonies. . .to contribute to the general Defence of the Country, & Annoyance of the Indians, by raising and employing such Numbers of Provincial Troops or Militia, as you shall find requesite."[38]

Bouquet and Amherst had always believed that experienced frontiersmen were necessary for wilderness campaigns. Bouquet noted, "without a certain Number of Woodsmen, I can not think it adviseable to employ Regulars in the Woods against Savages, as they can not procure any Intelligence; and are open to continual Surprise. Nor can they pursue at any distance this Enemy when they have routed them. . . ."[39]

General Thomas Gage, who had recently replaced Amherst as acting commander in chief (see chapter seven) was in agreement, replying, "It is as you observe next to Impossible, to March in Woods with Regulars alone without being every moment Subject to A surprize, from which a Body of good Woodsmen would Affectually Secure you."[40]

Unfortunately, due to the legislative squabbling and the fast approaching winter, Stephen eventually had to write Bouquet, "there is no hopes of Executing your favourite Plan this Season."[41]

Thus, Gage and Bouquet had no alternative but to delay the campaign until next year. Gage wanted to follow Amherst's intended plan for winter quartering of the Regular troops at the frontier outposts, but, due to the troop reductions, it was impossible for the 42nd and other troops to advance to Presque Isle and Detroit. This resulted in the following disbursement for the winter of 1763–1764:

1) Of the nine companies of the 42nd Regiment, eight would garrison the posts along the communication between Fort Pitt and Philadelphia, while the company at Niagara was sent to New York.

2) The 77th Regiment was disbanded, and those with remaining service time were sent to New York.

3) The 80th Regiment was to have been entirely disbanded, but since reinforcements were not available, "Major Gladwin was empowered to keep up the 80th Regiment," and they remained at Detroit for the winter.

4) The 60th Regiment was reduced to two battalions with the reduction of the 3rd and 4th Battalions. Three companies were sent south to garrison posts in South Carolina and Georgia, as the three South Carolina Inde-

pendent Companies were also disbanded. The remaining Royal American Companies were at Detroit, Niagara, and with Bouquet in Pennsylvania.

5) The 46th Regiment was at Fort Niagara.

6) The 55th Regiment had remnants disbursed at Detroit, Niagara, upper New York, Albany, Oswego, and Crown Point.[42]

With the matter of the winter quartering of troops finally settled, Gage's attention turned to his plans to take possession of the Illinois Country posts. Indeed, 1764 would, in many ways, be a most trying year for both sides.

A nineteenth-century depiction of Fort Detroit under siege, by Frederick Remington. Private collection.

Chapter VII
The Uprising Loses Momentum and the Changing of the Guard
Fall 1763 to Winter 1764

I am brought into a scrape, and left in it;
things are expected of me that cant be performed. . . .
Major Henry Gladwin

The Siege of Detroit Breaks Down

ALTHOUGH THE BATTLE OF BLOODY RUN at Detroit was a tactical victory for the Indians, it did not yield any long-term strategic gains. Gladwin now had a significant number of reenforcements and was emboldened to try some offensive moves of his own. The fort was not even close to being captured, and Pontiac's supporters were growing increasingly weary of the siege. As summer turned into autumn, they had to begin thinking about preparing for the coming winter.

After the Battle of Bloody Run, groups of Indians stood watch around the fort every night hoping to catch more soldiers outside the walls, but they were largely unsuccessful. One night, Gladwin sent sixty men out under Captain Grant to wait in the houses that the Indians were using for cover during the day, hoping to catch them by surprise. As it turned out, the Indians did not appear that morning, and the effort was unsuccessful.

After a harrowing and sometimes exciting captivity, John Rutherfurd escaped back to the fort on August 5. On the sixth, the schooner *Huron* returned safely from Niagara, further raising the garrison's spirits by bringing provisions and another sixty men. In the early morning fog of the eighth, Captain Hopkins led a force by boat to attack the Potawatomi village, but his boats became separated in the fog and the attempt was unsuccessful. On the thirteenth, both the *Huron*

and the *Michigan* sailed for Detroit, and the Indians did not contest their departure. The ships carried fifteen of the most seriously wounded soldiers and a number of traders whose goods had been lost to the Indians.

On August 17, Pontiac moved a large portion of his village south of the fort by the River Rouge so that they could better intercept any reenforcements coming upriver. Two hundred more warriors had recently joined him, but the defection of most of the disenchanted Potawatomies largely offset these numbers. On the eighteenth, the Chippewa chief Wasson sent a letter to Gladwin again demanding that he surrender the fort, which of course was ignored.

On August 20, Captain Hopkins and Lieutenant James Rogers led a combined force of the Queen's Rangers and Rogers' Rangers to set up an ambush on a road between two of the Indian camps. Even though four bateaux were sent in the opposite direction as a diversion, the Rangers were discovered and had to return to the fort empty handed. On August 23, the Indians drove in one of the fort's advanced pickets, so Robert Rogers was sent out to retake the position. These operations showed that Gladwin was not content to just sit in the fort and submit to the Indians' siege—he was more than willing to take the offensive when the opportunity was right.

Through the rest of August and into September the siege continued without any dramatic developments. There were occasional skirmishes in which both sides suffered casualties. On August 31, a Chippewa chief was killed, and on September 1, the nephew of an Ottawa chief was lost. Gladwin kept hoping for a major reenforcement so that he could mount a large enough offensive to break the siege once and for all.

On September 2, two Frenchmen from Fort de Chartres reached Detroit. They said that there still was no official word of a peace treaty between England and France and that Major de Villiers was giving the local Wea Indians lead and gunpowder. This news gave Pontiac renewed hope that French help would eventually arrive. That same day, the *Huron* arrived at the mouth of the Detroit River and dropped off six Mohawk emissaries from Sir William Johnson, who went to speak with Teata's Wyandots. The next morning, two Frenchmen were allowed on board the schooner to sell the crew vegetables. On board, they easily saw that the crew consisted of only twelve men including the captain. Either they or the Mohawks let Pontiac know what an easy target the ship was. That night, the Mohawks were detained in the Wyandot village, and some 340 Indians in canoes silently paddled toward the schooner in the darkness. It had moved upriver near Turkey Island, in an area where rushes concealed the approaching Indians, and they were not discovered until they were only one hundred yards away. The alert crew managed one shot with the bow gun before the Indians got too close, and they were forced to use their small swivel guns and their muskets. As the Indians started to climb up the ship's sides, the captain and one soldier were killed, but the others fought back fiercely with their edged weapons. The attackers tried to chop holes in the stern with their tomahawks, and they did manage to cut the anchor cable, setting the ship adrift. It swung around in the current and brushed many of the canoes aside. The confusion allowed the remaining crew to go back to their muskets and swivel guns, and they were ready to fight to the end, the mate crying out for the last man to blow up the ship. Someone among the Indians understood and

gave warning, causing them to give up the attack and race for the shore. Besides the two killed, the crew suffered four wounded, while the Indians had eight killed and twenty more wounded. These were extremely high losses by Indian standards.

When the noise of the battle was heard at the fort, four armed boats were sent to assist, but they arrived too late to help. Captain Hopkins and twenty men remained on board, and the *Huron* made it safely to the fort the next day with its much-needed cargo of supplies, including 47 barrels of flour and 160 of pork. Gladwin awarded the ten surviving crew members one hundred dollars for their bravery, and General Amherst was so impressed that he ordered medals struck for them. At the same time, he chastised Major Wilkins at Fort Niagara for sending the ship out with so small a crew. He wrote that "Nothing could be more thoughtless and unaccountable than permitting the Master to sail without any guard for the defence of the vessel, when he was going to the jaws of the Savages who would certainly take every occasion they could to attempt it. The Master's permitting the Mohawks to go on shore was not less inconsiderate and imprudent, like our trusty, faithful friends (as all Indians are) they, as they ever will do, certainly told the savages everything they knew of the vessel, and as soon as they heard that there were but twelve men on board and loaded with provisions, it could not fail to indice them to make the attempt."[1]

This debacle did not do anything to enhance Pontiac's already weakening reputation. His followers had suffered heavy casualties with nothing to show for them. In frustration, they burned Pierre Reaume's barn, which contained a thousand bushels of wheat that they feared the garrison might use.

Pontiac's grip on his followers continued to weaken as more and more began to look toward providing for their families in the coming winter. Holding the alliance together over the summer to maintain the siege of Detroit, as well as his part in orchestrating the attacks on the other posts, was nothing short of remarkable. Still, it would mean

Preparing to Meet the Enemy, by Robert Griffing. A group of woodland warriors prepare for battle.
Courtesy of Robert Griffing and Paramount Press.

little if Detroit held out and the English were able to maintain their presence in the Great Lakes. On September 9, about seventy Potawatomies from Saint Joseph arrived at Detroit, but their purpose was to talk peace with Gladwin. By the nineteenth, all had departed. The Chippewas, and even some of the Ottawas were beginning to doubt Pontiac's leadership. He sent one last appeal to de Villiers at Fort de Chartres, asking him to ignore the peace treaty and send him help.

Even with Pontiac's weakened position, the siege continued and the garrison was still in danger. A sergeant was killed outside the fort on September 24, and a soldier was killed when a patrol boat was attacked. On October 2, Lieutenants Abbott, Brehm, and Hay were sent up to the mouth of Lake Saint Clair to see about getting firewood from Hog Island (Belle Isle). They were also to try to recapture the boat that the Indians had taken from Captain Robertson on his depth-sounding mission. The Indians fired on their boats from the shore and then gave pursuit in canoes and bateaux. Brehm fired a round of grapeshot from a four pounder into one of the war canoes at close range. Of the approximately fifteen occupants, only two were able to paddle away. This demonstration convinced the other Indians to withdraw. On the way back, after completing their mission, the soldiers challenged the Indians to come out after them again. The only response was a few musket shots from the shore. The soldiers had one man killed and three wounded, two of which were very minor.

On October 3, the *Huron* returned from Niagara, bringing news of the loss of the *Michigan*. This was bad news for Gladwin. Now with only one ship to bring him men and supplies, he had only three-weeks' supply of flour on hand, and like his adversaries, he too had to worry about food for the coming winter. He immediately sent the *Huron* back to Niagara for more supplies. On board were Captain Gray and Lieutenant Brown, who had both been wounded at Bloody Run, as well as Lieutenant MacDonald, who was to settle long-neglected matters with the paymaster. Gray, who had served bravely and well, was eventually appointed as aide-de-camp to General Amherst to replace Dalyell.

For all of the strength and determination that he had shown, the strain of the siege was beginning to wear on Gladwin. On October 7, he wrote to Sir William Johnson, "I am brought into a scrape, and left in it; things are expected of me that cant be performed; I could wish I had quitted the service seven years ago, and that somebody else commanded here."[2]

Then on November 1, he confided to Colonel Bouquet, "I am heartily worried of my command, and I have signified the same to Colonel [William] Amherst; I hope I shall be relieved soon, if not, I intend to quit the service for I would not chuse to be any longer exposed to the villainy and treachery of the settlements and Indians."[3]

In spite of his own self-doubt, Gladwin's determination and military skill had been the largest single factor in Detroit's ability to hold out, and no one could justly criticize him for what he had accomplished. He was the perfect example of the British officers who came to North America, did their best to learn the new ways of warfare, and served their king and country with unswerving loyalty and devotion to duty.

On October 11, 12, and 13, Wabbicomigot, a Mississaugi Chippewa chief from Toronto, met with Gladwin to discuss peace terms. The importance of this conference is that Wabbicomigot claimed that he also spoke for many of the other Chippewas and even some Ottawas. On the fourteenth, the Chippewas turned over six prisoners as proof of their desire for peace, and more conferences were held in the fort. The day also brought the first snow of the season, emphasizing to the Indians the urgency of looking after their families.

About this time, a Frenchman from the Illinois Country brought word that a detachment of French troops and forty packhorses loaded with supplies were on the way. This was obviously a ploy that some of the habitants made up to keep the war going. Although it may have encouraged Pontiac, the last of the Potawatomies, and many of the Chippewas and Ottawas, still left for their fall hunt. The French too were at a turning point. Those who had been reluctant before started to supply the garrison with needed supplies, while those who had supported and profited from the war began fleeing to the Illinois Country to escape what they foresaw as inevitable retribution.

On October 20, Pontiac held one last grand council. Although there are no records of exactly what was said, Lieutenant Montresor counted sixty canoes headed toward Pontiac's camp to attend. Pontiac's pleas were at best only partially successful. On October 23, a party of the Chippewas went back to the fort to continue their peace talks, while others loyal to Pontiac did what they could to keep up the siege. On the twenty-ninth, four inches of snow and a hard frost helped many of the remaining Indians to make their choice.

That night, Pontiac's final hope disappeared when a messenger from de Villiers appeared, carrying letters to Pontiac, the habitants, and to Major Gladwin. De Villiers informed Pontiac that the French had indeed made peace with the English, and he asked that all Indians do likewise. He

Facing page. *On the Great Trail,* by Robert Griffing. The Great Trail was the primary land route between Fort Pitt and the Great Lakes posts, and it was of great importance during the Pontiac Uprising. Courtesy of Robert Griffing and Paramount Press.

promised that the French would never abandon
them, but they would now supply their needs
from the west side of the Mississippi. This was the
end of Pontiac's dream. It was the end of the what
he had worked so hard and sacrificed so much for.
One can only imagine the hopelessness and
exhaustion that he must have felt, knowing that he
had failed. Without help from the French, Pontiac
could not hope to prevail against the might of the
English. In his letter to the habitants, de Villiers
confirmed that peace had been signed and that
Fort de Chartres would be turned over to the
British. Any of the French who did not wish to
become British subjects were told to move to the
lands west of the Mississippi that had been ceded
to Spain.

On October 30, the messenger, Cadet Louis
Cesaire Dagneau Dequindre, delivered de Villiers'
letter to Gladwin. De Villiers assured the British
commander that he had sent out messages to the
Indians advising them of the peace and that he
stood ready to turn over Fort de Chartres as soon
as British troops could reach there.

Pontiac had no choice but to accept the reality
of his situation. He sent a note to Gladwin that
read:

> My Brother
> The word which my father has sent me to
> make peace I have accepted; all my young men
> have buried their hatchets. I think you will for-
> get the bad things which have taken place for
> some time past. Likewise I shall forget what
> you may have done to me, in order to think of
> nothing but good. I, the Saulteurs [Chippewas],
> the Hurons, we are ready to go speak with you
> when you ask us. Give us an answer. I am send-
> ing this council to you in order that you may
> see it. If you are as good as I, you will send me
> a reply. I wish you a good day.
>
> Pondiac[4]

Gladwin replied that he did not have the
power to end the war, only General Amherst did.
He would notify the general of Pontiac's message
and let him know as soon as he received a reply.
Gladwin did not agree to Pontiac's request to meet
with him in the fort. It was probably for Pontiac's

John Montresor Chief Eng:

Lieutenant John Montresor, from a portrait by John
Singleton Copley, ca. 1771. Tim J. Todish collection.

own safety, for it would have been difficult to protect him from all those who held grievances
against him.

Although he was glad that the siege was over,
Gladwin regretted that he would not have the
chance to send a large enough force out to deci-
sively defeat the Indians in battle. He understood
that if the British now punished the Indians too
severely, they would move west of the Mississippi,
and British trade would suffer. On November 1, he
wrote to Amherst that if the general wanted to
punish them, "it may be easily done without any

General Thomas Gage, by John Singleton Copley. Courtesy of the Yale Center for British Art, Paul Mellon Collection. Signature from Benson Lossing's *Field Book of the American Revolution*. Tim J. Todish collection.

expense to the Crown, by permitting a free Sale of Rum, which will destroy them more effectually than Fire & Sword." His personal advice was to meet with them in the spring, when "the Savages will be Sufficiently reduced for want of Powder, and I don't imagine there will be any danger of their breaking out again, provided some Examples are made of our good Subjects, the French, who Set them on." Continuing the war would serve no good purpose, Gladwin continued, and would only drive the Indians to the west, which would "render it extremely difficult (if not impossible) for us to possess that Country, as the French have

promised to Supply them with every thing they want."[5]

On November 2, Gladwin arrested Jacques Godfroy and Mini Chesne for the part they played in the treacherous attack on Fort Miami. As for the actions of the other habitants, Gladwin merely took testimony from witnesses and sent the affidavits to Amherst for his action.

With his dream collapsed and many of his own people now turned against him, Pontiac could no longer stay at Detroit. In mid-November, he left with Dequindre for the Illinois Country. Gladwin, who was hoping to be relieved, received word that he would have to spend the winter at Detroit. There was much for him to do. His garrison was now much larger than he could support over the winter; both provisions and adequate barracks were lacking. On November 20, Rogers, Hopkins, Montresor, and 240 men were sent back east. About 250 soldiers remained at Detroit for the winter.

Gage Replaces Amherst

One other major change was taking place. At long last, after repeated requests to the home government, General Jeffery Lord Amherst (he had recently been knighted), the conqueror of Canada, had finally been granted permission to return home to England. General Thomas Gage was appointed acting commander in chief in his absence. Some authors have made much of how badly Amherst handled the Indian war, claiming that he was recalled in disgrace because of it. The truth is that as early as June 1760, he had asked to return home, but was refused permission. It was finally granted shortly before the recent outbreak of hostilities, which again forced him to delay his departure. While some criticism of his attitude toward the Indians is warranted, the picture of Amherst going home in disgrace does not do him justice.

In an era when self-betterment was almost an expected fringe benefit of public service, Amherst was a dedicated soldier with a very strict sense of right, wrong, and duty to his country. His attitudes toward the Indians were similar to those of many other British officers, and there was some foundation for those beliefs. He is often criticized for advocating what we now hold to be cruel and inhumane tactics, but such actions were commonplace in the eighteenth century. Even Sir William Johnson, recognized as the Indians' champion, called for harsh measures for those who participated in the war. According to Amherst, "He [Johnson] thought the Senecas, Delawares, and Shawnese deserved the most severe punishment, and he said *should be tortured as they do our people.*"[6] [Authors' emphasis.]

In conquering Canada, Amherst succeeded where several other commanders had failed. In victory, he showed compassion and understanding for the conquered Canadians, although he continued his predecessor General James Abercromby's policy of holding the French military accountable for the atrocities committed at Forts Oswego and William Henry.

In dealing with the Indian uprising, Amherst was faced with a situation never before seen on the continent—a widespread, well-coordinated alliance involving a people previously known for their strong individualism and reluctance to engage in prolonged warfare. Certainly he made some mistakes, and as supreme commander he was ultimately responsible for the mistakes of his subordinates. Yet, it is also true that when the war began, the inevitable postwar reductions and the ravages of tropical diseases contracted during the Caribbean campaigns severely weakened his once powerful army..

Amherst was not without detractors. For example, in October, George Croghan had a heated argument over policy disputes with Amherst. He eventually resigned his position as deputy superintendent of Indian affairs and went to England, where he successfully persuaded the king to make changes in that department.[7]

General Amherst's long-sought request to return to England was finally granted, and General Thomas Gage informed Colonel Bouquet that

"the Command of His Majesty's Troops in North America has devolved on me."[8] When Amherst sailed for England on the sloop of war *Weasle*, on November 10, 1763, it can hardly be said that he returned home on the waves of victory, but neither did he return home in disgrace. Much of his quiet reception at home was due to the political turmoil in England at the time. The new king, George III, was young and inexperienced, and various political factions were vying for his favor. Secretary of State for the Southern Department William Pitt, a strong Amherst supporter and one of the primary architects of the war in America, had fallen from power. His successors were not anxious to lionize one of his proteges.

Parliament, Lord Halifax, and the king were not happy with the recent setbacks in America, and although Amherst would have to defend his policies, he was not severely criticized for the actions he had taken. Some historians have contended that Thomas Gage was a much better commander in chief. Gage, however, had his own faults, prejudices, and petty jealousies, which tainted many of his decisions. He was also just as determined as Amherst to make the Indians pay the consequences for the war and most of all for the atrocities committed against innocent people on the frontier.

All in all, Amherst had been able to put together a strategy and a makeshift army that relieved the sieges of Forts Pitt and Detroit and broke the fighting spirit of the Indians' remarkable alliance in about six month's time. Furthermore, the recent defeats at Devil's Hole and Buffalo Creek, along with the Lake Erie storm disaster, were obviously not Amherst's fault, but rather the actions of war and nature beyond his control.

Part of Amherst's desire to return home was because he needed to get the family estate in order. His wife and his older brother were seriously ill, and both died soon after he arrived home. Amherst officially remained the commander in North America until 1764. He continued to serve the army in important capacities, including as commander in chief of the entire British army. His successful strategies extended well beyond his time in North America. During the American Revolution, he was asked to return to America to command the crown forces, but he refused. When he died in 1797, he was a field marshal, the highest rank in the British army.[9]

Although Pontiac had sued for peace and Amherst had returned to England in late 1763, there was still much work to be done in the coming year before the peace would become a reality.

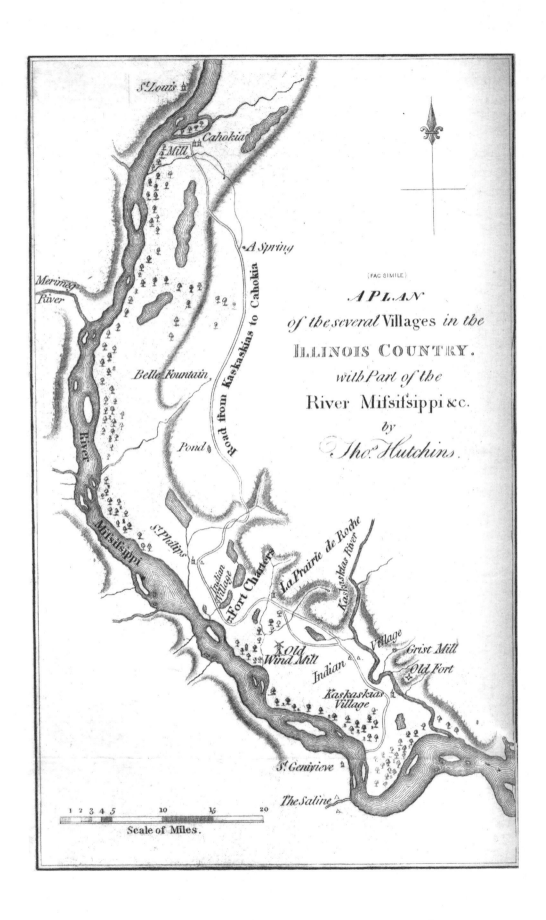

Chapter VIII
The "Forgotten" Campaign—the British Attempt to Take Possession of the Illinois Posts and the Ambush at Roche a Davion
Winter to Spring 1764

I am sorry to Acquaint You, We could not Proceed to Our Intended Destination at the Illinois; The Savages having been Determined to oppose Us, Posted themselves at an Advantageous place, Called the Roche D'Avion. . . .

Major Arthur Loftus

The Challenges of the Illinois Country

WITH THE CESSATION OF HOSTILITIES over the winter of 1763–1764, the British turned their attention to taking possession of the Illinois posts the Treaty of Paris had ceded. At the time of the Pontiac Uprising, "the *Illinois Country* usually meant the settled areas on both sides of the Mississippi, running from Saint Louis on the north to Kaskaskia on the south, including the communities of Cahoka, Saint Philippe, Fort de Chartres, Prairie du Rocher, and Sainte Genevieve."[1]

The 1763 uprising delayed the British takeover of the French posts in the region, which adversely affected the fur trade and also caused concern that the Illinois Country could be used as a source of support for the Indians if the uprising resumed in 1764. By garrisoning these posts and settlements, the British hoped to secure the region for trade and as a restraint on renewed Indian hostilities.

Both the British and French made sincere efforts to improve relations with the different tribes and mend the underlying resentment in an effort to restore the trade that was beneficial to all parties. The French and Indian War had a devastating effect on the French economy as well as the British, and it was particularly evident in New Orleans and its dependent posts. The war "ruined many New Orleans merchants, created shortages, and led to a raging inflation."[2]

This scarcity resulted in French attempts to reestablish and strengthen Indian trade on the west side of the Mississippi River. Several merchants were granted trading monopolies for this purpose, and in February 1764, Pierre de Laclede and associates established the settlement and trading post of Saint Louis. Later that year, Laclede and other French inhabitants in the upper Louisiana–Mississippi region were stunned to learn that the French government had actually ceded it to the Spanish as part of the 1762 Treaty of Fontainebleau, knowledge of which had been withheld from the French governor and officials in New Orleans. It would be another two years before Spain would complete the Louisiana transition.[3]

Although there was some optimism that the

Facing page. *A Plan of the Several Villages in the Illinois Country with Part of the River Mississippi &c,* by Thomas Hutchins. Tim J. Todish collection.

Chippewa Indian Warrior, by Dirk Gringhuis.
Courtesy of Mackinac State Historic Parks.

peace would carry over the winter, Gage continued to plan offensive campaigns for 1764. The Indians had ceased hostilities in the fall for want of ammunition, the need to provide for their families, and, to some extent, weariness of the war. However, while some tribes were ready to sue for permanent peace, there was still a substantial number intent on renewing hostilities in 1764. Although Pontiac had pledged peace, he was secretly working in the Illinois Country and farther south to raise support for renewed violence in 1764. That

Pontiac could not be trusted to keep his word is why many British officers were so vehemently against him—a justifiable resentment that modern-day historians sometimes ignore.

Both the French and British military officers realized that peaceful relations with the Indians were necessary for the recovery of the western trade. Even Gladwin encouraged ending the war because he was concerned about further alienating the western tribes and how that would affect trade and the economy. The French commanders also understood the best interests of not only their own country's economy, but that of the Indians as well. As early as September 1763, the French commandant at Fort de Chartres tried to persuade the Indians to make a formal and lasting peace with the British:

> Neyon De Villieres major Commandant at Fort Dechart: to the Indians Sept 27, 1763
>
> To all my Children the Irequois, or Six Nations, Abenaekees, Shawanese, Ottawas, Chippawas, Hurons, Powtawatamies, Kickapouts, Macoutins, Mimis, Ouyatonons, Peanguicheas Illenois, Sachias, Foxes, Folliovanines, Ozags, Kanzas, Missauris, Panis, and to all Red Men—
>
> My dear Children—
>
> As none of you can reproach me with Lying, I promised to communicate to you the news, and desire you to listen to my Speech, Lo! Here it is, my Dear Children. Open your Ears, that it may penetrate even to the Bottom of your Hearts. The great Day is come at last, whereon it has pleased the Master of life to inspire the great King of the French and him of the English to make Peace . . . Sorry to See the Blood of Men Spilt so long. What Joy will you have in seeing the French & English smoking with the same Pipe, and Eating out of the same Spoon, and finally living like Brethren. You will see the Roads free, the Lakes, and Rivers unstopped: Ammunition, and Merchandize will abound in your Villages, your Women, and Children will be Clothed as well as you. . . .
>
> The French are free even as You. They change the Land when the King orders it. He has not given yours; he has only Ceded those which he had amongst you, in Order to avoid

War for the future, and that you may always enjoy Tranquility, and have Abundance of Merchandize in your Village. I depend on you that you will not make me Lie, and that your Young Men will not quit their Rattles, and Playthings to take up the Hatchet, but to carry it amongst Savage Nations from whom you expect no Succour, and who live only on Earth to embroil it. . . .Our Hearts are now but one. You cannot strike at present the one without having the Other for an Enemy, so if you continue Hostilities you will have no Supplies, and it is from them, that your are to expect them. You will be always in my heart, and those of the French, who will never abandon you.[4]

Although peace seemed possible, the British military still had concerns over the possible renewal of Indian hostilities. One problem was how Indians would react when the British took possession of the Illinois posts, which included Fort de Chartres (the largest and strongest fort), Cahokia, Fort Kaskaskia, Fort Massac, and the settlements at Sainte Genevieve, Prairie du Rocher, and Vincennes.[5]

The uprising delayed the takeover of these posts. When an expedition again became feasible, the British began planning the route from the south beginning at New Orleans rather than through the Great Lakes as originally intended. They hoped that this would prevent, or at least deter, the northern Indians from obtaining supplies and ammunition from French or Spanish traders should the Indians renew hostilities later in the year.

In late July 1763, while the sieges of Fort Detroit and Fort Pitt were in their waning stages, other British troops prepared for the occupation of the former Spanish posts at Saint Augustine, Pensacola, and Mobile.[6]

John Stuart, superintendent of Indian affairs for the Southern District (counterpart to Sir William Johnson in the north), along with the governors of Virginia and North and South Carolina, held a large conference with the Creeks, Choctaws, Chickasaws, and Cherokee at Augusta, Georgia, on November 3, 1763. They discussed reopening the trade and a cession of land to Georgia by the Creeks.[7]

In preparation for the council, in spite of the austerity program, British officials purchased presents as customary to show good faith. For example, Lieutenant Colonel Augustine Prevost of the 60th Regiment at Pensacola purchased from William Satterthwaite a multitude of goods for the Creek and Choctaw Indians, which included "31 Blanketts, 12 Looking glasses, 1 Saddle, 2 box knives, 1 Bagly Bulletts, 1 Trading Gun Painted, 1 ps Blue Cloth, 1 Laced hatt, 1 Bagy Small Shott, totaling £126. . . ."[8]

Stuart received some £2,966 in payment for goods purchased for the Indians at Saint Augustine and the surrounding area.[9]

Even as the Indian conferences were in progress, planning was also underway for the proposed military expedition into the Illinois Country. Lieutenant Colonel Robertson (who oversaw the transport of the Platoons from New York to Albany back in September) was sent south to oversee these operations. He noted that he "traveled to St. Augustine, Pensacola & Mobile and Charles Town, South Carolina, being payed for his expenses at this in regulating [sic] Fixing the troops in these garrisons Three hundred and three pounds Sterling."[10]

These transactions suggest that the British were intending to open a fair trade with the Indians and were trying not to alienate them further. While in Mobile, Robertson made arrangements with William Hugh, master of the brigantine *Nancy*, for transportation of the troops to New Orleans.[11]

On the surface, it appeared that the plans for the Illinois expedition were progressing satisfactorily. However, British officials would soon learn otherwise.

The Indians did not receive well the change to British authority in the southern region. This was because the French traditionally aligned with and supported most of these tribes. In December and January, reports from de Villiers at Fort de Chartres and French officers at the outlying posts began to reach New Orleans and were eventually forwarded to the British commanders.[12]

As previously noted, after leaving Detroit, Pontiac was actively pursuing the Illinois Country Indians, who in turn influenced the Mississippi and Louisiana tribes to join in stopping the British expedition—showing that he still had hostile intentions.

Like de Villiers at New Orleans, both the previous governor of Louisiana, Louis Billonart (Bellouart) Chevalier de Kerlerec, and his successor (the last French governor of Louisiana), Jean-Jacques-Blaise d'Abbadie, did everything in their power to encourage the Indians to accept the transfer of power and accept the friendship of the British. They also tried to alleviate the French inhabitants' fears about how the new rulers would treat them.[13]

The population of the region was sparsely dispersed among six settlements, Kaskaskia, Fort de Chartres, Saint Philippe, Prairie du Rocher, Cahokia, and Saint Genevieve. The 1752 French census listed approximately 1,380 persons, with 785 whites, including missionaries, soldiers in garrison, and their wives, 446 Negro slaves, and 149 Indian slaves.[14]

Despite these efforts and the conference that Superintendent Stuart held in November, many tribes, particularly the Choctaws, remained hostile toward the British. Governor d'Abbadie encouraged Choctaw Chief Mastabe to remain peaceful, even after the British expedition left New Orleans in March 1764. The governor wrote:

> that the English were today our brothers, that there was no longer any question of war and that it was necessary that the white and red men should live together in harmony, and that they should work. I further told him that the English would provide for their needs by the traders, and that everything tended, as far as I saw, to inspire them with sentiments of peace and tranquility. According to the custom it was necessary to make them some small presents. On the fourteenth I received news from Mobile informing me that fourteen English traders had been killed among the Alibamu, and some oth-

ers had been sent back to Mobile all naked; that four hundred Choctaw were at Mobile and were demanding present. . . . I fear that if these promises are not fulfilled, it is going to cost the English something. I have been informed that two hundred and thirty Mobile savages, Taenasa, and other little nations from around Mobile are coming here to demand that they be established on our territory.[15]

Governor d'Abbadie went out of his way to insure that his commanders provided the utmost assistance to the British, including helping them secure provisions and bateaux. They were also to assist in planning the route of the expedition and provide information about the terrain, potential hazards, the posts, the inhabitants, the Indian tribes, and even what weather to expect.

Major Arthur Loftus of the 22nd Regiment was to command the expedition. He arrived in New Orleans on January 23, and d'Abbadie received him well. In his journal, d'Abbadie described the arrival of the British troops:

> On the eighteenth, an English bateau from Mobile arrived at the bayou with ten men and three officers. I permitted them to enter. The bateau which the English commandant, who is going to ascent to the Illinois, had selected to carry the garrison for the Natchez must be transported by land from the bayou to the Mississippi. I do not wish to appear to refuse my consent to this arrangement, but on account of the impossibility of the undertaking, the bateau will be obliged to return the way it came.
>
> On the twentieth, I permitted the English officer, who is here for the purpose of storing the ammunition of the bateaux of the convoy to send a boat to the Balise in order to be better informed about the arrival of the troops who are to go to the Illinois and are expected to come by way of the mouth of the Mississippi.
>
> M. Loftus, sent to command at that post, and several other officers who have profited by this occasion to ascent to the town came to my house upon their arrival (on the 23rd of Jan) On the next day, the twenty-fourth, I gave them a dinner. After the dinner, I had M. Loftus come to my office; in the presence of MM. Loftus, Dolsay, [Lieutenant Phillip] Pittman, another

English officer, I had read to him and interpreted by M. [Captain Charles Philippe] Aubry the letters of M. De Villiers, containing all the information he has given me particularly in regard to the Illinois savages; finally I told him how much I desired that he go to this post, since it was daily of more importance to evacuate it for the king's interest.[16]

Eventually the remainder of the British troops who were to comprise the expedition arrived, and the French commandant permitted them to encamp on "the bank of the [Mississippi] river, a little above the city" during the course of the next three weeks while preparing for the expedition.[17]

In 1766, British engineer Captain Harry Gordon described New Orleans, then under Spanish rule:

New Orleans is but a small Town, not many good Houses in it, but in general healthy & the Inhabitants well looked; Its principle Staple is the Trade for furs & Skins from the Illinois, their want of Negroes keeps back the Indigo making; They have attempted Sugar. . .they have now five Plantations that produce it, but they do not make it turnout to great amount. There is only a stockade round the Place with a Large Banquet; their dependance for Defence is the difficulty of Approach, that up the River is tedious, & easily opposed, particularly at the Detour d' Anglois, & there is only 12 feet Water at the Bar.[18]

In January, once he was aware of the British plan, d'Abaddie began sending letters to the various French commandants at the upper posts, including M. Desmazellieres at Pointe Coupee, the nearest post above New Orleans, M. De Cabaret de Trepi commandant at the Arkansas post beyond, and M. de Villiers at Fort de Chartres, instructing them to provide all necessary assistance when the time came to evacuate the forts. The governor's letter to de Trepi on January 25, 1764, typifies his mandates to these officers:

I notify you of the arrival of the English here, where they are preparing to ascend to the Illinois. Their convoy is to be of eight or nine boats which will carry four hundred and fifty men to relieve the French garrison. I recommend that you procure them the assistance they may need, especially warning them of the activities of the Indians of which you may have knowledge. Warn your Indians that the English are now our friends and that the intention of the great emperors is that we live in peace.[19]

Although, according to d'Abbadie, Loftus could be arrogant at times, d'Abbadie complimented the British officer on his control and handling of his troops during this difficult period. Many of the British soldiers were apprehensive due to the reports they received about unrest among the Illinois Indians. This resulted in some desertions, which added to the already existing tension during the three weeks of hard work involved in securing provisions, boats, equipment and additional personnel for the expedition. D'Abbadie had even stopped all work on French projects to provide more workmen for the British efforts. It is interesting to note the purchase of osnaburg "to cover the Troops going up the Mississippi from Muschetto's [Mosquitos] as was practiced by the French when they sent up Convoys in the hot Season."[20]

During this time, d'Abbadie informed Loftus about the letters he had received from de Villiers at Fort de Chartres concerning the Indians' attitudes toward the British. Many of the French inhabitants in the upper country still were fearful of British rule and were requesting permission to relocate to areas that were still under French authority. In fact, during the first year of the new settlement at Saint Louis, some forty families relocated there from Fort de Chartres and nearby Cahokia.[21]

Many other habitants, however, chose to remain in the Illinois Country, where they found that they would receive fair treatment from the British, just as the French inhabitants at Detroit and Michilimackinac did.

Finally, by February 27, the expedition was ready to depart. D'Abbadie recorded in his journal that he was well satisfied with the restraint the English troops had shown. He added that despite doubling the guard at the river levee, "There has not happened here the least little thing that has given me cause to complain," which put to rest his concern over "what undertakings the English could have attempted here."[22]

Watch was kept on the transport *Salomon*, where several canon were loaded with grapeshot. In spite of the discipline the English maintained, twenty men deserted. The French commandant expected more desertions before they arrived at Pointe Coupee, saying, "these people are frightened at the difficulties of the passage and are afraid of the savages: some of the officers are not much more reassured." In order to avoid difficulties and put an end to the disputes that may occur among the inhabitants, d'Abbadie sent an officer on half-pay, M. Baurans, to accompany them as far as Pointe Coupee to serve as a guide and interpreter. The governor deemed it "necessary, as much for them [the British] as for our subjects, that there should be a reliable Frenchman with them during their voyage. . . ."[23]

Again he warned Loftus to prevent his troops from molesting the inhabitants along the river, which Loftus promised to do.[24]

The contingent consisted of eleven boats with about 420 persons, which included "three hundred and sixty men, seventeen officers, thirty women, twenty-eight children and some servants, in all."[25]

Ambush at Roche a Davion

After leaving New Orleans on February 27, the expedition arrived at Point Coupee, the first French outpost, on March 15. During that time, despite rigid discipline, Loftus had more than fifty men desert and seven soldiers die.[26]

Captain Gordon later described the settlement at Point Coupee as consisting of "110 Families, who live much at ease; their produce at present only Tobacco & Corn. . . . Their situation is low, & are obliged to have Levees of Earth to keep off the Flood. . .there is here a small ruinous Stockade Fort with 1 officer & 10 men in it."[27]

While at Point Coupee, an incident occurred where d'Abbadie felt Loftus acted improperly by

giving shelter to a fugitive slave. An alleged Indian slave of a New Orleans habitant joined the expedition under the pretense of being a free man. Apparently the French at Point Coupee recognized him, and a dispute arose because Loftus believed the Indian's claim. D'Abbadie, despite his good intentions of helping the British and keeping the peace, was showing his own cultural bias in this situation, as it was essentially one man's word against the other's, and there is no mention of any legal documentation for the slavery claim. As commanding officer, Loftus would have had the authority to make such a decision for an official member of his force. This is another example in which some British officers were sympathetic toward the Indians, as Loftus was showing compassion and giving his man the benefit of the doubt.

Site of the ambush at Roche a Davion, near modern Fort Adams, Mississippi. Although the course of the Mississippi River has changed over the years, the ambush site is believed to have been near the curve in the river in the upper-right section of this aerial photo. Courtesy of the Upper Midwest Environmental Sciences Center and the United States Geological Survey Section of the Department of the Interior.

The interpreter-guide Baurans left the English expedition at Point Coupee to return to New Orleans. Loftus and his troops then proceeded onto Roche a Davion, named for a huge rock near the former site of Father Antoine Davion's mission at present-day Fort Adams Landing, Mississippi, some forty leagues from the Iberville River. About seven o'clock in the morning, on March 20, the convoy encountered a surprise attack by a force of French-allied Tunica, Ofogoula, Choctaw, and Avoyelles Indians, who appeared suddenly on both banks of the river, catching the troops in a crossfire.[28]

While the previously discussed attacks at Devil's Hole, Bloody Run, and Buffalo Creek are more familiar, this lesser-known skirmish is evidence that the uprising was still very much alive during the winter. In a letter to General Gage, Major Loftus described the harrowing action:

I Beg leave to Inform you, that we left New Orleans the Twenty Seventh of February But I am Sorry to Acquaint You, We could not Proceed to Our Intended Destination at the Illinois; The Savages having been Determined to oppose Us, Posted themselves at an Advantageous place, Called the Roche D'Avion, on the East Side of the River, about Seventy leagues from New Orleans, & at a Convenient Point on the West side; we had certain Intelligence several Days before, of our being Attacked at that Place, or near it; So that You may Imagine, we took all the Care we Could, both on Shore, & in our Boats. The only precaution we could take in the Boats, was keeping them One a head of the other, as Close as they Conveniently could, and to have their Arms ready beside them, while they Rowed; As we had not men Enough to Supply the Oars, it made it very Fatiguing to them; this was Occasioned by the great Desertion we had, & Death & Sickness; The Twentieth of March, about Seven in the Morning, the two light Boats which I always Sent a head to look out, were attacked on the West side, all our Boats being on the Same Side, I had given Orders to the Boats in case any of them were Attacked, to Cross over to the other side; But these two Boats were Entirely Disabled the first Fire, for out of Fifteen men that was in both Boats, there was Six Killed and Four Wounded, [one of d'Abbadie's letters stated six killed, with seven wounded; however, Loftus' eyewitness account is most likely more accurate] so that they could not Cross over, but falling down the Stream to Us, we took them in tow, &

Crossed over to the Other side; But finding the Savages were possessed of both Sides of the River, I Apprehended it was in Vain to proceed; for We could not See One of them, nor could we get on Shore, for the River was so high, that it Overflowed it's Banks, So that in many places the Trees were as thick in the River Fourteen or Twelve Yards from its Banks, as they were on the Land, besides, we Could not keep out of the reach of their Shot, the River not being Wide enough, & if it had, we could not Row against the Stream in the middle of it. I Therefore Ordered the Boats to Retire, & this was the Unanimous opinion of Every Officer with me; [not surprising because d'Abbadie had already noted that the officers were nervous and apprehensive about the Indians from the beginning]. If the Savages had not fired on the first Boats, but have let them pass, & not attacked until our last Boat had come within their Party, they would have Killed on half of us, as by that means every Boat would have Received a fire, & we had not the least Cover, and were Obliged to keep as near the Shore as the Trees would allow us, to avoid the Strength of the Current; by a general fire they made on Seeing Us Retire, I Judged there could not be less, than Two Hundred of them [French sources claim there were only thirty attackers], which was Enough to Stop Two Thousand Men in open Boats; I Returned to New Orleans, where, I was in hopes of getting all our Boats & Stores, over-Land to the Bayou, in the Lake Portchartrin, a thing Commonly done there, and I had agreed with a Merchant there to Carry them over; in which Case, we could have proceeded to Mobile where I Intended to go, without danger, or any further Expence; But Mr. D'Abbadie the Governour would not Allow it; Indeed I did not Expect any great favor here; For while we Remained before Orleans, Several of the Savage Chiefs who had Attacked Us, made their Publick Entry into the Town; I was therefore Obliged to find Some other Way, & fortunately One of the Transports that brought us from Mobile, was in the River; I sent an Officer down to Stop her, & take her into the Service; and I went down the River to the Belire [Balise] with all our Boats & Stores, and putting as many Men & Stores on Board the Vessel, as She could

Carry, Proceeded to Pensacola, as the most likely place to get Assistance.[29]

In letters recounting the action to fellow French officers, d'Abbadie criticized Loftus, citing the fact that French convoys had suffered more severe attacks and had gone on in spite of them. He felt that the British officer should have gone on to Natchez because it was closer than returning to New Orleans, suggesting that the British could have eventually completed the mission. Additionally, he claimed that some British officers disagreed with the retreat, even though Loftus reported the opposite in his letter to Gage. There is an apparent lack of documentation supporting d'Abbadie's claim.[30]

It is apparent that d'Abbadie's assessment is unrealistic for several reasons. French officers knew the country well, while Loftus was unfamiliar with it and did not know the exact strength of the Indian attackers. It is fair to state that he made the appropriate decision to return to New Orleans rather than risk the destruction of his entire convoy with further loss of life and provisions. Such a situation out on open water is entirely different from fighting to the death in an enclosed fort or blockhouse, as Bouquet and Amherst advocated the summer before to the officers commanding the small British posts. Furthermore, it is absurd that d'Abbadie would claim the British convoy would have been safe at Natchez, as he had reduced the French garrison there to only fifteen men and previously recommended, back in August 1763, that post be abandoned because "the lawful buildings of which are entirely fallen in ruins and the fortifications of which are not much better. . . ."[31]

Regardless of his opinion about the British retreat, d'Abbadie chastised the Indians involved when the chiefs visited him two days after the engagement and told him about the fight. Inquiring why they had attacked the party after promising d'Abbadie that they would not, the principal chiefs Perruquier and Bride le Boeuf replied that the British were responsible for the smallpox epidemic that recently killed most of their children. Also, they felt the British were intent on building

more forts and planned genocide on the Indians and the French. In a clearly defiant attitude, the chiefs also challenged the French commander to "have us put in irons and send us to the great chief; we shall see if he will have us put to death."[32]

They added that they would wait for the British at Point aux Ecors. If the British returned, they would drive them away again. Loftus apparently did not include in his letter to Gage that they had fired several shots from swivel guns at the Tunica Indian village during the retreat to New Orleans, which further enraged the Indians. This could partially account for the hostile attitude of the Indians when they visited the French governor in New Orleans. De Villiers and others later confirmed that much of this attitude was also due to the fact that Pontiac encouraged the local Indians to join the uprising.[33]

By late May, Gage had been informed of the failure of the expedition, as well as received the information from d'Abbadie and de Villiers about Pontiac's activities to undermine the peace effort. This included de Villier's comment that the chief "has destroyed in one night what I had accomplished in eight months."[34]

When Gage forwarded this information to Sir William Johnson, he added, "This fellow [Pontiac] should be gained to our Interest, or knocked in the head, He has great Abilities, but his Savage Cruelty destroys the regard we Should otherwise have for him."[35]

British efforts dragged on as both Lieutenant Pitman and Major Loftus unsuccessfully attempted to organize additional efforts later in the year. Pitman did meet with the Indians on a few occasions, particularly during July with the Tunicas who had attacked Loftus. Chiefs Perruquier, Latanache, and Bride le Boeuf related that they had attacked the British because they were "afraid of the English making them slaves but were now sorry," and they of course stated their expectation of receiving presents.[36]

The British would never establish any new posts in the Illinois or Mississippi Country, but rather kept only those the French had ceded, just as they had promised. In fact, in 1771, long after the Pontiac Uprising had subsided, General Gage prohibited granting lands in the Illinois Country to individuals in the interest of promoting and protecting the fur trade enterprises of both parties.[37]

The ambush at Roche a Davion caused a setback for the British in taking possession of the region, which would not occur until late October 1765, when troops of the 42nd Regiment marched into Fort de Chartres.[38]

Even as late as December 15, d'Abbadie received news from Captain Louis Groston de Saint Ange de Bellerive, the new French commander at Fort de Chartres, that "the disposition of the savages and of Chief Pontiac is in no way favorable to the English in their project to ascend the river to the Illinois."[39]

While de Villiers had not thought the conspiracy to be general in nature and expressed his hopes for a sincere peace between the French, British, and Indians, it was more than obvious that the natives had other ideas. Indeed the British had to deal with the uprising back on the eastern frontier in the later months of 1764, as will be seen in the Bradstreet and Bouquet campaigns. Perhaps d'Abbadie described it best when he commented back on May 16, to Major Robert Farmer, the British commandant at Mobile: "it is with pain, sir, that I entertain you with these details at moments when we ought to be enjoying the sweets of the peace which unites us. . . . It is not the first time that I have the honor to say it to you and they are only evil and vile souls who can suspect anything different. . . ."[40]

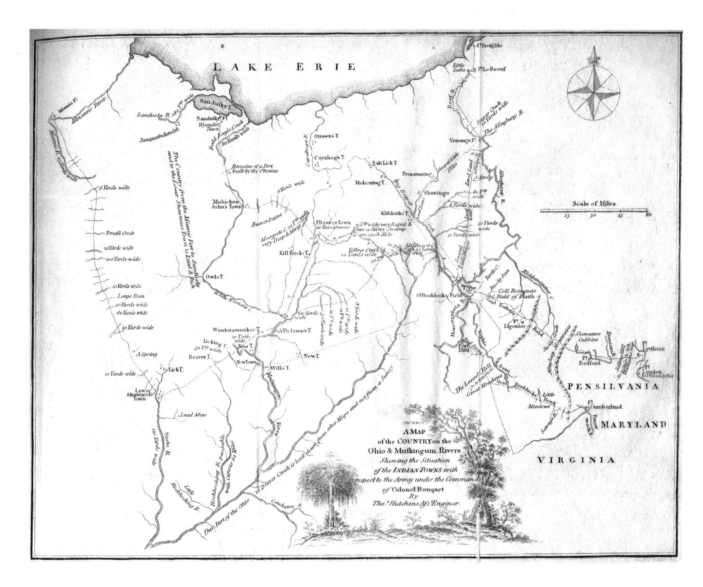

A Map of the Country on the Ohio and Muskingum Rivers Showing the Situation of the Indian Towns with respect to the Army under the Command of Colonel Bouquet, by Thomas Hutchins. Tim J. Todish collection.

Chapter IX
End of the Uprising
Summer to Fall 1764

You have by an admirable Conduct, reduced and humbled them as they deserved; and thereby made a Peace upon a Solid Foundation, and greatly added to the Reputation of His Majesty's Arms, amongst the Indian Nations.
General Thomas Gage to Colonel Henry Bouquet

Bradstreet's Expedition

IN THE SPRING OF 1764, General Gage simultaneously had to direct his attention to plans for campaigns against the Indians on the Great Lakes and eastern fronts and also for an expedition to take possession of the French posts in the Illinois Country. His strategy for dealing with the northern Indians essentially followed that which Amherst and Bouquet had begun the previous year. In correspondence with Bouquet, Gage discussed a two-pronged move to bring the hostile Indians into final submission in 1764.[1]

Colonel John Bradstreet would command the first prong. He would push from Niagara across Lake Erie to relieve Fort Detroit and subdue the tribes along his route of march. The second force, under the command of Colonel Henry Bouquet, would drive through the interior of the Ohio Country, stamping out any remaining Indian resistance among the Ohio tribes, especially "against the settlements of the Barbarians, either on the heads of the Sioto or Muskingham" Rivers.[2]

Although there is some dispute about the specifics of Gage's orders to Bradstreet, it is clear that he was to relieve the still-besieged garrison at Detroit and either attack or make peace with the various Indian tribes along the way, especially the Shawnee and Delaware at Sandusky and along the Scioto River. From Detroit, he was to send a detachment to reoccupy Michilimackinac, while the smaller posts of Saint Joseph, Miami, Ouiatenon, and La Baye would not be regarrisoned.

From the beginning, Bradstreet had some apprehension about his mission. On July 12, he wrote to General Gage from Niagara, "Had we the numbers of Troops first intended for this Service and that in time so as to be made in some degree fit for it, we might push forward & leave a proper number here for the Security of this place during the Stay of those Savages who are here talking of peace; but. . .the Season advanced & the Enemy apprais'd in every quarter of our being here leaves little hope of our Success against them unless they may think proper to give us Battle instead of drawing out of the way. . . ."[3]

Although there would be some additions and subtractions along the way, Bradstreet's force initially consisted of approximately twelve hundred men. According to Lieutenant Thomas Mante, Bradstreet's aide-de-camp, the force had the following breakdown:

243 men from the 17th Regiment
98 men from the 55th Regiment
344 New York Provincials
213 Connecticut Provincials
209 New Jersey Provincials
73 Boatmen[4]

About 250 Indians also joined the expedition,

including a number of Iroquois, whose services were secured with the help of Sir William Johnson.

The expedition had considerable logistical problems to overcome, and Bradstreet, who had made a name for himself in that area during the French and Indian War, energetically set about getting his army ready to advance. Lieutenant John Montresor, an engineer officer assigned to the expedition, recorded two interesting details about the preparations in his journal: "I ordered 124 Tents out of the Store for to be painted with Tar, also sent to Capt. Standish to make Rocket and fire works for my signals and sent him up Sulphur and Antimony."[5]

One of the major challenges of getting supplies to the western forts had always been carrying them up the steep Niagara Escarpment along the portage road between Fort Niagara and Fort Erie. By 1764, the British had built a unique tram railroad to ease the burden of transporting the supplies up this steep incline. Using a series of inclined planes called "cradles," they used windlass power to move boats and supplies up the escarpment in three different stages. A small stockade was built to protect the top of the escarpment.[6]

To safely get the men and supplies across the many miles of water that the trip would cover, a new kind of forty-six-foot boat was designed that would carry twenty-seven men and three weeks' provisions.[7]

There also were personnel problems to be dealt with. On May 17, Lieutenant Montresor recorded, "A fight occurred this day between a Captain of a Quebec Company and a Lieutenant of the Montreal Companies. The Captain was wounded in the Sword arm. I put 'em both under an arrest." He further noted that in general the men were "indolent, careless of their arms & slovenly service, falling sick daily overeating themselves and sleeping in the Sun on the bare ground."[8]

While Bradstreet and Bouquet were preparing their expeditions into the interior, Sir William Johnson held a grand council at Niagara. In all, over seventeen Indians attended, and over a period of three weeks, agreements were reached with delegations of Chippewas, Ottawas, Wyandots, and Senecas. As successful as this conference was, there were still a significant number of Indians that had not come, most notably the still-hostile Delawares and Shawnees.

The Niagara Escarpment from the Niagara River. It was near this spot along the Niagara Portage that the British built the ingenious tram railway to assist in getting goods up and down the incline. Photo by Tim J. Todish.

On August 8, Bradstreet's force left Fort Schlosser at the south end of the Niagara Portage and proceeded west on Lake Erie. On the twelfth, at l'Ance-Aux-Feuilles (Montresor called this the "Cove of Peace"[9]), on the south shore of the lake, a group of emissaries from the hostile Shawnees, Delawares, Wyandots of Sandusky, and the Five Nations of the Scioto Plains met Bradstreet. They claimed that they represented their tribes and came to negotiate for peace with the British. Bradstreet, apparently believing in their sincerity, offered them preliminary terms that basically required the following:

1. They would meet him at Sandusky in twenty-five days to finalize the terms.
2. They would bring all of their white captives and deserters to Sandusky and turn them over to him.
3. They would give up claims to all forts and other posts in their country and further agree to the establishment of as many new ones as necessary for trade. Land the distance of a cannon shot around each post would be included for the purpose of raising provisions.

4. If an Indian killed a British subject, a jury made up of six Englishmen and six Indians would try the Indian under English law.

Six of the emissaries were to remain with Bradstreet as hostages, while the rest, accompanied by a British officer, would return to their tribes to gather up the white captives and prepare for the meeting at Sandusky.

Bradstreet reached Sandusky by August 23, but there was no sign of the Indians and their captives. Another delegation met Bradstreet and asked for more time, and because the agreed upon twenty-five days had not yet expired, he agreed.

About this time, Bradstreet decided that he would send an officer to Fort de Chartres to notify the French and the local Indians of the preliminary treaty and warn them against any hostile acts against British soldiers in the region. Captain Thomas Morris of the 17th Regiment was selected for this dangerous mission. The party embarked from Cedar Point on the south side of Lake Erie on August 26. In addition to Morris, it consisted of two French Canadian guides, two servants, seventeen Indian warriors, and two chiefs. The chiefs were Attawang of the Ottawas, and Wasson, the Chippewa chief who had treacherously murdered Captain Campbell at Detroit.

On August 27, they reached an Ottawa village where they met a less-than-friendly reception. There, Pontiac himself confronted Morris. As Morris related in his journal, Pontiac asked "whether I was come to tell lies, like the rest of my countrymen," and stated "That Ononteeo (the French king) was not crushed as the English had reported, but had got upon his legs again."[10]

Pontiac then showed Morris a letter in French saying that the British troops who had gone to take possession of Fort de Chartres had been defeated and that a French army that had landed in Louisiana would drive the British out of the country. This letter was obviously a forgery, but a still-defiant Pontiac was using it to rally continued support for his cause.

The next day, Morris addressed the assembled chiefs in council, where some of the Indians refused to believe that the French had surrendered to the English. After the council though, Pontiac said, "I will lead the nations to war no more; let 'em be at peace if they chuse it: but I myself will never be a friend to the English. I shall now become a wanderer in the woods; and if they come to seek me there, while I have an arrow left, I will shoot at them."[11]

Afterward, Pontiac said to the other chiefs present, some of whom were in favor of killing Morris, "We must not kill ambassadors: do we not send them to the Flatheads, our greatest enemies, and they to us? Yet these are always treated with hospitality."[12] This shows a significant change in attitude from when he allowed the Chippewas at Detroit to take and kill Captain Campbell.

On August 29, the leader of the Mohawks accompanying Morris ran away after selling two barrels of rum to the Ottawas and stealing other supplies. A number of the Ottawas got drunk, and one young warrior attacked Morris with a knife. One of the French Canadian guides, Jacques Godfroy, intervened and saved his life.[13] Morris and his two guides were forced to flee the village and hide in a cornfield until, eventually, Attawang sent his two sons to guard them. Although tensions remained high, none of the party was injured. On the thirtieth, one of the chiefs presented Morris with a volume of Shakespeare's plays, most probably a captured war trophy, and asked for a little gunpowder in return. When the party continued, a former drummer in the French army, identified only as Saint Vincent, joined them. The drummer proved to be of great service to them. On September 3, Pontiac's nephew and two young Ottawas, who had been sent to escort them, overtook them, making their total number now twenty-four. On the fifth, they met an Indian who was riding a white horse that was said to have been taken from General Braddock at the Battle of the Monongahela in 1755.

On September 7, the party arrived at the former site of Fort Miami, where the local Indians met them in a very threatening manner. A delegation of Shawnees and Delawares had just visited the village and presented the chiefs with wampum belts in an attempt to keep them involved in the war, and anti-British feeling was running high. Leaders of the Kickapoos, Weas, and Mascoutens, who were at the village, all declared that they would kill the Englishmen if the Miamis allowed them to proceed. At one point, two Indians-grabbed Morris and dragged him to a lodge where he was stripped and tied to a post. Morris was certain that he was about to be tortured to death, but at that moment, Pacanne, a young Miami chief, rode up on horseback He intervened, telling the Indians, "If you want meat (for they sometimes eat their prisoners) go to Detroit, or upon the lake (meaning go face your enemies the English) and you'll find enough. What business have you with this man's flesh, who comes to speak with us?"[14]

Morris spent the night in the home of one of the French inhabitants, still in danger of the unfriendly Indians harming or killing him. The next day, the Indians in Morris' party spoke in council to the Miamis, who returned with their answer the following day. Although Morris wanted to proceed to Ouiatenon, he was advised that he must leave the Indian country immediately, or he would be put to death. Deciding that he had no other choice, Morris conceded. Saint Vincent agreed to deliver Bradstreet's letter to the commander of Fort de Chartres. The English gave all of their blankets and shirts to the Indians who had been loyal to them, and Morris gave Saint Vincent, Pacanne, and Pontiac's nephew letters attesting to the loyal service they had given him. The party then began a tense but largely uneventful return to Detroit, where they arrived on September 17. In conducting this mission, Morris exhibited courage and resourcefulness that is typical of many of the British officers who served on the frontier, but for which they are often given too little credit.

After dispatching Morris on his expedition, Bradstreet continued on to Detroit. He arrived on August 26, much to the relief of the beleaguered garrison, which had essentially been under continuous siege since May 1763. Major Gladwin was more than happy that Lieutenant Colonel John

Captain Thomas Morris of the 17th Regiment of Foot. Private collection.

Campbell and seven companies of the 17th Regiment had relieved him. Captain William Howard, also of the 17th Regiment, was promptly sent to reestablish the garrison at Fort Michilimackinac.

On September 5–7, Bradstreet held a conference with the Detroit Indians—Ottawas, Wyandots, Chippewas, Potawatomies, and Miamis. Chippewa chief Wasson, speaking on behalf of his tribe, the Ottawas, and the Miamis, declared:

> We are extremely glad to find ourselves so well received, and hope you will give us peace. . . .
>
> Last year, God forsook us. God has now opened our eyes, and we desire to be heard. 'Tis God's will our hearts are altered. . . . 'Tis God's will also, there should be peace and tranquillity all over the face of the earth and of the waters. . . .
>
> You have forgiven us; but our offences are

Colonel John Bradstreet, by Thomas McIlworth, 1764. Reproduction of this little-known portrait is courtesy of the William Reese Company. Signature from the George A. Bray III collection. Used with permission.

so great, we must again ask it, in the names of our wives and children. We also pray, that all your troops, will have compassion on them and us. . .and we thank the Great King for allowing you to forgive us, and grant us peace.[15]

After the Indians finished speaking, Bradstreet replied:

The ingenuous confession of your folly last year, without any provocation from the English, affords me pleasure, as it gives me reason to believe your submissions sincere, and that your requests for mercy and forgiveness come from your hearts. I shall take compassion on your distress, and grant you peace on the following terms. . . .[16]

Among the terms Bradstreet then stipulated were:

1. The Indians must acknowledge that they were subjects of King George III.
2. If any of the tribe violated the peace, the remaining tribes must join the British in their war against them.
3. If any Indians under the peace plundered or killed any British subjects, they must be delivered up to be tried under English law.
4. All white prisoners and deserters must be promptly delivered up.

Although he originally intended to demand that Pontiac be given up as a prisoner, Bradstreet abruptly changed his mind. No doubt he realized that this was an impossible demand, and he specifically pardoned the chief so that he could come to the conference at Sandusky without fear for his safety.

This treaty was negotiated on September 5, and under normal custom, it should have been ratified on the sixth, but as Lieutenant Montresor reported, "The Ottawas and Jibbeways [Chippewas] incapable of attending Council to sign the Articles of Peace agreed on, through Excess of liquor."[17]

Consequently, the treaty was not formally ratified until the September 7.

While Bradstreet was at Detroit, word arrived on September 13 that the Shawnees and Delawares were still raiding along the frontier, and he realized that their false promises had duped him. These tribes, among the most warlike on the frontier, never intended to honor the terms of the preliminary peace agreement. Rather, they hoped only to stall long enough to prevent the British forces from being able to attack their towns that season. During his march, reports were regularly received about how the Indians were planning to attack Bradstreet's force or commit other depredations on the frontier.

Bradstreet was anxious to leave Detroit as quickly as he could complete his business, as the weather was having a bad affect on the health of his troops. Lieutenant Montresor noted "Extreme heat & the season dry. The 80th Regt. sickly—the camp in general subjected to fevers, agues & Flux-es."[18]

On September 13, Bradstreet received word that eight hundred Indian warriors had assembled at Sandusky, but their purpose was to keep the British troops from landing rather than to ratify the peace treaty.[19]

On the morning of the fourteenth, Bradstreet's force left Detroit and reached Sandusky on the eighteenth. The Shawnee and Delaware emissaries had not arrived, so Bradstreet granted them seven more days. On the nineteenth, a few delegates appeared, and in council "'twas full explained that no dependance was made on the Belt sent, that the Delawares in particular had forfeited their word long since."[20]

Despite his agitation, Bradstreet had no choice but to agree to the time extension. At the same time, he moved his force up the river to the site of the village Dalyell and Rogers had burned on their way to Detroit the previous year. This would not only allow him to meet the Indian representatives sooner, it would also put him in a better position to attack their villages if it became necessary.

When Gage and Bouquet heard about the proposed peace that Bradstreet had negotiated with the Delaware and the Shawnee, both of them were furious. On August 27, Bouquet wrote to Gage:

> I received this moment advice from Col: Brad-street, of his having granted Peace to all the Indians living between Lake Erie & the Ohio: The Terms he gives them as such as fill me with Astonishment. After the massacres of our Offi-cers and Garrisons, and of our Traders & Inhab-itants, in Time of a profound Peace: After the Immense Expence of the Crown, and some of the Provinces to punish those infamous Mur-derers, not the least Satisfaction is obtained.[21]

On September 2, Gage answered Bouquet, telling him that he too had received dispatches from Bradstreet, "which to my great Astonishment contained Articles of Peace which He has taken upon Himself to conclude, with the Shawnese and Delawares. A Peace that obtains not the least Satis-faction for the Cruelties those Barbarians have been guilty of; That adds Dishonour to our Arms

amongst the Indians, and can Serve no Purpose; but be the Basis of future massacres."[22]

On the same day, Gage angrily wrote to Brad-street:

> To offer Peace, I think can never be construed a power to conclude and dictate the Articles of Peace. And you certainly know that no such Power could with Propriety be Lodged in any Person but in Sr Wm Johnson, His Majesty's Sole Agent and superintendent for Indian affairs. . . .
>
> The Peace you have thought proper to con-clude with the Shawnese and Delawares, you had no Powers to Conclude nor do I approve or will I ratify or confirm any Peace so derogatory to the Honor and Credit of His Majesty's Arms amongst the Indian Nations so unsafe to the future Peace and Tranquility of His Majesty's Subjects, and so apparently productive of future Wars.[23]

In a later letter, he again chastised Bradstreet severely:

> They have negotiated with you on Lake Erie and cut our throats upon the frontiers. . . . Had you only consulted Colonel Bouquet, before you agreed upon any thing with them. . .you would have been acquainted with the treachery of those people, and not have suffered yourself to have been thus deceived, and you would have saved both Colonel Bouquet and myself the dilemma you brought us into.[24]

Gage clearly stated that he would not honor the terms of this unauthorized treaty and again ordered Bradstreet to move against the hostile Delaware and Shawnee tribes.

About this same time, Bradstreet received a copy of Morris' report from his expedition, further reenforcing how he had been tricked. Instead of marching on the hostile villages as directed, he decided that, for a combination of reasons, such a move was not possible. Part of the problem was the reluctance of his Indian allies to assist with any such attack. On September 27, Lieutenant Montre-sor noted in his journal that a planned attack by part of Bradstreet's force was cancelled because the Indians "declined, saying 'that they were sent out to make Peace.'"[25]

Instead of marching on the hostile Indians, Bradstreet began to march his army back to Niagara.

The return trip was filled with difficulties, sickness, and a frequent shortage of provisions. Lieutenant Montresor noted, "Several men yet swelled up prodigiously both by touching & burning the poison Vine[probably poison ivy]."[26] Then on October 31, "Two men of the 80th poisoned by eating a root resembling that of the parsnip, one of which immediately died."[27]

While camped on the shore of Lake Erie one night, a severe storm destroyed nearly half of the force's boats, and many of the others were so badly damaged that they could barely be kept afloat. Six six-pound artillery pieces, quantities of muskets, lead balls, and other supplies had to be secretly buried because there was no way to transport them.[28]

When the storm finally abated three days later, it was necessary to send many of the troops home in a very difficult overland journey. The main body of Bradstreet's army finally arrived at Niagara on November 17.

Many authors have just accepted Gage's condemnation of Bradstreet's actions, but a close examination of all of the facts shows that there were two sides to the story. It is true that Bradstreet had an abrasive personality and had a tendency to irritate superiors and subordinates alike. At the same time, he was a tough, talented, and dedicated soldier with many accomplishments to his credit. It is only fair that both sides of the story be presented here.

First, it must be clarified that Bradstreet's terms were only *preliminary*, which was understood throughout the army. Lieutenant Montresor wrote in his journals that peace was "Granted Conditionally as per the articles of the Terms of Peace."[29]

In order for the peace to become binding, the Indians had to meet certain conditions within fifteen days, and these were not met. Therefore, the proposed treaty automatically became void.

Next, one must look closely at the relevant parts of the orders that Gage initially issued to Bradstreet.

In the third article of his orders, Gage writes that he *recommends* an attack on the Wyandots at Sandusky, but of the Delaware and Shawnee, he says, "I must require likewise, that you make an attack on the Delawares and Shawanese, who are retired on the Muskingham and Scioto rivers."[30]

In and of themselves, these statements seem clear and unequivocal, but when later sections of the orders are also considered, it becomes much more ambiguous.

In the eighth article of the orders, Gage writes, "You will give the Indians, in general, to understand, that you go with a body of troops to chastise such nations as shall continue in arms against us; to offer peace and his Majesty's protection *to those who shall conclude a lasting peace,* [authors' emphasis] and live in amity and friendship with us."[31]

There are no restrictions or qualifications to the clause "to those who shall conclude a lasting peace," and it can certainly be argued that Bradstreet was empowered to offer peace to all Indians who he felt deserved it. Also, there is no clear explanation in Gage's orders that the "offer" did not include the power to negotiate the terms. Gage concludes his orders with the statement: "You will be on the spot, and I must trust for the execution of every thing to your discretion and judgement."[32]

In addition, writing to Sir William Johnson, Gage directs Johnson to instruct the Iroquois who were to accompany Bradstreet, "to make war on such nations of Indians as did not sue for peace; and that peace was to be granted to all those nations who did ask it, without any exception."[33]

Certainly, as commander of the expedition, it can be reasonably argued that if Bradstreet was empowered to *grant* peace to all those nations who asked for it, as well, he was empowered to *offer* it.

Gage did in fact issue stronger orders to Bradstreet, but it was *after* the preliminary treaty had already been agreed to. On August 16, he wrote, "And in respect of the Shawnese and Delawares, who still bid us defiance, you will let nothing prevent your attacking them, at the time you have been told, that Colo. Bouquet will make his attack from the side of Fort Pitt." Even here, he equivocates, because later in the same letter he adds, "Nor will you suffer yourself to be amused by these Nations by Offers of peace unless they immediately deliver into your hands Ten of the Chief promoters of the War to be put to Death and agree in a proper manner to Sir Wm Johnson to sue for peace."[34]

Regardless of how specific Gage's orders of August 16, were, there is no way that they reached Bradstreet before he negotiated his preliminary peace on August 12, as they were not written until the sixteenth. Therefore, Bradstreet had only his initial orders to direct him, orders that, along with requiring him to attack the Delawares and Shawnees, gave him the power "to offer peace and his Majesty's protection to those who shall conclude a lasting peace, and live in amity and friendship with us.... " He conclude by saying, "I must trust for the execution of every thing to your discretion and judgement."[35]

Gage's later claim that Bradstreet's authority to *offer* peace did not give him the authority to actually *grant* it is an argument that is on weak ground. He seems to have forgotten that he had previously written to Sir William Johnson "that peace was to be granted to all those nations who did ask it, without any exception."[36]

Lieutenant Mante, Bradstreet's aide, was obviously sympathetic to Bradstreet's position, as was Lieutenant Montresor, who noted that Gage had written that his:

[D]isapprobation of the Peace concluded with the Delawares, Shawanese, Savages of the Scioto Plains and Hurons of Sandusky notwithstanding the Orders 'make Peace with those Savages who should offer it' and that Extraordinary Peace granted to the Senecas and that Branch of them called the Jennesees at Niagara [by Sir William Johnson] in August after that recent and most barbarous stroke Septr 1763 on the Niagara carrying place [the Devil's Hole Massacre]. . . .[37]

Bradstreet does deserve some criticism here,

because he clearly did not pursue the Delawares and Shawnee with as much energy as he should have, and he went beyond his authority when he advised Colonel Bouquet, a senior officer, to cease his advance because of the preliminary peace. At the same time, Gage's duplicity cannot be denied. A final proof of this is found in his September 2, letter to Bradstreet, where he writes, "I know of no Power given you to conclude a Peace with *any Nation* [Authors' emphasis]."[38]

Gage clearly had given Bradstreet the power to make peace with nations other than the Shawnee and Delaware, even if one accepts the view that these two tribes were excluded.

Bouquet's Expedition

While Bradstreet's expedition was well underway, Bouquet's had met with delays due to numerous factors. The original plan had been for both campaigns to commence simultaneously so that they could support each other and rendezvous near Sandusky at the end of the summer. However, due to difficulties in procuring provisions, equipment, and manpower, it was August before Bouquet was ready to even leave Philadelphia for Fort Pitt. The reluctance of Pennsylvania and Virginia to authorize the necessary Provincial troops caused the biggest delay. On May 31, Bouquet wrote to Sir William Johnson that "from the delays of this province [Pennsylvania] we have already lost the oppertunity of the high waters, & supposing the Ohio to remain Navigabel, the Muskingham or Sioto would be too Shallow" and that, even if possible to have the bateaux carry provisions with the troops marching along the shore, it would be too difficult "on account of the Craggy hills, Swamps, & high Weeds. . . ." The expedition was therefore forced to travel by land, and although Bouquet acknowledged that to go by such a route "with Pack horses & cattle is Certainly slow and expensive, the Woods at a Certain distance from the River are said to be open, no large rivers to obstruct the March. . . ."[39]

By late June, it was clear that Bouquet's expedition could not depart until sometime in the fall.

He wrote to Gage: "we have lost by their precedent Delays the great advantage of acting in concert with Coll Bradstreet, It becomes of less consequence to wait a little longer, as we could not without great Risk and difficulty, penetrate in Summer beyond the Ohio, where there are no Roads." Bouquet felt that by delaying the start until October, "The Leaves and Weeds decay, and the Woods are more open," and further, there would still be "Sufficient time. . .to do every thing we can expect, that is, go to the Lower Shawanese Town."[40]

Like Bradstreet, Bouquet had many logistical problems to overcome. He estimated that among "Regulars, Artillery People, Provincials, Indians, Volunteers, Drivers &ca We Shall have upwards of 2000 Persons to victual; which will require about 3000 Pack Horses to carry Six months flour. . . . The Ammunition, Stores & Baggage; 1600 Beeves, &ca." With such a huge entourage, Bouquet decided that several convoys were required to transport the necessary supplies along the route because it was "not possible thro' Such a Country, and no Roads. . . ."[41]

The supplies were divided into several convoys, and fifty men each were stationed at forts Loudoun, Bedford, and Ligonier to act as escorts. Bouquet also had made arrangements with Plumsted and Franks, the agents for the supplies, to hire contractors for hundreds of wagoners and drivers. Of course, this added to the overall expense of defending the frontier, which had been such a concern for Amherst. Bouquet commented that men from the province were hired as:

> Pack Horse Drivers and Waggoners, such Employs for which a Coward is as fit as a brave man: Will not people Say that they have found it easier to kill Indians in a Goal, than to fight them fairly in the Woods?
>
> I am the more concerned for that mean Spirited behaviour. . .as the Ministry at home appear greatly incensed at their past Proceedings, that hardly any Men of Property and character have joined the Expedition, that they will hereafter be lefft to fight their own Battles themselves; as while they are Exempted to pay their Proportion of Taxes The Government had

a more particular Right to depend upon their Personal Services; and that they would have made some amends for the large sums of money laid out chiefly for their Protection.[42]

Bouquet was referring to the brutal December 27, 1763, murder of fourteen Christianized Conestoga Indians, including women and children, who were sheltered in the Lancaster, Pennsylvania, jail. A group of Pennsylvania settlers known as the Paxton Boys killed them. Nine days earlier, the same group had killed six more of these peaceful Indians at their Conestoga Manor village, because they incorrectly suspected them of being spies for the hostile Indians.[43]

Bouquet was also critical of the Pennsylvania legislators for procrastinating and disregarding their obligation to protect their own frontier. In addition to the difficulty in raising troops, many of the volunteers that were raised deserted once the campaign got underway. In spite of these difficulties, the preliminary portion of the expedition was assembled at Carlisle and was ready to embark by August 9. Although the initial force was eventually comprised of just over 1,100 men, Bouquet wrote Benjamin Franklin that the Pennsylvania Provincial forces had been reduced to about 750 men due to desertion. Bouquet subsequently wrote to Colonel Andrew Lewis of Virginia requesting an additional 200 Virginians to replace the Pennsylvania deserters.[44]

The Virginia replacements eventually arrived, although not in the numbers hoped for. The Regulars of the 42nd and 60th Regiments, which suffered from desertion as well, would supplement them.

After leaving Carlisle on August 9, the expedition arrived at Fort Loudoun on August 13, and two days later, Bouquet sent the first convoy consisting of "900 Horses, Cattle, and Sheep. . .and an Escort of 150 Regulars and 300 Provincials" to Fort Pitt.[45]

Bouquet and the second convoy remained at Loudoun for about twelve days. While there, he received news of Gage's disapproval of Bradstreet's tentative peace with the Shawnees and

Delawares. The commander in chief instructed Bouquet to "proceed in your Operations. . . . Attack and use every means to extirpate the Shawnese and Delawares, and listen to no Terms of Peace, till they deliver the Promoters of the War into your Hands to be put to Death, and Send their Deputys to Sir William Johnson to Sue for Peace."[46]

Bouquet also learned from Sir William Johnson of the July 6, to August 6, Indian conference at Niagara, and that he supposedly had "settled Affiars with by much the Greater part of the Western Indians and made peace with the Senecas" in New York, who he also related "made a large cession of Territory to His Majesty of the Land between Lakes Ontario & Erie."[47]

Once again, disingenuousness of both Gage and Johnson emerges when one realizes Gage allowed Bouquet a greater degree of leeway with the Shawnee and Delaware, who were still committing "horrid Perfidies. . .as late as the 22nd Instant [August], killed six Men, and they taken four Prisoners on this Frontier/not to recall the Schoking and recent Murder of the Schoolmaster [Enoch Brown] and children. . . ."[48]

On August 26, a Delaware war party had murdered and scalped schoolmaster Enoch Brown and ten of eleven children at the schoolhouse near Greencastle, Pennsylvania. Bouquet was to attack and destroy those Indians and their villages *if* they did not completely comply with the mandates, whereas Gage gave Bradstreet no alternatives. As it will be seen, Bouquet did not follow his orders to the letter either. Yet, he was not reprimanded as Bradstreet was.

Also, at Niagara during the recent Indian conference, Johnson did not actually conclude a full peace with the western tribes because only the Wyandots and Genesee Senecas agreed to an armistice, while the Ottawas, Chippewas, Caughnawagas, Sacs, and Foxes refused to make any agreement at that time. Johnson also promoted farther encroachment upon Indian lands by forcing the Genesee Senecas to relinquish title to the Niagara Portage region, thereby validating the Indi-

ans' complaints about land loss.[49] Johnson might be excused to some degree because he may have felt this was justified in restitution for the hostile actions of the Senecas during the recent uprising.

Bouquet's convoy left Fort Loudoun after a nearly two-week stay there and arrived at Bedford on September 5. They were at Fort Ligonier by September 12, at Bushy Run Station on September 16, and proceeded on to Fort Pitt by the eighteenth. Shortly thereafter, the Virginia Provincials that replaced the Pennsylvania deserters arrived, and another large contingent from Virginia under Lieutenant Colonel John McNeill soon followed. This still amounted to less than the 250 men anticipated.

At Fort Pitt, Bouquet made the final preparations for the main portion of the expedition and also held a major conference with the Indians. The Delawares, Shawnee, Mingoes, and Senecas were well aware of Bouquet's plans, having kept close watch on the convoys as they slowly made their way to Fort Pitt. Bouquet's force of about 1,174 troops consisted of

316 men (6 companies) of the 42nd Highland Regiment under Lieutenant Colonel John Reid, including two staff officers—Captain John Small acting as major of the brigade and Lieutenant Nathaniel McCulloch acting as quartermaster.

113 men (2 companies) of the 60th or Royal American Regiment under Major Jacques Mark Prevost (brother of Augustine Prevost, who was commander of the 60th Regiment), including three staff officers—Captain Louis Ourry, Ensign Thomas Hutchins, and Captain George Etherington.

223 men (4 companies) of the 1st Battalion of the Pennsylvania Provincial Regiment under Lieutenant Colonel Turbutt Francis.

218 men (4 companies) of the 2nd Battalion of the Pennsylvania Provincial Regiment under Lieutenant Colonel Asher Clayton.

138 men of Lieutenant Colonel John McNeill's Virginia Volunteers. Due to illness, McNeill would not accompany the expedition beyond Fort Pitt.

82 men of Major John Field's Virginia Volunteers.

50 men of the Maryland Volunteers.

14 men of the Pennsylvania Volunteers.

20 Indians, with Indian agent Alexander McKee and interpreter David Owens[50]

One of Fort Pitt's original brick blockhouses, built under the direction of Henry Bouquet in 1764, still survives. Photo by Todd E. Harburn.

When they arrived at Fort Pitt, Delaware chiefs Captain Pipe and Captain Jacob, along with eight of their Indians, appeared on the far side of the Ohio River and asked to speak with Bouquet about the rumor that some of the Six Nation Indians had made peace for them. The next morning, Bouquet invited them over to the fort, but only three reluctantly accepted. Suspecting they were spies, Bouquet detained them as hostages. On September 20, he sent one of them to inform the Delaware chiefs that he received word from Colonel Bradstreet that they had asked for peace, but he was also aware of their open violation of that agreement. Since he could no longer trust their promises, he would attack them unless they honored his demands. By agreeing to his Bouquet's terms, the Indians could prevent your own destruction and save families. He further

informed them that if they did not allow two of his men carrying dispatches safe passage to and from Detroit, he would "Put all to Death."[51]

On October 1, two friendly Indians of the Six Nations delivered a reply to Bouquet, saying that the Delawares, Shawanees, Senecas, and Wyandots were "sincerely sorry for what they have done and were now collecting all their Prisoners form the Lower Shawanese Town to deliver them up at Sandusky." They tried to persuade him not to proceed with the expedition. In reply, Bouquet thanked them for "the Trouble you have taken in coming to me to make Peace between us & the four above mentioned Nations," but reminded them that he could not depend on the promises of the Delawares and Shawanees, and "if they have anything to say to me, I will hear them at Tuscorawas." He added that if they were inclined to agree with his terms for peace, he would "allow them to go to Sir William Johnson to conclude it."[52]

Bouquet's expedition finally left Fort Pitt on October 3. The order of the march and the precautions taken against surprise attacks are worth noting:

> A corps of Virginia volunteers advanced before the whole; detaching three scouting parties. One of them, furnished with a guide, marched in the center path, which the army was to follow. The other two extended themselves in a line abreast, on the right and left of the aforesaid party, to reconnoitre the woods. Under cover of this corps, the ax-men, consisting of all the artificers, and two companies of light infantry followed in three divisions under the direction of the chief engineer to clear three different paths, in which the troops and the convoy followed, viz.-
>
> The front-face of the square, composed of part of the 42nd Regiment, marched in a column, two deep, in the center path.
>
> The right face of the square, composed of the remainder of the 42nd and the 60th regiment, marched in a single file in the right-hand path; The 1st Battalion of Pennsylvanians composed the left face, marching in like manner in the path to the left of the center.
>
> The corps of reserve, composed of two pla-

toons of grenadiers, followed in the right and left faces of the square; The 2nd Battalion of Pennsylvanians formed the rear-face of the square, and followed the corps of reserve, each in a single file, on the right and left hand paths; all these troops covering the convoy, which moved in the center path.

A party of light horse-men marched behind the rear-face of the square, followed by another corps of Virginia volunteers, forming the rear-guard.

The Pennsylvania volunteers, dividing themselves equally, and marching in single file, at a proper distance, flanked the right and left faces of the square. . . . The ammunition and tools were placed in the rear of the first column, or front face of the square, followed by the officers' baggage and tents. The oxen and sheep came after the baggage. . .properly guarded. The provisions came next to the baggage, in four divisions of pack-horses, each conducted by a horse master.

The troops were ordered to observe the most profound silence, and the men to march at two yards distance from one another. When the line or any part of it halted, the whole were to face outwards; and if attacked on their march, they were to halt immediately, ready to form the square when ordered. The light horse were then to march into the square, with the cattle, provisions, ammunition and baggage. Proper dispositions were likewise made in case of an attack in the night: and for encampments, guards, communications between the sentries, signals, and the like.[53]

The expedition left Fort Pitt on October 3, but only covered about a mile and a half the first day. Thereafter, the column advanced in a series of numbered camps established each night, usually on a defensible ridge near a good water supply. The column averaged anywhere between seven

A sketch of an Indian council during Bouquet's 1764 Ohio Expedition, by Assistant Engineer Thomas Hutchins. This scene is a detail from *A General Map of the Country on the Ohio and Muskingham Shewing the Situations of the Indian Towns with respect to the Army under the Command of Colonel Bouquet*. From William Smith, *An Historical Account of the Expedition against the Ohio Indians, in the Year MDCCLXIV*. From the collection of Seymour I. Schwartz, M.D. Used with permission

and twelve miles per day depending on the terrain. A journal account relates each day's trek, often describing the beautiful scenery along the way.[54]

The column slowly hacked its way through the wilderness after leaving the Ohio River. One journal entry related: "The path after the army left the forks was so brushy and entangled, that they were obliged to cut all the way before them, and also to lay several bridges, in order to make it passable for the horses. . . ."[55]

Much of the country was described as "small hills and rich vales" and "fine land, watered with small rivers and springs; proceeding likewise through several savannahs or cleared spots, which are by nature extremely beautiful."[56]

The army passed several deserted Delaware, Shawnee, and Mingo towns along the way. On

October 13, they established Camp No. 12 on the main branch of the Muskingham River near the Tuscarawas, "a place exceedingly beautiful by situation, the lands rich on both sides of the river, the country on the north-est sides being an entire level plain, upwards of five miles in circumference."[57]

The following day, the two couriers who were sent to Detroit came into camp and reported that "they had been made prisoners by the Delawares, and carried to one of their towns sixteen miles from hence, where they were kept till the savages, knowing of the arrival of the army here, set them at liberty, ordering them to acquaint the Colonel that the head men of the Delawares and Shawanese were coming as soon as possible to treat of peace with him."[58]

The capture of these messengers is another example of the Indians not keeping their word, and there were also still sporadic attacks on the frontier. One can hardly blame the British for their determination to punish them. Back on October 1, Gage wrote to Bouquet:

> The vilanies of those perfidious Savages [the Delawares and Shawnee] are endless. The other Indians are Sensible of their Perfidy, and particularly the Hurons of Detroit observed to Sir Wm Johnson, the Necessity of punishing them. I believe the Six Nations are Jealous of the power of the Shawnese and Delawares, who have lately set them at Defiance. They are all of opinion, that those Indians at Presqu'Isle had no Authority to make Peace.[59]

Bouquet replied that he would "not be amused by their deceitful promises, I proceed with the Troops to Tuscorawas, and at all Events if the Delaware and Shawanese refuse to deliver the promoters of the War, I Shall attack them."[60]

Bouquet then moved his army two miles farther down the river and established Camp No. 13 "situated on a very high back, with the river at the foot of it, which is upwards of 100 yards wide at this place, with a fine level country at some distance from its banks, producing stately timber, free from underwood, and plenty of food for cattle."[61]

Messengers from the Delaware and Shawnee arrived three days later to inform the colonel that

they were ready to negotiate peace. Bouquet replied that he would meet them "the next day in a bower some distance from camp" and then "ordered a small stockaded fort to be built to deposit provisions for the use of the troops on their return; and to lighten the convoy."[62]

At the bower, on October 17, Bouquet held a conference with Seneca chief Kiyashuta and fifteen of his warriors, Delaware chiefs Custaloga and King Beaver and twenty of their warriors, and Shawanee chief Keissinautchtha and six of his warriors. The Indians again stated that the war was not their fault, as it was "owing to the Western Nations & our foolish Young Men, that this war happened between us." They sheepishly asked for clemency and peace as they had "taken now hold of the Chain of Friendship. . .& must likewise look up to God for his Assistance who now see's every thing that passes."[63]

Bad weather forced cancellation of the next day's conference, but when Bouquet did respond, he chastised the chiefs for their excuses and admonished that it was their responsibility to keep their young men in line "when they do wrong and not so Suffer yourselves to be directed by them." He further reminded the Indians it was they who broke the peace with Bradstreet by "continuing to Murder Our People on the frontiers and take prisoners to this day." He reminded them of their various attacks on traders, towns, and about Fort Pitt, and particularly the murder of the eleven school children near Greencastle. Referring to Bradstreet's September 5–7 Detroit treaty, he stressed that "their former Allies the Ottawas, Hurons [Wyandots], Tweegtweas [Miamis] &c; have made their Peace with us" and very strongly warned them that "if they did not stop their Perfidious Conduct and the Six Nations have joined us against you." It is "consequently in our Power to destroy you, but if I find that you execute faithfully the Conditions I shall require of you, I will not treat you with the Severity you deserve. I give you Twelve Days, from this Date, to deliver in my hands at Wakatawmiki, all the Prisoners in your Possession, with out any Exception, Englishmen, Frenchmen, Women, & Children whether adopted in your Tribes, married, or under any other Denomination whatever, and all Negroes, and to furnish all the Said Prisoners with Cloathing, Provisions, &c Stores to carry them to Fort Pitt." When that was completed, he would let them know "on what Terms you may obtain the Peace you Sue for."[64]

Bouquet informed Gage of these proceedings in a letter the following day and also mentioned being "reinforced yesterday with 43 Maryland Voluntiers, These Gentlemen have been of great Service, in enabling me to proceed on this Expedition."[65]

Over the next three days, the expedition moved further into the Ohio Country and established their last camp, No. 16, at the forks of the Muskingham on October 25. Here "Four redoubts were built opposite to the four angles of the camp; the ground in the front was cleared, a store-house for the provisions erected, and likewise a house to receive, and treat of peace with, the Indians, when they should return. Three houses with separate apartments were also raised for the reception of the captives of the respective provinces. . . ."[66]

Bouquet chose this spot as the most central and convenient place to receive the prisoners and conclude the agreements.

During the next seventeen days, Bouquet held final conferences with the chiefs. Messengers were sent back and forth concerning the delivery of prisoners and to finalize the terms of the peace. The "Articles of Agreements" as they were officially referred to, were three:

That the above Nations [Senecas, Delawares, and Shawenees] shall immediately stop all Hostilities and. . .Acts of violence on the persons, or Properties of any of His Britanick Majesty's Subjects.

2) That they forthwith collect all the English Prisoners, Deserters, Frenchmen, and Negroes; and any other Person of the White People living among them, under any Pretence whatsoever, and deliver them to Colonel Bouquet. . . . Providing them with Horses, Cloath's or Skins and Provisions to carry them to Fort Pitt.

3) That they do appoint Deputies from each Nation properly Authorized to Treat for them; and as soon as the said Nations have fully complied with the above Conditions, & convinced Coll Bouquet of their Sincere Intentions to give Satisfaction for what is passed; the said Deputies will be permitted to go to Sir William Johnson Baronet His Majestys Sole Agent & Superintendent for Indian Affairs to make Peace for their respective Nations.[67]

The Indians giving a Talk to Colonel Bouquet in a Conference at a Council Fire, near his Camp on the Banks of Muskingum in North America in Octr. 1764. Detail of an engraving after a painting by Benjamin West. From William Smith, *An Historical Account of the Expedition against the Ohio Indians, in the Year MDCCLXIV.* From the collection of Seymour I. Schwartz, M.D. Used with permission.

Bouquet also stipulated that each tribe provide six of their warriors to be designated as hostages to be held at Fort Pitt to assure these above conditions were met.[68]

On November 10–14, Bouquet met in conference with the delegates to complete the terms for the preliminary peace agreement and the final transfer of captives. Both sides gave elaborate speeches, with Bouquet finally able to secure a promise from the Indians to submit to the terms, although not without some reluctance on the part of the Shawnee. Some eighteen prisoners had already been released, and, thereafter, small groups were delivered to Bouquet on a daily basis. In all, 206 captives were returned (90 Virginians and 116 Pennsylvanians), with the Shawnee promising to bring the remaining 100 in the spring.[69]

Some of the former captives were understandably reluctant to return to white civilization, with the Shawnees being "obliged to tie them to bring them to us." A few women even managed to "escape and run back to the Indian towns," while still others had a very bitter and unhappy parting with their Indian families and "continued many days in bitter lamentations, even refusing sustenance." Likewise, many of the Indians were melancholy in giving up their family members and "shed torrents of tears over them."[70]

The Shawnee were particularly resistant to the peace because they had heard reports from French traders that British "had some bad designs against us" according to Red Hawk.[71]

Also, a soldier had been found murdered near the camp (remarkably, the only casualty suffered during the campaign), and the Shawnee thought Bouquet suspected them of his murder.[72]

The colonel, however, was able to convince them that his intentions were to have the "prisoners remaining in their Possession" delivered and peace offered under "the same terms as the Delawares."[73]

Although the initial plan was to attack and destroy the Shawnee and Delaware tribes if they did not comply with Bouquet's orders, the shortage of supplies and the lateness of the season forced him to accept reality. Circumstances forced him to make the return of as many prisoners as possible his first priority. As he wrote to General Gage:

> [A]t the Same time I was Sensible of the impossibility of obtaining the deliver of the Authors of the War, to be put to Death, unless I had Seized upon them myself, which would have been no Satisfaction, and that violence would have put it out of my Power to Bring afterwards the Savages to submit on my Terms; They would have dispersed themselves, and necessity would have forced them to fall upon our Frontiers, which must have remained exposed to their Depredations at least for another Year, as I had neither Troops nor provisions, to take Post in their Country. . . .
>
> The Shawnese have been very obstinate, and have given me a good deal of Trouble; They refused to submit on the above conditions, and were particularly averse to giving of Hostages; But being certain that if they were driven to Despair, they would have massacred 150 Prisoners then in their hand, I determined to make a last Effort with the Chiefs of their Warriors, who have the principal Authority among them, and in a private Conference, I convinced them of their Folly. . . . They have delivered about 40 Prisoners, and have given me Six of their People as Hostages: I have Sent Parties to their Towns to assist in collecting, and bringing to Fort Pitt the remainder of their Captives: and as soon as they are all given up They will Send Deputies to Sir William Johnson.[74]

This again shows Gage's double standard. He should have given Bradstreet the same latitude that he gave Bouquet. After Bradstreet's preliminary agreement was broken, Gage allowed Bouquet to "relax your Demands upon them for Satisfaction; and get as good Terms as you can. . .if you are assured of their Sincerity, and real Desire of Peace."[74] Gage admitted this in letters to Bouquet on October 21, and again on December 7, relaying his congratulations on the success of the Ohio expedition. In fairness, this same courtesy should have been afforded to Bradstreet.

he Indians delivering up the English Captives to Colonel Bouquet near his Camp at the Forks of Muskingum in North America in November, 1764. Detail of an engraving after a painting by Benjamin West. From William Smith, *An Historical Account of the Expedition against the Ohio Indians, in the Year MDCCLXIV.* From the collection of Seymour I. Schwartz, M.D. Used with permission.

Bouquet arrived back in Philadelphia on January 5, 1765, the same day nine former Shawnee captives arrived at Fort Pitt with the Virginia Volunteers.[77] He spent the winter attending to military and private affairs.

The Royal Americans from Bouquet's expedition were designated to garrison "Posts on the Communication to Ontario" and Niagara. However, due to the severe weather, Bouquet "ordered the Royal Americans to halt in the Barracks at Lancaster to fit their Cloathing, which could not be done during the Campaign" and requested Gage to allow them to "wait there till the Season is more moderate."[78]

In spite of the peace, tension still existed on the frontier. One of the Maryland Volunteers murdered and scalped an Indian near Pittsburgh, and dissension between tribes was also beginning to reemerge.[79] Captain Murray received intelligence from an Indian informant of "Warriors having been sent from Detroit to Skalp or make Prisoners of any of the Shawanise or Delaware's they mett."[80]

Following the departure of the 60th Regiment, all the volunteers of the Pennsylvania regiments were sent to Philadelphia and mustered out of service. During the winter of 1764, the 42nd Regiment garrisoned Fort Pitt and its communication, with five companies at Fort Pitt, a company each at Fort Ligonier and Fort Bedford, and half companies each at Fort Cumberland and Fort Loudoun. All the captives were sent to the colonies they were taken from, and the six Delaware hostages were confined at Fort Pitt. Of the Shawnee hostages, two were left sick back in the Ohio Country, one was sent, "with a Delaware to the Ouabache [Wabash], & the Miamis, to acquaint those Nations of the Peace," and three were sent as

Their business with the Ohio Indians concluded, Bouquet and his expedition left Camp No. 16 on November 18, and made the journey back to Fort Pitt in ten days. A party of the Virginia Volunteers was allowed to accompany the Shawnees to Lower Shawnee Town to attempt to secure their remaining captives. In a lengthy letter to Gage on November 30, Bouquet recorded all that had occurred during the past month. He commented on the poor decisions that had led to "this dispendious War," including the issue of presents. But he was more critical of the colonies for having "consumed themselves in a feeble, and useless defensive, while one half of the money they have Spent, might have fitted out an Expedition, that would have cut the Evil by the Root." Bouquet was also prophetic in that he didn't expect the regiment ordered up the Mississippi to succeed, "while there is a Nation to oppose them, owing to the facility and Safety they will find to Fire at them every day with Impunity."[76]

deputies to Sir William Johnson for "concluding Peace with these Two Nations at the Same time, rather than to give the trouble of a Separate Treaty, by waiting for their [other] Deputies who are to come with the Captives. . . ." Seneca chief Keyashuta went to the Great Lakes to convince the Wyandots to deliver the remainder of their prisoners to Fort Pitt. Bouquet wrote, "For the Mingoes, They have behaved as usual, and after Stealing upon the March Seven or Eight of our best Horse, They are run off: That Vermin is not worth treating with them; We Shall however have Two other Hostages of these Banditties, when their Chief returns from the Lakes, where I have Sent him to give an Account of the Peace."[81]

Although some of the Seneca continued to be recalcitrant, Keyashuta, who previously led the violence in western Pennsylvania, was now amenable to the peace agreement. The Shawnees brought in additional captives when they met at Fort Pitt on May 9, 1765. There would be further difficulties among the Delawares, Senecas, and Wyandots before the final peace could be negotiated with Sir William Johnson.

So ended the Bouquet Expedition of 1764. In spite of the conditions and hardships of the expedition, Bouquet had successfully deterred further major hostilities and recovered a significant number of captives.

Both the British and the Indians were tired of the war, and the influence of Pontiac, Neolin, and other hostile leaders had waned. While both sides obviously did not want to lose control of their destinies, there was now hope for peace and a resumption of the fur trade.

While 1765 would see some sporadic and isolated raids, due in part to Pontiac's remaining influence, there were no further major organized hostilities. While the British had their faults, in many ways they really tried to trade fairly and deal peaceably with the Indians. Still, the violence and treachery of the recent war was not easily forgotten. Bouquet made this clear when he wrote to Gage that only "The Dread of English Power is, in my opinion, the Sole motive capable of making a Solid Impression upon their Minds."[82]

Bouquet was hailed as a hero upon his return to Philadelphia. The Pennsylvania Provincial Assembly, the *Philadelphia Gazette*, and the majority of the people there rained accolades upon him, thanking him for his efforts. Gage wrote to Bouquet:

> The Peace you have made, does great Honor to yourself, and must give the greatest Satisfaction to His Majesty, as well as to every Person who wishes well to his Services. Nothing but the Steps you have taken, of marching into their Country, and prescribing your own Terms, with that Firmness and Resolution which you have shewn thro' all your Transactions with the Savages, would ever have brought those Savages, to a Serious Peace. You have by an admirable Conduct, reduced and humbled them as they deserved; and thereby made a Peace upon a Solid Foundation, and greatly added to the Reputation of His Majesty's Arms, amongst the Indian Nations.[83]

Captain George Etherington, former commandant of Michilimackinac, served during the Ohio Expedition and was now back with the Royal Americans in Lancaster. He expressed the heartfelt approbations of the officers who served under Bouquet and the outpouring of admiration the people of the province had for him at the conclusion of the campaign:

> Tho' I allmost despair of this reaching you, before you sail for Europe, yet I cannot deny my self the pleasure of giving you Joy on your Promotion; and can with truth tell you, that it gives great Joy to all the Gentlemen of the Battalion for two reasons, first, on your Account, and secondly our own, as by that means we may hope for the pleasure of continuing under your command. You can hardly imagine how this place rings with the News of your promotion, for the Towns Men, and Boors stop us in the streets, to ask If it is true that the King has made Colonel Bouquet a General and when they are told it is true; they march off with great Joy. . .for sure I am that all the people here are more pleased with the news of your promotion then they would be if the Government would take off all the Stamp Dutys &C &C. . . .[84]

Etherington's congratulatory message to Bouquet was in reference to the British government rescinding a long-standing rule preventing foreign officers from being appointed to the rank of general. The Swiss-born colonel had become the first to achieve this rank, and he also was appointed commander of the Southern District and the forces in east and west Florida.[85]

However, Bouquet would not be afforded the opportunity to enjoy the fruits and challenges of his new promotion, as he prematurely died at Pensacola, Florida, of yellow fever on September 2, 1765.[86]

Thus, a tropical disease from a mosquito, rather than an Indian arrow, brought an end to the career of perhaps one of the British army's greatest and most respected officers. Although of foreign birth, Bouquet's dedicated service to Great Britain—his military expeditions as well as his diplomatic efforts—had done much to put an end to both the French and Indian War and the Pontiac Uprising. His courage, and also his diplomatic and logistical skills were in a large part responsible for the fact that, by the end of 1764, the major Indian threat to the frontier had been quelled.

Johnson Hall, Sir William Johnson's Mohawk Valley home and the site of many important Indian conferences. Photo by Todd E. Harburn.

Epilogue

I have no complaint whatever against the English. It is only my young men who have shamed me. This has obliged me to leave my village. It is solely against my own nation that I am offended, by the several insults that they have made me, saying that I was never chief.

Chief Pontiac

English Rule Restored

THE CONCLUSION of the Bradstreet and Bouquet campaigns essentially brought an end to the Pontiac Uprising. Although General Gage expressed optimism that Bouquet had made a lasting peace, he was not so naive as to think that the Indian troubles were over for good. Negotiating the peace was one challenge; enforcing it was another. Tensions on the frontier continued, and in some ways it contributed to the colonists' break from the mother country a decade later. Many of the continuing developments west of the Appalachians can be seen through the later lives of two of the main figures in the uprising—Chief Pontiac and Major Robert Rogers.

In spite of the Proclamation of 1763, unauthorized settlers continued to push onto Indian lands, with resultant acts of violence on both sides. British attempts to get the colonies to share in the costs of the wars against the French and the Indians and the necessary maintenance of troops were met with increasing hostility. In an event reminiscent of the Paxton Boys incident on March 6, 1765, one hundred Pennsylvanians led by James Smith attacked a convoy of goods intended for the restoration of the Indian trade at Sideling Hill, and then later fired on the British garrison at Fort Loudoun. Their actions became known as the Black Boys Rebellion because the attackers disguised themselves by blackening their faces.[1]

At this same time, the provincial governments continued their squabbling over expenses. Virginia refused to pay their own militia who served with Bouquet, saying the troops were raised to complete Pennsylvania's quota, and Pennsylvania eventually did pay them.[2] The infamous Stamp Act especially incensed the independently minded colonists, and their protests influenced nearly every area of British-colonial relations.[3] The seeds of revolution were fermenting.

Attempting to address some of the problems that led to the colonial unrest, the British government changed its policies on the regulation of Indian trade. Through the influence of Sir William Johnson and George Croghan, they granted full authority over the trade to the Indian Department. Croghan had resigned his position in a dispute with Amherst and went to England to plead his case. While there, he publicly disparaged Amherst in social circles and privately gloated over Parliament's debate. In favoring Indian Department autonomy, Croghan had an underlying personal agenda, as he was seeking a large portion of this authority for himself. The administrators ultimately decided that Sir William Johnson and John Stuart would continue as superintendents for the Northern and Southern Departments respectively, with deputy agents appointed to assist them.[4]

Croghan returned to Fort Pitt with an appointment "to take the sole management of that Department" as one of Johnson's agents, assisted by Alexander McKee.[5] The fundamental problem with this policy was that by excluding the military entirely, there was no one to enforce the regulations or deter illegal activities by those conducting the trade. Certainly the Indian Department did not have the manpower to do it. In response to this issue, Bouquet wrote, "The Licenciousness of the Frontier Inhabitants in general is carried to a high degree, and unless Severe Measures are taken to restrain them with proper Bounds, and Hunting beyond the Allegheny Mountains is expressly forbid to them, It will be impossible to preserve Peace with the Indians."[6]

This also raised questions about maintaining the frontier garrisons. If the military was not involved in the trade regulation, it was foolish to continue the expense of maintaining the posts, yet the Indian Department could not perform all of the duties currently assigned to the military. Bouquet had already expressed his concern about potential abuse by unscrupulous traders and even by government agents such as Croghan, who had secretly contracted with the partnership of Baynton, Wharton, and Morgan to provide some £20,000 worth of goods for the Illinois Country. Such actions certainly supported the fears of illegal profiteering and trading. Although Croghan claimed that his official position in the Indian Department justified his behavior, it was actions like this that led to the Black Boys Rebellion.[7]

The Eastern Tribes Make Peace

Regardless of these policy disputes, it was still necessary for Sir William Johnson to officially end the uprising by finalizing the tentative peace agreements. This would prove to be a difficult task, particularly with the still-hostile Illinois tribes, partly because the British had not yet taken actual possession of the posts in the region.

In spite of their promises, the Delaware, Shawnee, and Seneca delayed coming to Fort Pitt to meet with Johnson to conclude the peace, partly due to the severe winter weather, but also because there had been disagreements among themselves about how to proceed with the negotiations. The conference was finally held on May 8–11, 1765. The delegates spoke of their desire for a lasting peace, although there remained many "Jealousys & disputes amongst themselves, each

Nation wanting to lead the other. . . ." Croghan mentioned that Neolin, the Delaware prophet, claimed that he "had been up to Heaven, & being directed there to make their Peace with the Quakers" as opposed to the British, but that "the other Nations pay no regard to their nonsense. . . ."[8]

While Neolin would have a degree of spiritual influence among the Delawares for a few more years, like Pontiac, his influence had waned. Ironically, he eventually embraced Christianity and the ways of the white man, which he so staunchly had opposed in earlier years. What ultimately happened to him after 1766 is unknown.[9]

The Indians' internal jealousies would be their ultimate undoing, as their inability to work together undermined their efforts to resist white expansion into their territory. The Ohio Delawares, the Senecas (under Kyashuta), and the Shawnees all sent representatives to meet at Johnson Hall on July 13 to concluded the formal peace agreement. The Shawnees never returned all of their captives as promised, and moreover, sent only one representative who spoke for just one group of the tribe. Other factions, under the influence of Charlot Kaske, a Shawnee and ally of Pontiac, remained hostile to the British.[10]

Many of the Illinois tribes also resisted British attempts to negotiate peace, occupy the former French posts, and restore trade. In fact, it was not until October 9, 1765, that a force under Captain Thomas Stirling was able to finally take possession of important Fort de Chartres.[11] The redcoat garrisons did not occupy the remaining Illinois Country posts until 1766.

On June 8, eighty Kickapoo and Mascouten Indians ambushed Croghan and a contingent of Delaware, Shawnee, and Seneca delegates from Fort Pitt. "[T]he Stroke of a hatchett on the Head," wounded Croghan.[12] Three of the Shawnee delegates and two white men were killed, and the rest were taken prisoner. Fearing the revenge of other tribes, Croghan and the survivors of his party were soon released and continued on to Fort Ouiatenon, where they met with Pontiac. The Indians agreed to British occupation of the posts in the

Major Robert Rogers. In spite of being one of the most famous men in colonial America, no authentic portrait of Rogers is known to exist. This drawing by Arthur S. Armour is based on the Ranger figure in Benjamin West's painting *Death of General Wolfe* ca. 1771. Courtesy of Dr. David A. Armour and Mackinac State Historic Parks.

region, pledged friendship, and expressed a desire to reopen the trade. Pontiac, however, insisted that the British compensate the Indians for the forts and land because the French had never paid for those, but "had been there only as tenants, not as owners."[13]

Pontiac also agreed to go to Fort Detroit, where between August 23 and September 4, he met with Croghan, commandant Lieutenant Colonel Campbell, and various Indian chiefs. The usual complaints and agreements were discussed and the

Indians ultimately agreed to meet Sir William Johnson the next spring for the final peace treaty.[14]

The final peace treaty was not concluded until late July 1766. In the process, Pontiac again crossed paths with Major Robert Rogers and then finally met Sir William Johnson at Fort Ontario at Oswego.

Rogers Appointed Governor of Michilimackinac

Robert Rogers, intrepid Ranger and hero of the Battle of Bloody Run, played a larger part in the continuing development of the Great Lakes region than any of the other principal British participants in Pontiac's Uprising. Continually plagued by debts largely incurred as a result of his wartime service, like many other reduced officers he petitioned the government to have his just expenses reimbursed and also hoped for a suitable appointment as a reward for wartime contributions. On August 3, 1765, the London *Public Advertiser* reported, "The gallant Major Rogers is lately arrived from America to solicit some Preferment from the Ministry. This gentleman was the first Person in America who raised a Body of Troops at his own Expence, and headed them against the Indians who were in the Service of Our Enemies— His Regard for the Welfare of his Country, however, utterly exhausted his private Fortune. . . ."[15]

Rogers traveled to England to make his case to the government in person. While in London in 1765, he had two books published, his French and Indian War *Journals* and *A Concise Account of North America*, which was a geographical history. Critics and readers alike received both of these titles very well. A third volume, a play entitled *Ponteach, or the Savages of America*, was attributed to Rogers, but it is likely that someone else wrote at least part of it. Published in 1766, the critics justifiably panned it, but the book nonetheless showed a remarkable understanding of the Indians' plight. That Robert Rogers exhibited such empathy for the Indians' way of life is not surprising. Although he had proven himself to be a ferocious Indian fighter when required, he also had always shown great respect for them and had several Indian companies in his French and Indian War Ranger corps.

Rogers returned from London with instructions for General Gage, the new commander in chief, to commission him as a captain in the 60th Regiment and to appoint him commandant of the important post of Michilimackinac, including a superintendency over the local Indians. If, for some reason, Gage could not appoint Rogers to the Michilimackinac command, he was to give him another suitable position and was further instructed to settle Rogers' outstanding accounts quickly and fairly.[16]

General Gage and Sir William Johnson both had a strong dislike for Rogers, largely because he was threatening their own ambitious interests. Gage was a strong proponent of the development of Light Infantry units to replace the American Rangers. To Gage's disappointment, the Light Infantry was never able to fully replace the Rangers, despite the Light Infantry's many successes. Johnson jealously guarded his almost total control over Indian affairs in the Northern District, and Roger's success with Indians, and the respect they held for him, had not gone unnoticed by Johnson. Both men also had large financial stakes in the development of the land recently acquired from France and the inevitable commerce that would follow.

The result was that both Gage and Johnson conspired to control Rogers to make sure that he did not succeed in his new assignment. One particular concern was that the fur trade at Michilimackinac generally worked through Montreal, dealing out Johnson and the Mohawk Valley Iroquois as middlemen. On hearing of Rogers' appointment, Johnson wrote to Gage that he was "astonished that the Government would have thought of Such an Employment for him but since it is so, I am of Your opinion he should be tied up in such a manner as shall best prevent him from doing Mischief. . . ."[17]

Taking advantage of a clause in his orders allowing him to make "any equivalent appoint-

ment for him," Gage only made Rogers commander of Michilimackinac and did not give him a commission in the 60th or any power over the Indians except through Johnson.[18] He also tied up the review of Rogers' financial claims in bureaucratic red tape and eventually approved only a very small portion of the total submitted.

A major reason Rogers sought command at Michilimackinac was so that he could pursue the search for the Northwest Passage, the fabled route to the wealth of the Orient. There was a standing reward of £20,000 for the first person to make this discovery. While in London, Rogers submitted a proposal for a three-year expedition that would cost an estimated £32,000. The government deemed the plan too expensive for the turbulent times, but Rogers still hoped that by making some preliminary explorations, he could eventually gain the necessary support.

Pontiac and the Western Tribes Make Peace

As Rogers was preparing to go to Michilimackinac, Pontiac went to Detroit to join a combined British and Indian negotiating party headed to meet with Sir William Johnson at Oswego. While at Detroit, Pontiac was involved in an altercation where he stabbed Chief Makatachinga (Black Dog), an incident that would eventually lead to his death.[19]

At Fort Erie on June 28, 1766, Rogers once again met his old rival Pontiac, who had arrived from Detroit as the major was heading west. Exactly what they talked about is not known, but they did smoke a pipe, drink a bottle of wine, and parted "with the usal Ceramonays of Shaking hands &ca."[20]

From Fort Erie, Rogers continued on to Michilimackinac, while Pontiac and his group went to Fort Niagara, where Indian commissary Benjamin Roberts gave them tobacco and rum. At the same time, Pontiac almost certainly had a reunion with his old acquaintance Captain Thomas Morris, who was now in command at Niagara.

On July 1, the group left Niagara, and arriving at Oswego on the third. There, on July 23, they began talks with Johnson. After eight days of talks, they formally concluded the tentative peace of the year before. Then gifts were distributed, including silver medals for each chief, all of whom pledged lasting peace and friendship to Great Britain. Pontiac assumed a dominant role in these negotiations, which created further animosity between him and the other chiefs.

Rogers' Controversial Term as Governor of Michilimackinac

On August 10, 1766, Robert, along with his wife Elizabeth, who had agreed to accompany him to the distant post, finally arrived at Michilimackinac aboard the schooner *Gladwin*. Quickly beginning his official duties on the twelfth, he met with a group of local merchants and traders who welcomed him and expressed their hope that under his command the formerly restrictive trading conditions would improve. The prior commandant, Captain William Howard, had severely limited trade and had allowed only a select few traders to winter among the Indians. Rogers relaxed these policies, which made him very popular among both the traders and the Indians. On August 24, Captain Lieutenant Frederick Christopher Spiesmaker (Spiesmacher) and one hundred men of the 60th Regiment relieved Howard and his men of the 17th Regiment.

Even though Rogers did not have official approval for his Northwest Passage search, he still planned to send out a preliminary expedition in the hopes that it would stimulate further support. He chose one of his trusted Ranger captains, James Tute, as the leader, with Jonathan Carver, a former Provincial captain and veteran of the 1757 siege of Fort William Henry, as the expedition's chief mapmaker and surveyor, and James Stanley Goddard as secretary. Interestingly, Rogers sought the assistance of one of his old adversaries, the noted French partisan leader Charles Langlade. Langlade had moved from Michilimackinac to

Green Bay, and Rogers wrote him, "I have the pleasure to write you by Captain Tout your auld acquaintance—and as he is to go beyond the bay and further Into the cuntry I shall Esteme it oblidging in you to give him any Intelligence you can of it."[21]

On September 3, Carver headed west with a party of traders who were going to winter among the Sioux on the Mississippi River. Tute and the rest of the party soon followed, carrying Rogers' detailed orders, which read in part:

> Instructions to Captain James Tute Esqr. Commanding a Party for the Discovery of the north West Passage from the Atlantic into the Pacific Ocean, if any such Passage there be, or for the Discovery of the Great River Ourigan that falls into the Pacific Ocean about the Latitude Fifty.[22]

They were to spend their first winter on the Mississippi and then proceed west to Fort La Prairie, 250 miles west of Lake Winnipeg, for the second winter. In the spring of 1768, they were to explore the chain of lakes that was said to lead to the "Great River Ourigan," which in turn was believed to lead to the Atlantic Ocean and the route to the Orient.

Unfortunately, this plan would never be fulfilled. The party spent their first winter on the Mississippi near the Falls of Saint Anthony (Minneapolis, Minnesota). When the promised supply convoy did not appear in the spring of 1767, Tute and Carver decided that they would head east to the Grand Portage on the west end of Lake Superior to meet it. When the canoes finally did arrive, they carried far fewer supplies than expected. The supply shortage and the failure of Rogers to gain additional financial support forced them to return to Michilimackinac. Although Rogers never had official authorization to organize this expedition, Carver later claimed that while in London, he was told that had it not been for changes taking place in the government at that time, the plan *would* have been approved.[23]

Rogers never gave up, and kept working on getting approval and funding until the outbreak of

Robert Rogers Launches the Northwest Passage Expedition from Fort Michilimackinac,
September 17, 1766, by Gary Zaboly. Courtesy of Tim R. Todish and Gary Zaboly.

the American Revolution brought his dream to a final end. If he had gained the necessary support, he very likely would have been the first to cross the continent, fifty years ahead of Lewis and Clark.

With his Norwest Passage expedition underway, on August 18, Rogers invited the local Ottawa chiefs to a council at his commandant's quarters. They had generally been loyal to the British, and he asked them for continued peace. In return, he promised more open trade policies and presented them with the traditional beaded wampum belt. The chiefs retired to consider his words and returned the next day, giving Rogers a beaded belt along with promises of peace and friendship. They then presented Elizabeth with a decorated beaver blanket, saying, "We thank your wife for coming along with you, we see by her coming that she had no fear, and that she thought the Ottawas here were quiet. Here is a bed we give her, she may sit down upon it Quietly without any fear."[24]

On September 20, Rogers met with the more hostile Chippewas, giving them essentially the same message. They replied that they had never been able to trust Captain Howard, but now that Rogers was in command, they hoped that things would improve. As a symbol of their good will, they turned a war belt over to him that the Shawnees and the Delawares had sent calling for a resumption of hostilities that very summer.

The next day, Rogers continued his peacekeeping efforts by going to the large Ottawa village at L'Arbre Croche on the Lake Michigan shore.

There, the chiefs advised him of rumors that a French army had returned to Louisiana and would soon strike north against the British. Rogers replied that the French had been driven away for good and that all tribes should embrace the British. A few days later, he repeated this message in another council at Michilimackinac.

Rogers was well received at all of these conferences and he was seeing good results, but protocol required that at each meeting he present gifts to the Indians. Although necessary, it forced him to technically violate Gage and Johnson's orders that he operate with strict economy. On October 10, 1766, Gage wrote to Secretary of State Lord Shelburne, "by the last Accounts from the Detroit, the Indians in general in those parts were never in better Temper, or more inclined to Peace; enjoying a plentiful Trade, and everything they can be in need of."[25]

In a later letter, even Gage acknowledged the necessity of allowing traders to go and live among the Indians, which had previously been prohibited. He said that "greater Quantitys of Peltry would be obtained if they were not confined to trade in particular Places, and that their being debarred the Liberty of going amongst the Nations, gives the Opportunitys to the French Traders from the Mississippi to reside with them," and he noted that even Spanish traders were having a harmful effect on British interests.[26]

In his dealings with the Indians, Rogers had shown himself to be firm but fair, and he recognized their basic character and needs. Although Gage's statements to Shelburne were but a grudging acceptance of the success of Rogers' policies, it shows that the higher authorities were not totally oblivious to what had been a principle cause of Pontiac's Uprising just a few years before. Rogers certainly had one of the most difficult jobs of any of the frontier officers. He was the military commandant of the most important of the western posts, responsible for Indian trade and relations, and he also governed over the British and French civilian populace. All in all, he handled it with amazing diplomacy and success. His success,

however, placed him at even greater odds with Gage and Johnson, who saw him as a formidable threat to their own interests.

To further control Rogers' actions and to keep a better eye on him, Johnson sent an Indian commissary to Michilimackinac, who was supposed to take over most, if not all, of the Indian affairs. Rogers was ordered to incur no more expenses on his own—hardly a realistic demand. Benjamin Roberts, the appointed commissary, was a favorite of Johnson's, but he could not have been worse suited for the job. A reduced lieutenant from the 46th Regiment and a former member of Rogers' 1757 Cadet Company, Robert's quarreled and caused trouble wherever he went. He arrived at the post in June 1767, and soon he demonstrated that he had no intention of submitting to Rogers' authority.[27]

Rogers was frustrated by the attempts to control his every move and prevent him from doing what he felt was necessary in his position. On May 27, 1767, he submitted a petition to the Board of Trade asking that Michilimackinac be set up as a separate colony with himself as governor, answerable only to the king and the home government. By the time his request arrived in England, Gage had already had Rogers arrested on allegations of treason, and no action was ever taken on it. Many historians see this as an audacious and self-serving move by Rogers, but several other colonial leaders made similar requests. In fact, Gage himself was involved in a plan to set up a colony in the area around Fort Pitt, yet one more example of the double standard that he applied in his treatment of Rogers.[28]

That summer, Rogers planned a large Indian conference, bringing together as many of the western tribes as possible. On July 2, representatives of the Menominee, Winnebago, Sauk, Fox, Ottawa, Missisauga, Chippewa, and Sioux all met at Michilimackinac and professed their friendship for the English. Of particular importance was establishing peace between the Chippewa and the Sioux, who had been at war with one another for over forty years. Lieutenant James Gorrell, who had been commander of the post at LaBaye, noted of this rivalry, "This nation [the Sioux] is always at war with the Chippewas, those who destroyed Mishamakinak. They told me with warmth, that if ever the Chippewa, or any other Indians, wished to obstruct the passage of the traders coming up, to send them a bolt, and they would come and cut them off from the face of the earth, as all Indians were their slaves or dogs."[29]

Ending their warfare would greatly benefit English trade and help to thwart the growing French and Spanish influence in the region. Successfully negotiating this treaty was Rogers' greatest success while at Michilimackinac. To close the conference, not only did he present the Indians with presents to be paid for with public funds, but the local traders also donated £300 worth of gifts from their own pockets.

In spite of the importance of Rogers' accomplishments, Gage and Johnson still did their best to undermine him and plotted to get him relieved of his post. As commandant, Rogers not only spent money for gifts to the Indians and the Northwest Passage Expedition, he also had to procure necessary food and supplies for the fort garrison. Rogers' counterpart at Fort de Chartres, Edward Cole, spent as much as Rogers, if not more, with far fewer accomplishments, and yet his accounts were paid. Using the excuse that Rogers' position was a civil appointment rather than a military one, Gage refused even to pay him his salary as commandant, just as he had refused him his pay for

The Grand Council At Michilimackinac, July 2, 1767, by Gary Zaboly.
Courtesy of Robert J. Rogers and Gary Zaboly.

service during the Pontiac Uprising, as Amherst specifically ordered him to do. Claiming that his position was civil to avoid paying him shows the depth of Gage's animosity toward Rogers, as well as the general's own lack of integrity. In his orders to Rogers on January 10, 1766, Gage wrote, "I do by these Presents appoint you to be Captain Commandant of the Garrison of Michilimackinac, and you are hearby Authorized to take the Command of the said Garrison, and *the Officers and Soldiers that compose the same are required to obey you as their Commanding Officer.* . . . [Author's emphasis]"[30]

That Gage would later claim that these words did not imply military command was ludicrous. Commissary Benjamin Roberts continued to defy Rogers at every opportunity, and even his personal secretary, Nathaniel Potter, turned against him. After a bitter feud, Potter left Michilimackinac on August 29, intent on getting revenge for his alleged grievances. After dictating a damning but largely unsubstantiated deposition in Montreal, he boarded a ship bound for England and died at sea during the voyage.

Before Rogers even took command at Michilimackinac, Gage had received copies of letters written by Captain Joseph Hopkins, who, feeling slighted for his services during the siege of Detroit, had defected to the French. On April 9, Hopkins mailed Rogers a letter from Saint Domingo (Hispaniola). The rambling missive recognized that Rogers had been ill rewarded for his loyalty and hinted that if he joined Hopkins in the French service, he would be justly compensated.[31]

The letter addressed to Rogers was one of several similar ones Gage intercepted. Saying that they were men of good character, Gage never revealed the names of the other recipients, and subsequent historians have been unable to uncover their identities. Even though there had been considerable friction between Hopkins and Rogers at Detroit, Gage readily accepted the letter's authenticity. After making copies of the letter and forwarding one to Johnson, he had it resealed and sent on to Rogers. Rogers, in turn, notified Gage of his receipt of the letter from Hopkins, but did not comment on the contents. When he later sent the letter itself to Gage, it was lost in Lake Huron when the bateau carrying it sank.[32]

Benjamin Roberts, who had been shown the copy of the letter before he took his post, later reported back to Johnson and Gage that Rogers appeared to be preparing to defect to the French. This was the excuse that Gage had been waiting for, and on October 19, he issued orders for Captain Spiesmaker to place Rogers under arrest: "And I do hearby order and require you, and you are hearby Ordered and Authorized and required immediately upon receipt of this to Seize the Person of the said Major Robert Rogers as a Traitor to his King and Country, and to hold him in sure and safe custody, till a proper opportunity offers of conveying him with a sufficient Escort either to Montreal or Detroit. . . ."[33]

Spiesmaker received this order on December 6, and immediately placed Rogers under close arrest. He was confined in irons in the fort's guardhouse throughout the winter, often without adequate food, heat, or clothing. The local Indians and traders were furious at Rogers' arrest. Gage himself reported to Lord Hillsborough, "Some disturbance happened at Missilimakinac, on the Occasion of sending Major Rogers from that Fort, to the Detroit; a disorderly tribe of the Chippewas, went there with their Arms; and threw their English Belts into the Lake, and invited other Nations to join them to release the Major from his Confinement."[34]

On May 21, Rogers was transported to Detroit, then to Niagara, and then on to Montreal for trial. Ironically, he left aboard the *Gladwin*, the same schooner that had first brought him to Michilimackinac filled with hope for his future. Of his trip, he testified at his trial, "my unrelenting keepers threw me (Still in Irons) upon the Ballast Stones, in the Hold of a Vessell, and sent me on a Voyage of Ten days to Detroit, having first deprived me of my most Material Papers, and keeping back my Witnesses who ought to have attended my Trial."[35]

Ignoring his own clear attempts to prevent

Rogers from having adequate means for his defense, with typical duplicity, Gage wrote to officials in the home government, "the strictest Enquiry will be made into it, and every Evidence called upon who can Serve to prove or disprove the crimes, wherewith Major Rogers stands accused."[36]

Rogers arrived in Montreal on July 17, and his trial began on October 20, 1768. Despite the disadvantages Gage placed on him, Rogers rendered an eloquent defense, and the court found him not guilty. Lieutenant Colonel Valentine Jones of the 52nd Regiment, president of the court-martial, wrote:

"The Court, having taken into consideration the Articles of Accusation preferred against Major Robert Rogers, together with the Evidence in Support of the Charge, as well as what the Prisoner had to offer in his Defence, is of the Opinion, that Major Robert Rogers is not Guilty of any one of the Articles laid to His Charge; and therefore doth acquit him of the same."[37]

Although it is beyond the scope of this book to fully explore Rogers' career after the siege of Detroit, two points must be made. Both Gage and Johnson appear to have done their best to thwart him at every opportunity, largely because his success threatened their own personal interests. Gage's treatment of Rogers is similar to that he gave Colonel Bradstreet in 1764. John Cuneo puts it mildly when he wrote of "Gages proclivity to trim his sails to conform with winds from home. . . ."[38]

Robert J. Rogers, a direct descendant of Robert's brother James, suggests that Gage and Johnson never really intended for Rogers to go to trial—that their real expectation was that the harsh weather and poor treatment would result in him dying in custody awaiting trial. The weakness of the case against him lends considerable credence to this theory.[39]

Despite the verdict, Gage refused to reinstate Rogers in any position. He wrote, "after a Mature Deliberation of every thing that has happened, I can not answer to reinstate Major Rogers in the Actual Command of Missilimakinac or of any other Fort in the Indian Country."[40]

Furthermore, although Rogers was acquitted on October 31, 1768, Gage did not even order him freed from close confinement until February 1769, and he was not given his full release until June 3.

After the trial, even though acquitted, Rogers never recovered his reputation. Still heavily in debt, he again went to England to seek redress and support for his Northwest Passage dream. He returned to America on the eve of the Revolution. As a half-pay British officer he was looked upon with suspicion, and his offers to serve the American cause were rebuffed. He eventually accepted a British commission and served with some distinction, but he also appears by then to have fallen victim to heavy drinking. His marriage to Elizabeth ended in divorce. He returned to England at the war's end and lived out his remaining days in poverty and obscurity—a sad end for one of the most heroic and visionary soldiers of early America.

Pontiac's Final Days and Death

And what of Chief Pontiac after the uprising? For the most part, his life was much simpler than Major Rogers'. Although he always retained a small band of loyal followers, his prestige diminished significantly. He mainly lived quietly in the Midwest and the Illinois Country, and he worked to support his family. Once he finally reconciled himself to peace with the English, he did his best to keep it and encouraged other Indians to do so as well. It is known that he spent the winter of 1767–1768 hunting in the area below Fort Ouiatenon.

In the spring of 1768, Lieutenant Jehu Hay requested that Pontiac come to Detroit. His answer, written on May 10, with the help of a local Frenchman, tells much of his situation at that time. As this is probably the last record we have of any of Pontiac's words, it is reproduced in full here:

My father:
    I have no complaint whatever against the

English. It is only my young men who have shamed me. This has obliged me to leave my village. It is solely against my own nation that I am offended, by the several insults that they have made me, saying that I was never chief. I have replied to them, 'You are chiefs like me; make arrangements to command the village. As for me, I am leaving it'

I have spoken to Sir William Johnson. He had bound me to him, and I am still united with him.

My father, it appears that you have sent to see me. I will go next spring. I am hunting at present in order to pay my debts. I am going to Illinois to find the brothers of my wife. On my return next spring, I repeat, I will go to Detroit.

My father, I am loyal. I never listen to the bad birds and never pay attention to those who speak against me.

My father, if I go to the Illinois it is of my own free will. No one calls me there. It is only to get some shot. Do not think I go there to complain. Sir William Johnson and I have put away all bad happenings.

My father, I always hold fast to your hand, as you tell me to by your belt and twist of tobacco, which I have accepted and which is proof I have never acted to perpetrate any bad affairs. I tell you goodbye until next spring and I hold you ever by the hand.

Ouiatenon, May 10, 1768, in presence of Mr. Maisonville and several other Frenchmen.[41]

Sometime later in 1768, a mysterious incident happened to Pontiac in the Illinois Country. Although it is not known exactly what it was, he reportedly vowed to return the next year to get

The Death of Pontiac, ca.1870. Artist unknown. Tim J. Todish collection

revenge on those who had wronged him. In April 1769, the Peorias agreed in council to assassinate him. A nephew of Chief Makatachinga (Black Dog) was assigned the task, possibly because Pontiac had stabbed Makatachinga in 1766 on the way to Detroit for the conference with Croghan.[42]

On April 20, Pontiac was in Cahokia, east of Saint Louis, at the trading post of Baynton, Wharton, and Morgan. When he left the store, a Peoria warrior followed the unarmed chief into the street. Suddenly the Peoria struck him on the back of the head with a war club and then finished the job by stabbing him with a knife. The once powerful Pontiac died almost immediately. His murder by such treachery outraged Indians and the local French alike.

The Peorias quickly realized the folly of their action, and with more than some justification feared that the Ottawas and other tribes seeking revenge would attack them. The French commandant at Saint Louis, Captain Saint Ange, spread the rumor that the English had been responsible for Pontiac's murder, but he refused to let the Peorias camp near his fort for fear that the French would be drawn into any resulting violence. When word of the council authorizing Pontiac's assassination spread, the Peorias fled to Fort de Chartres, where they appealed to the commander for protection. To show respect for the slain chief, Lieutenant Colonel John Wilkins (the former commandant of Niagara) immediately ordered an unknown trader at Cahokia to see that Pontiac was properly buried in the Indian manner.

It is possible that Pontiac was buried in Cahokia, but it seems more likely that Saint Ange had his body brought over to Saint Louis for burial. His exact resting place remains unknown, and over the years there have been many different legends. One interesting story that persisted until at least the mid-twentieth century is that he is buried on Apple Island in Orchard Lake, southwest of Pontiac, Michigan.[43]

Of all the alternatives, the most likely place, in the opinion of these authors, is that Pontiac lies in an unmarked grave somewhere in what is now downtown Saint Louis. Thus ended the life of one of the most influential Indians in American history.

Pontiac is believed to have been killed on the site of the parking lot behind the motel seen across the street in Cahokia, Illinois. Photo by Todd E. Harburn.

Appendix A

Chronology of Major Events

September 8, 1760 French Canada is surrendered to the British at Montreal.

September 12, 1760 Major Robert Rogers receives secret orders from General Jeffery Amherst, British commander in chief, to take an expeditionary force to accept the surrender of Fort Detroit and the other western French posts.

October 25, 1760 King George II dies and is succeeded by King George III, his grandson.

November 7, 1760 Rogers meets with Pontiac near Presque Isle on Lake Erie.

November 25, 1760 Colonel Henry Bouquet takes command of Fort Pitt.

November 29, 1760 Rogers accepts the surrender of Fort Detroit.

December 16, 1760 Rogers is forced to abandon his attempt to reach Michilimackinac due to bad weather, but other detachments are able to secure French posts at Ouiatenon and Miami.

February 14, 1761 Rogers returns to New York and reports to General Amherst.

November 19, 1760–February 13, 1761 British take possession of the former French forts at Presque Isle, Le Boeuf, and Venango.

June 16, 1761 Captain Donald Campbell, the commander at Detroit, learns of a proposed Seneca plot against the British.

July 26, 1761 Senecas complain to Sir William Johnson about land encroachment along the Niagara Portage area by traders and former British army officers.

September 9, 1761 Captain Henry Balfour's expedition leaves Fort Detroit to take possession of the remaining western French posts at Michilimackinac, La Baye, and Saint Joseph.

August 16–September 18, 1761 Sir William Johnson and George Croghan hold a Grand Council with the Indians at Detroit to hear grievances and set fair prices for trade goods.

November 28, 1761 Fort Sandusky, an important stopover post on the Great Trail between Forts Pitt and Detroit is completed.

January 16, 1762 General Amherst reissues orders for the prohibition of the sale of rum and regulates the distribution of trade goods and ammunition to the Indians.

August 23, 1762 Major Henry Gladwin takes command of Fort Detroit.

September 30, 1762 Captain George Etherington is in command of Fort Michilimackinac.

April 27, 1763 Pontiac holds a council with Ottawas, Potawatomies, and Wyandots near Fort Detroit, discussing Neolin's message and encouraging the Indians to act against the British.

May 6, 1763 Pontiac begins the Siege of Fort Detroit with his attack on the Davers party.

May 13, 1763 Lieutenant Abraham Cuyler's relief column is attacked at Point Pelee on Lake Erie.

May 16, 1763 Fort Sandusky is attacked and taken.

May 17, 1763 Fort Miami is attacked and taken.

May 25, 1763 Fort Saint Joseph is attacked and taken.

May 28, 1763 Initial siege of Fort Pitt begins with the attack on the Clapham plantation.

June 1, 1763 Fort Ouiatenon surrenders.

June 2, 1763 Fort Michilimackinac is attacked and taken.

June 2, 1763 Fort Ligonier is attacked.

June 3, 1763 Fort Bedford is besieged and receives an influx of panicked settlers from the outlying regions.

June 6–June 13, 1763 Amherst orders a relief expedition to Fort Pitt, under Colonel Bouquet, and another one to Detroit, led by Captain James Dalyell.

June 21, 1763 Fort Edward Augustus (La Baye) is abandoned.

June 16, 1763 Fort Venango is attacked and taken.

June 18, 1763 Fort LeBoeuf is attacked and abandoned.

June 20, 1763 Fort Presque Isle is attacked and surrenders.

June 23, 1763 Amherst is now aware of the serious nature of the uprising and orders available troops for the relief efforts of Forts Pitt and Detroit.

July 28, 1763 Siege of Fort Pitt intensifies.

July 31, 1763 Battle of Bloody Run at Detroit.

August 5-6, 1763 Battle of Bushy Run near Fort Pitt.

August 10, 1763 Siege of Fort Pitt ends with the arrival of Bouquet's relief column.

August 10–August 15, 1763 Amherst sends the Platoons to Niagara to subdue the local Senecas and to eventually relieve Detroit.

September 14, 1763 Devil's Hole Massacre along Niagara Portage.

October 7, 1763 King George III issues Royal Proclamation of 1763.

October 20, 1763 Battle of Buffalo Creek near the entrance to Lake Erie.

November 1, 1763 Siege of Fort Detroit is lifted as Pontiac withdraws south for the winter.

November 7, 1763 A major storm on Lake Erie destroys a relief expedition en route to Detroit from Niagara.

November 17, 1763 His longstanding request to be relieved is granted, and Amherst sails for England. General Thomas Gage becomes acting commander in chief.

December 27, 1763 Paxton Boys Incident occurs in Lancaster, Pennsylvania.

February 27, 1764 Major Arthus Loftus leads an expedition from New Orleans to attempt to take possession of the French posts in the Illinois Country.

March 20, 1764 Loftus Expedition is attacked on the Mississippi River in the Battle of Roche a Davion.

July 6–August 6, 1764 Sir William Johnson holds a grand peace council at Fort Niagara; the Senecas agree to peace and cede Niagara Portage land to the British.

August 8, 1764 Bradstreet's Detroit Expedition leaves from Fort Schlosser at the south end of the Niagara Portage.

August 9, 1764 Bouquet's Ohio Expedition leaves from Carlisle, Pennsylvania.

August 26, 1764 Bradstreet sends Captain Thomas Morris to Fort de Chartres to notify the French commandant of the Treaty of Paris.

August 26–September 7, 1764 Bradstreet arrives at Detroit, holds conferences with the western tribes, and negotiates a controversial preliminary peace agreement.

September 18, 1764 Bouquet arrives at Fort Pitt.

October 25–November 18, 1764 Bouquet holds a series of conferences with the Ohio tribes on the Muskingham River and concludes a preliminary peace agreement to be finalized with Sir William Johnson.

January 5, 1765 Bouquet arrives back in Philadelphia.

March 6, 1765 Black Boys Rebellion occurs in Pennsylvania.

May 8–11, 1765 Croghan holds peace conferences with the Ohio Indians at Fort Pitt as a follow up to Bouquet and Bradstreet's agreements.

June 8, 1765 Croghan and a contingent of Ohio Indians are ambushed while en route to the Illinois Country, where they meet with Pontiac.

July 4–13, 1765 The Ohio tribes and eastern Indians conclude final peace agreements with Sir William Johnson at Johnson Hall, New York.

August 23–September 4, 1765 Pontiac meets with Croghan and commandant Lieutenant Colonel John Campbell at Detroit for peace discussions.

September 2, 1765 Henry Bouquet dies in Pensacola, Florida.

October 9, 1765 The British finally take possession of Fort de Chartres in the Illinois Country.

June 28, 1766 Rogers meets with Pontiac at Fort Erie.

July 23–July 31, 1766 The uprising is formally concluded at Fort Oswego when Pontiac and the principle chiefs of the western tribes meet with Sir William Johnson and agree to final peace terms.

July 2, 1767 Rogers holds an important conference with the western tribes at Michilimackinac, resulting in the end of a long war between the Chippewa and the Sioux.

December 6, 1767 Rogers is arrested at Michilimackinac on questionable allegations of treason.

October 31, 1768 Rogers is acquitted of all charges after a court-martial in Montreal.

April 20, 1769 Pontiac is murdered in Cahokia, Illinois, by a Peoria Indian.

Appendix B

Posts, Commanders, and Garrison Strength of the British Posts: Spring 1763

Note: These totals are for British Regulars only. They do not include Provincials, local militia, or the civilian traders who were part of the garrisons at some of the posts.

THE WESTERN POSTS

Fort Detroit and Its Dependencies,
from *A Return of the Detachment of the Royal American Regiment and the Returns of the Queens Royal Independent Company*, January 25, 1763, in TNA, MG 13, W.O. 34/49, f.150
(copies in the collections of the authors).

1) Fort Detroit, Detroit, Michigan
Commandant: Major Henry Gladwin, 80th (Gage's) Regiment of Light Armed Foot.
Garrison: 60th (Royal American Regiment): 1 captain, 3 lieutenants, 1 surgeon's mate, 5 sergeants, 3 drummers, 123 rank and file.
Queen's Independent Company of American Rangers: 1 captain, 1 ensign, 1 sergeant, 1 drummer, 22 rank and file (the remainder of this regiment is listed as 1 lieutenant, 13 sergeants, 1 drummer, 82 rank and file at Fort Niagara).
Royal Artillery: 1 gunner, 1 matross.
The initial attack on the Robertson-Davers party was on May 6; the actual siege ran from May 7 through October 31.

2) Fort Michilimackinac, Mackinaw City, Michigan
Commandant: Captain George Etherington, 60th Regiment.
Garrison: 60th or Royal American Regiment: 1 captain, 1 lieutenant, 1 sergeant, 1 drummer, 35 (possibly 37) rank and file.
By the start of the uprising, Lieutenant Jamet and his men from the Post at Saint Mary's had increased the garrison. This was because a disastrous fire had consumed the Post at Saint Mary's. Also, there is some discrepancy as to number of soldiers in the garrison. At least thirty-five privates are known to have been present. For further details on this discrepancy, see Harburn, *In Defense of the Red Ensign at Michilimackinac 1763*.
Attacked June 2, over half of the garrison is killed. The survivors are eventually exchanged and make safe passage to Montreal.

3) Post at St. Mary's or Fort Repentigny, Sault Sainte Marie, Michigan
Commandant: Lieutenant John Jamet, 60th Regiment
Garrison: 60th or Royal American Regiment: 1 lieutenant, 11 rank and file.
Fire destroys fort on December 10, 1762; garrison transferred to Michilimackinac, February 1763.

4) Fort La Baye or Fort Edward Augustus, Green Bay, Wisconsin
Commandant: Lieutenant James Gorrell, 60th Regiment
Garrison: 60th or Royal American Regiment: 1 lieutenant, 16 rank and file.
Fort never attacked, but abandoned on June 22; garrison joined survivors of the Michilimackinac garrison.

5) Fort Saint Joseph, Niles, Michigan
Commandant: Ensign Francis Schlosser, 60th Regiment
Garrison: 60th or Royal American Regiment: 1 ensign, 17 rank and file.
Attacked and destroyed May 25; commander and 3 soldiers taken prisoner, later exchanged at Detroit in July.

6) Fort Ouiatenon, West Lafayette, Indiana
Commandant: Lieutenant Edward Jenkins, 60th Regiment.

Garrison: 60th or Royal American Regiment: 1 lieutenant, 19 rank and file.

Fort is besieged and surrendered on June 1; garrison is taken prisoner to the Illinois Country. Commander and several soldiers later escaped safely to Mobile, Alabama, in 1764.

7) Fort Miami, Fort Wayne, Indiana

Commandant: Ensign Robert Holmes, 60th Regiment

Garrison: 60th or Royal American Regiment: 1 ensign, 16 rank and file.

Attacked and surrendered on May 17; commander killed and garrison taken prisoner.

THE EASTERN POSTS

Fort Pitt and Its Dependencies, from *Return of the Detachment Military and Civil of the Royal Artillery*, Fort Pitt, January 24, 1763, in TNA, W.O. 34/40, f. 209B, D.S., also printed in BP, Volume VI, p. 152. Also Ecuyer to Bouquet, June 2, 1763, BP, Volume VI, pp. 202–203.

1) Fort Pitt, Pittsburgh, Pennsylvania

Commandant: Captain Simeon Ecuyer, 60th Regiment

Garrison: 60th or Royal American Regiment: approximately 115 rank and file (including the Grenadier Company) .

Royal Artillery: 20 total: 1 lieutenant, 1 sergeant, 1 bombardier, 2 gunners, 9 matrosses, 1 drummer, 1 conductor, 1 carpenter, 1 cooper, 1 collarmaker, 1 smith.

The initial siege began May 29, after Colonel William Clapham and family were killed on their plantation the day prior. The siege continued throughout the summer, with the most intense period being July 28, through August 1. Bouquet's column relieved the garrison after the battle of Bushy Run.

2) Fort Presque Isle, Erie, Pennsylvania

Commandant: Ensign John Christie, 60th Regiment

Garrison: 60th or Royal American Regiment: 29 rank and file.

Attacked on June 20, and surrendered the following day.

3) Fort Le Boeuf, Waterford, Pennsylvania

Commandant: Ensign George Price, 60th Regiment

Garrison: 60th or Royal American Regiment: 13 rank and file.

Attacked June 18, and abandoned that evening; garrison escaped to Pitt.

4) Fort Venango, Franklin, Pennsylvania

Commandant: Lieutenant Francis Gordon, 60th Regiment.

Garrison: 60th or Royal American Regiment: 15 rank and file.

Attacked and destroyed on June 16, or 17; entire garrison killed.

5) Fort Ligonier, Ligonier, Pennsylvania

Commandant: Lieutenant Archibald Blane, 60th Regiment.

Garrison: 60th or Royal American Regiment: 8 rank and file.

Initially attacked on June 2, held out until relieved on July 9.

6) Fort Bedford, Bedford, Pennsylvania

Commandant: Captain Louis Ourry, 60th Regiment.

Garrison: 60th or Royal American Regiment: 3 corporals and 9 rank and file.

Royal Artillery: 1 conductor.

 Initially besieged on June 2–3; held out until relieved on July 11.

7) Fort Sandusky, Sandusky, Ohio

Commandant: Ensign Christopher Pauli, 60th Regiment.

Garrison: 60th or Royal American Regiment: 1 sergeant, 1 corporal, 14 rank and file.

Attacked and destroyed on May 22; commander taken prisoner and garrison killed.

8) Small Intermediate Posts

Juniata Crossings, Stoney Creek, and Fort Burd were abandoned in early June with the latter's garrison sent to **Fort Cumberland** in Maryland (also a dependency of Fort Pitt).

Juniata had a small contingent of four Royal Americans (including a sergeant).

  Provincial troops garrisoned **Stoney Creek, Fort Burd, and Fort Cumberland**.

The other provincial posts, **Fort Loudoun** and **Fort Lyttleton (Littleton),** were not garrisoned at the beginning of the uprising, but Provincial and Regular troops occupied them later in the conflict.

Appendix C

THE FORTS TODAY

The French originally built some of the Pontiac War forts, which were turned over to the British after the French and Indian War. The British built and occupied others. Some remained in service well after Pontiac's Uprising. The brief sketches presented here are not intended to tell the entire history of each site. It should be noted that there were other British forts that were in use during the uprising, but we have chosen to present only those that were substantially involved in the conflict.

THE WESTERN FORTS

Site of the commandant's quarters at Fort Detroit, in the heart of modern-day downtown Detroit, Michigan. Photo by Todd E. Harburn.

1) Fort Detroit, Detroit, Michigan.

The French, under Antoine de la Mothe Cadillac, built the first fort at Detroit in 1701. In 1778, the British built a new fort named Fort Lernault on the hill above the original fort and village site that had endured the 1763 siege. Unfortunately, nothing exists of either fort today. However, several historical markers on Jefferson Avenue at the Ponchartrain Hotel, near the Cobo Convention Hall, identify the locations The fort boundaries encompassed the area within and around present-day Washington Boulevard, and Larned, Griswold, and Jefferson Avenues. Salvage archaeology was done at the Fort Lernault site in the 1960s during construction of a large bank building, the findings of which are stored at Wayne State University. No major excavations have been conducted on the original 1701 fort site. About a mile from the original fort, the Battle of Bloody Run is marked on the Detroit Players Club building on east Jefferson Avenue. Detroit's historic Elmwood Cemetery, which contains the only remaining portion of Parent's Creek, is nearby.

Top. The water gate and north stockade wall of reconstructed Fort Michilimackinac in Mackinaw City, Michigan. Above. Inside Fort Michilimackinac. In 1763, Michilimackinac was primarily a fortified fur-trading village. Photos by Tim J. Todish.

2) Fort Michilimackinac,
Mackinaw City, Michigan

Originally built by the French in 1715, the British took possession of the fort in September 1761 and later enlarged it. During the American Revolution, the fort was moved to nearby Mackinac Island, where Fort Mackinac was built in a more defensible location. Fort Michilimackinac has been reconstructed on its original site under the auspices of Mackinac State Historic Parks. Currently, "Colonial Michilimackinac," as it is called, is the longest ongoing archeological project in the United States, with annual excavations every summer since 1959. Many of the original ruins have been preserved, thousands of artifacts discovered and displayed, and the fort has a daily military and civilian interpretive program during the summer months. The library and collections of M.S.H.P. are located at its nearby office complex. The annual Fort Michilimackinac Pageant is held each year on Memorial Day weekend. Mackinaw City residents and reenactors from around the state depict the fort's history and the 1763 attack on the original site. It is the longest-running free pageant in the country. Historic Mackinac Island, a longtime tourist destination, and several other nearby historic sites make a visit to this region very worthwhile.

The site of Fort Repentigny, or the Post at Saint Mary's, as it was called by the British, in Sault Sainte Marie, Michigan. Photo by Todd E. Harburn.

3) The Post at Saint Mary's or Fort Repentigny, Sault Sainte Marie, Michigan

Originally built by the French in 1750, Fort Repentigny was merely a small trading post surrounded by a stockade. The British called the fort "The Post at St. Mary's" due to its location at the rapids of the

Saint Mary's River connecting lakes Superior and Huron. The British only occupied the post for two short months, from October to December 1762, when it was destroyed by fire. Although nothing remains today, Michigan State University and Lake Superior have conducted several archaeological excavations of the original site Historical plaques mark the area in a beautiful city park. In 1822, the U.S. Army built Fort Brady on the same location. The site has been excavated and a portion of the stockade reconstructed. The famous Soo Locks comprise a portion of this park, as do several other historic buildings in various stages of restoration. Nearby museums tell the history of the Sault from the time of the early Jesuits and the fur trade through the Civil War and the eventual building of the world's largest locks. The Fort Repentigny site is only fifty miles north of Colonial Michilimackinac and the famous Mackinac Bridge, which connects Michigan's Upper and Lower Peninsulas.

The site of Fort La Baye in modern-day
Green Bay, Wisconsin.
Photo by John Fenner. Used with permission.

4) Fort La Baye (Fort Edward Augustus),
Green Bay, Wisconsin

Like Fort Repentigny, the British only occupied this original French fort for two years. It was abandoned in 1763, when the garrison left to join the survivors of Michilimackinac during the Pontiac Uprising. Fort Howard, a U.S. military post, was built on the site in 1816. Unfortunately, nothing remains today. Industrial construction during the late nineteenth and early twentieth centuries essentially destroyed the site, and it is currently being renovated as a park. Some of the original buildings from Fort Howard have been moved and preserved at nearby Heritage Hill Historic Park. The local Neville Public Museum contains information pertaining to the history of the fort and the Green Bay area.

The site of Fort Saint Joseph in Niles, Michigan. Much of the original fort site is believed to be now under water due to the changing course of the Saint Joseph River. This photo was taken during the 2002 archeological excavations at the site and shows part of the PVC pipe system that was used for drainage. Photo by Todd E. Harburn.

5) Fort Saint Joseph, Niles, Michigan

Originally built by the French in 1691, Fort Saint Joseph was perhaps the smallest of the posts that the British took over. After more than a century of searching, the original fort site has recently been rediscovered along the Saint Joseph River, through the determined efforts of Support the Fort, Inc. (STF), an organization of dedicated citizens, amateur and professional historians, city administrators, reenactors, and history buffs. In conjunction with archaeologists at Western Michigan University, several excavations have been conducted since 1998, yielding tremendous results, including some of the fort's internal structures. The nearby Fort Saint Joseph Museum, which the City of Niles operates, has an extensive collection of fort artifacts, along with other objects relating to the history of Niles. Future plans call for a reconstruction of the fort on or near the original site, with its Jesuit mission and Indian village, an interpretive center, and a new museum.

The original site of Fort Ouiatenon along the Wabash River near West Lafayette, Indiana. Photo by Todd E. Harburn.

6) Fort Ouiatenon, West Lafayette, Indiana

In the late 1960s and early 1970s, archaeologists from both Indiana University and Michigan State University, in conjunction with the local Tippecanoe County Historical Association (TCHA), conducted extensive excavations of the site of Fort Ouiatenon, originally built in 1717 by the French on the Wabash River. Stockade sections and many artifacts were discovered. Although nothing more has been done at the original fort site since the late 1960s, its history has been celebrated in late September or early October at the Annual Feast of the Hunter's Moon Thousands of spectators and participants attend this event. The Feast, which is a huge trade fair with pageantry, parades, and demonstrations of eighteenth-century military and civilian life, is sponsored by the TCHA on nearby grounds that include a replica blockhouse built in the 1930s. Some artifacts from the excavations are on display, and many others are in the possession of the TCHA and Michigan State University.

Although nothing remains today, the area on the right side of this photo shows the original site of Fort Miami in modern-day Fort Wayne, Indiana. Photo by Todd E. Harburn.

7) Fort Miami, Fort Wayne, Indiana

Nothing exists of Fort Miami today, but the site is marked with a plaque along the Saint Joseph River at the intersection of Delaware Avenue and Saint Joseph's Boulevard, in an older residential section of the city. In 1750, the French constructed Fort Miami, one of five forts built in the present city of Fort Wayne. It was abandoned after it fell in 1763, and the British never regarrisoned it. Historic Fort Wayne, an authentic reproduction of the fort the U.S. Army built just after the War of 1812, stands in a nearby park and is open to the public.

THE EASTERN FORTS

Original footings from the walls of Fort Pitt
in downtown Pittsburgh, Pennsylvania.
Photo by Todd E. Harburn.

1) Fort Pitt, Pittsburgh, Pennsylvania

The remains of Fort Pitt, one of the largest and most
expensive posts the British built in North America, are
truly impressive. Although modern highways and
bridges hover over a portion of the site, the remains are
preserved in beautiful Point State Park in downtown
Pittsburgh, where the Allegheny and Monongahela
Rivers form the mighty Ohio. It is also the site of two
other forts associated with the French and Indian War,
Forts Duquesne and Mercer. An original 1764 blockhouse survives. Extensive excavations were conducted
during the 1940s, 1950s, and 1960s, and several bastions
have been preserved, including a reconstructed one
containing the Fort Pitt Museum. The large museum,
operated by the Pennsylvania Historical and Museum
Commission (PHMC), contains impressive exhibits
depicting the history of the fort, including its part in the
Pontiac Uprising. During the summer months, a recre-
ated Royal American reenactment unit demonstrates
British military drills for the public on Sunday after-
noons.

2) Fort Presque Isle, Erie, Pennsylvania

Although nothing remains of this important post,
the site is well marked. The British built the fort in 1760,
replacing the one the French destroyed on the same site
near the end of the French and Indian War. It was basically a large blockhouse surrounded by a stockade.
There is a newly renovated curbside park with historic

plaques and flagpoles at the end of Parade Street at
Sixth Street, near the Old Soldier's Home. The site over-
looks the Presque Isle Peninsula and Lake Erie. Railroad construction during the late-nineteenth century
destroyed part of the location. There have been some
excavations at the original site under the auspices of
local Mercyhurst College.

Above. The site of Fort Presque Isle in Erie, Pennsylvania. Photo by Tim J. Todish. Below. Site of Fort LeBoeuf
in modern Waterford, Pennsylvania. Photo by Todd E.
Harburn.

3) Fort Le Boeuf, Waterford, Pennsylvania

The British rebuilt this post in 1760, on the site of an
earlier French fort. The location is now in downtown
Waterford. Across the street from the museum is a park
with a newly refurbished statue of George Washington
and plaques commemorating his mission to Fort Le
Boeuf in 1753. History staff from nearby Edinboro State
University maintains the small Fort Le Boeuf Museum.
It is generally open on weekends during the summer
months, but it is advisable to call ahead to be sure.
Some archaeological excavations were conducted several years ago.

The site of Fort Venango, or Michault as the French called it, in Franklin, Pennsylvania. Photo by Tim J. Todish.

4) Fort Venango, Franklin, Pennsylvania

The British built Fort Venango in 1760 near the old French Fort Michault. Nothing remains today, but a historical marker on Eighth and Elk Streets in a residential area marks the original site along the Allegheny River near the mouth of French Creek. The fort consisted of a large blockhouse on a raised earthen mound with a surrounding ditch. The local library, within walking distance, has substantial information on the history of the fort.

5) Fort Ligonier, Ligonier, Pennsylvania

An authentic reconstruction of the post, operated by the Fort Ligonier Association, stands on the original site in the town of Ligonier, southeast of Pittsburgh.

Extensive excavations have been conducted, not only of the stockaded fort, but more recently of the field hospital and many outlying structures such as breastworks, hornworks, and other entrenchments. Ligonier was originally built in 1758 as the last fort along General John Forbes' line of march in his expedition against Fort Duquesne. A new museum and a visitor's center have replaced older structures. They contain an excellent collection of fort artifacts and original portraits pertaining to the period of the fort. In October, the annual Fort Ligonier Days reenactment and living history weekend celebrates the fort's history.

Above. Reconstructed out-works at Fort Ligonier, in modern-day Ligonier, Pennsylvania. Photo by Tim J. Todish. Below. The site of Fort Bedford, in Bedford, Pennsylvania, showing where the covered way led down to Juniata Creek. Photo by Todd E. Harburn.

6) Fort Bedford, Bedford, Pennsylvania

Built at Raystown in 1758 by the British, Bedford was a substantial fort on the Raystown branch of the Juniata River. Unfortunately, nothing remains of the fort today, although there is a historical marker, replica blockhouse, gift shop, and small museum (with a model of the fort) on the original site in town. Nearby is Old Bedford Village, an impressive collection of restored historical buildings open to the public that offer summer interpretive programs.

The original site of Fort Sandusky in Venice, Ohio, is about one thousand feet out into Sandusky Bay from the bridge where this photo was taken. Photo by Todd E. Harburn.

Above. Stone marker on the site of Fort Loudoun, in modern Loudoun, Pennsylvania. Photo by Todd E. Harburn. Below. Site of Fort Lyttleton, in modern Littleton, Pennsylvania. Photo by Todd E. Harburn.

7) Fort Sandusky, Sandusky (Venice), Ohio

Built in 1761 by the British, the fort was a stopover post on the Great Trail, the land route between Fort Detroit and Fort Pitt. Similar to the other small posts, it consisted of a substantial blockhouse surrounded by a stockade, although it also had several outbuildings. After its destruction in the 1763 attack, it was never rebuilt, and nothing remains today. However, several years ago, the original site was thought to have been seen when the waters of Sandusky Bay were unusually low. The site is approximately three miles west of the city of Sandusky proper on Route 6 (Fremont Avenue) and U.S. Route 99, at Venice, Ohio. A state historical marker marks the intersection. A replica of the fort blockhouse and an information plaque is in the Frontier section of the nearby Cedar Point Amusement Park, and the Sandusky library has a collection of information on the fort's history.

8) Fort Loudoun, Loudoun, Pennsylvania

Built in 1756 by the colony of Pennsylvania for the protection of settlers, the British maintained the fort from 1758 until it was abandoned in 1765. After extensive excavations at the site in the 1980s, the fort has recently been reconstructed on its original location, about one and a half miles southeast of Loudoun, and the Pennsylvania Historical and Museum Commission maintains it. The fort was basically a squared palisade around the small Patton house, a private dwelling, and a few other small structures.

9) Other Small Pennsylvania Forts

These were built along the communication route between Pittsburgh and Philadelphia during the French and Indian War that were then used during the Pontiac Uprising. Three such posts were **Fort Burd**, near Brownsville, Pennsylvania, on U.S. Route 40, **Fort Lyttleton**, on U.S. 522 in Littleton, Pennsylvania, and the post at **Juniata Crossings,** on U.S. 30 on the Raystown branch of the river east of Everett, Pennsylvania. Pennsylvania Historical and Museum Commission markers mark all.

10) Fort Niagara, Youngstown, New York

This fort and trading center, originally built by the French in 1726 at the juncture of the Niagara River and Lake Ontario, was one of three major western British posts that did not fall during Pontiac's Uprising.

Although it was never even attacked during the conflict, it played an important part in defending the critical Niagara Portage, across which vital supplies had to pass on the way to the upper forts. Fort Niagara remained active during the American Revolution, the War of 1812, the Civil War, and beyond World War II. Original structures dating to the Pontiac period and before still remain. Old Fort Niagara is maintained by the Old Fort Niagara Association and is open to the public. Its museum depicts the fort's history and several reenactment weekends during the summer months, including one of the largest French and Indian War events in the country. Other nearby historic sites associated with Pontiac's Uprising, such as Devil's Hole, Fort Erie, Fort Schlosser, and the famous Niagara Falls, make this a worthwhile visit.

11) Fort Schlosser (Little Niagara), Niagara Falls, New York

Rebuilt by the British in 1761 near the site of an earlier French fort just above Niagara Falls, Fort Schlosser was a small yet important supply post along the carrying place, as the Niagara Portage road was called. Although a modern expressway destroyed the site of Fort Schlosser, a portion of one of its original chimneys (later used as a British trading house) still survives. It is preserved in a small park on Front Street in Niagara Falls along the river and the Niagara Parkway. It is a little-known, yet impressive, reminder from this period.

Top. View of Old Fort Niagara in Youngstown, New York, from the Niagara River. Photo by Tim J. Todish. Above. This chimney from the two-story Duncan-Sterling-Stedman trading house is all that remains today of the Fort Schlosser complex in Niagara Falls, New York, which once guarded the north end of the Niagara Portage. Photo by Todd E. Harburn.

Appendix D

Records Relating to the Platoons from the *Gage Warrants* in the William L. Clements Library at the University of Michigan

These records from the *Gage Warrants* are part of the manuscript collections of the William L. Clements Library at the University of Michigan. They provide a rare glimpse of some of the individual soldiers who served in the British army during the Pontiac Uprising. They are of particular interest because they deal with the Platoons, a little-known temporary force organized to assist with the relief of the western posts. They are reprinted here with the kind permission of the Clements Library.

Box 7:38

1) Pay Bill to Lieutenant Sutherland, Acting Paymaster of the Platoons:

By His Excellency The Honble: Thomas Gage, &tc, &tc.&tc.

You are hereby directed and required, out of Such Monies as are or shall come to your hands for the Extraordinary Expences of His Majesty's Forces under my Command to Pay or Cause to be Paid to Lieutenant Erick Sutherland Acting Paymaster to the Platoons that was Raised by order of His Excellency Sir Jeffery Amherst; for the Service against the Indians, or his Assigns with deduction, the Sum of Two Hundred Eighteen Pounds Six Shillings & Three Pence Half Penny Sterling; Being for the Subsistence of Said Platoons from the 25th of August 1763 to the 12th Day of December following; Being from the Day of their Enlistments, to the Day the last of them was Discharged; as per the Pay Bills Annexed to the Warrant And for so Doing, this, with the Acquittance of the Said Lieutenant Erick Sutherland; or his Assigns, shall be your Sufficient Warrant and Discharges

Give &tc, New York, 13th Feby:1764
To Abraham Mortier, Esqr
Dep: Paymr: Gen:

2) Pay Bills of the Platoons:

£218.6.3 1/2 Sterling: Being for the Subsistence of 5 Platoons from the 25th Augt to the 12Decr 1763 Dated New York 13th Febry 1764

Lieutenants Stoughton's Platoons	Sterling	£43..5..4
Sinclair's		40..1..0
Magra's		52..12..6 ?
Sutherland's		54..9..9
Paynter's		27..17..8
		£218..6..3 1/2

3) Pay Bill of Lieut Stoughton's Platoon, New York, February 8th, 1764:

[Left to right:]
Mens Names Commencing (all 25 Aug 1763)
When left the service & for what reason
No. Days at what Per Day
Total Amount

Serjt. Monro	Discharged 13, Jan, 1764	98	1sh	£ 4..18
Corpl Wakmen	Drowned 7th Nov 1763	75	.8	2..10
Josp Porter	Dischard 13 Jan 1764	98	.6	2..9
Wm. Graham	"	"	"	
Geor Robison	"			
Owen Cowley	"			
Wm Meeks	"			
Robt McCauley	Drowned 7 Nov 1763	75	6	1..17..6
Wm Preston	"			
Josp William	Sick at Niagara 30th Nov	98	6	2..9
Jno Williamson	Dischard Jan 13, 1764	"		
Jno Achmerty	Sick at Niagara 30th Nov	"		
Jton: Horsstottle	Discharged 13 Jan 1764	"		
Jno Shemalgas	Dead 20th Novr 1763	88	6	2..4
Rich'd Mead	Discharg'd 12th Decr 1764	110	6	2..15
Michl Vaughan	"			
Jno Jameson	Deserted 22 Aug 1763			1..7..8
Jno Branch	Do. Do			0..19..8

N: B: The sums of the above Account Charg'd to Jameson, and Branch, was advanced for Necessarys by Order Stoughton Lieut

4) Pay Bill of Lieut Patrick Sinclair's Platoon from 21 September 1763 to 30th Nov. Inclusive

John Brodie, Serjt (all 21st Sepbr 1763) Discharg'd December 12th 1764   83 1 lb £ 4..3..

Corporal Ridem	Drownd'd 7th Novr 1763	48 8	1..12..
George Holding	Discharg'd Dec 12th 1764	83 6	2..1..6
George Burford	Discharg'd 12th Jan 1764	71 6	1..15.6
James Winter	Listed 80th Regiment 30th Nov 1763	"	"
Jacob Reyter	Discharged 12th Jan 1764	"	"
Felix Quin	"		
Cristopher Pall	"	83	2..1..6
Michael Kelly	"	71	1..15..6
John Wilson	Sick at Niagar 30th Novr 1763	"	
John Scot	Discharg'd 12th Decr 1764	83	2..1..6
Robert Ervin	Discharg'd 12th Jan 1764	71	1..15..6
John Dogherty	"		
John King	"		
Michl Culverwell	Discharg'd 12th Dec 1763	83	2..1..6
William Hudson	Deserted Agu 31, 1763	———	
Charles Burns	"		
William Doghill	Killed October 20th, 1763	30	6..15..
Moris Wallace	"		
Daniel Hoggan	Drownd'd 7 Novr 1763	48 6	1//4..
Hugh Mirney	"		
Rolin Kendal	"		
Daniel Ross	"		

Total £36..6..6

To Money lost by Sergt Brodie, Michl: Culverwell, John Scot, Chris: Pall & Geo Holding, Soldiers in Said Platoon 3..14..6

Sterling   £40..1..0

Who being sent down to New York Sick, and there discharged, did not Credit their officers for the necessaries they had been Supplyed with, & not having funds of Non Effectives, or Contingencies to make good the Same, hope the Gerneral will not let them be the loser, as they took upon them that Service Voluntarily and without any allowance equal to defraying their Expences.

5) Pay Bill of Lieut [Redmond] Magra's [22nd Regiment] Platoon from ye 25th August 1763 to 30th Novr Inclusive

James Rushin Serjt. (All August 25th: 1763)		[Sterling]
The 22nd Regiment	98 1/	£ 4..18..0
Heny: London Corpl Do Do		
Discharged Nov 30 1763	98 0/8	3..5..4
Godfry Redingbough		
	"	98 2..9
Andw Dill	"	" "
Jos: Morris	"	" "
Jno Phillipson	"	" "
Philp Broadstreet	Listed 17th Regt. Dec 8	98 6 2..9
Moses Davise	Do	" "
Danl Christy	Left at Little Niagara	" "
Jos: Badaly	At N;Y: not Paid	110 6 2..15
Petr Peely	Disch'd Decr 12th 1763	" "
Jas Dougherty	"	" "
Noah Flood	At N; York not paid DCharg'd to the 12 Dec'r	
Frans Nichless	"	" "
Thos Swords	"	"
Anthy Bell	"	" "
Willm Arston	"	" "
Patk MucBebroy	"	" "

Total 50..1..4

To Money lost by James Dougherty & Peter Peely soldiers on said Platoon 2..`` 2 ½

Who being sent down to New York Sick, and there discharged, did not Credit their officers for the Necessary's they had been supplied with, and not having funds of non Effectives, or Contingencies to make good the same hope the General will not let them be the loser, as they took upon them that Service Voluntarily, and without any allowance equal to defraying their Expences.

6) Pay Bill of Lieut. Erik Sutherland's Platoon from 25th August 1763 to 30th November Inclusive

Mens Names		No. Day	[Sterling]
James Clark, Sergt Major Royal Highlanders			
	Aug 1, 1763	122	£6..2..
Moses Ibbot Sergt			
	Aug 25th 1763 Discharg'd 12th Jan 1764		
	98	1	4..18
John Boyle, Corporal Listed 80th Regt.			
	30th Nov 1763	98 8	3..5..4
Thos Pero	Drownded 7 Nov 1763	75 6	1.17..6
John Chandler	All rest are Aug 25th		
	Discharged 12th Jan 1764	98 6	2..9
John Duggan	"	"	
James Legg	Drownded 7th Nove 1763	75 6	1..17..6
John Came	Discharg'd 12 Dec, 1763	110	2..15
Jabox Twiney	Discharg'd 12 Jan 1764	98	2..9
Ephraim Phelps	Drownded 7th Nov, 1763	75	1..17..6
Patrick Irvine	Drownded 7th Nove, 1763	"	
Richd Fairwalker[Fairweather]			
	Discharg'd 12th Decr 1763	110 6	2..15
Simon Fraser	"		
Thomas Hill	Drownded 7th Nove 1763	756	1..17.6
Thomas Beins	Discharg'd 12th Jan 1764	98 6	2..9

Samuel Lansford Drownd'd 7th Novr 1763   75 6   1..17..6
John Valintyne   Discharg'd 12th Jany 1764   98 6   2..9
Simon Binnes   "   "   "
George Keatsbrough   "   "   "

Total £50..18..4

To Money lost by Simon Franser John Came, & John Fair-
weather Soldiers in Said Platoon

3..11..5

Sterling   £ 54..9..9

Who being sent down to New York Sick, and their discharged,
did not Credit their officers for the Necessarys they had been
supplied with, & not having funds of non Effectives or Contingencies to make good the Same, hope the Genl: will not let
them be the loser, as they took upon them that Service Voun-
tarily, and without any Allowance equal to defraying their
Expences.

7) Pay Bill of the Deceased Lieut. Paynters Platoon from 25th August to 30th November Inclusive

Mens Names			[Sterling]
James Trimble, Serjt All 25th Aug 1763			
Drownd'd 7th Novr, 1763	75 1		£ 3..15..
Cornelius McCore, Corpl		"	2..10..
John Levie	"	"	1..17..6
Henry Gustavus Hance	"	"	"
John Dixon	"	"	
Patrick Tool	"	"	
William Dark	"	"	"
George Devine	"	"	"
Peter Holden	"	"	"
John Lafferty	"	"	
John Obrien	"	"	"
Patrick Eyres	"	"	
John Cavannah Finley Deserted		....	
Domnick McCormick			
8th Augst 1763 Discharg'd 30th Novr 1763			
	115 6	2..17..00	
	Total 27..17..8		

Box 7:39

**1) Warrant to pay Lieutenant Erick Southerland Acting pay-
master to the Platoons raised by order of His Excellency Sir
J A for the Service against the Indians** for Fifty Five Pounds
Eight Shllings Sterling Being for the Batt and Forrage Money
for the Command officer of the Platoons; and to make up the
officers Half Pay Full Pay from the 25th Day of July 1763 to
the 12th of December following; as per the Annexed
Accounts; and for so doing, this, with the Acquittance of the
Said Lieutenant Erick Sutherland; or his Assigns, shall be
your Sufficient Warrant and Discharges
Give &tc, New York, 15th Day of Feby:1764
To Abraham Mortier, Esqr
Dep: Paymr: Gen:

**2) Warrent to pay Mrs. Joyce Johnston, Widow of the Lte
Lieutenant James Johnston, formerly of Gorham's Late
Corps of Rangers and was on Service with the Platoons** that
was Raised by Order of His Excellency Sir Jeffery Amherst,
for the Service against the Indians, and was Killed by the Savages on the 22nd Day of October 1763: or her Assigns without
deduction the Sum of Six Pounds Fifteen Shillings & Four
Pence Sterling: Being to make up the Late Lieutenant John-
son's Half Pay, Full Pay from the 25th Day of August 1763 to
the 22nd Day of October following, both Days Inclusive,
Being Fifty Eight Days at Two Shillings & Four Pence & Day;
And for so doing, this, with the Acquittance of the Said Mrs.
Joyce Johnston, or her Assigns, shall be your Sufficient War-
rant and Discharge.
Given under my Hand at Head Quarters in New York, this
22nd Day of February, 1764 Gage
To Abraham Mortier Esqr
Dep: Paymr: Gen:

Appendix E

John Rutherfurd's Indian Captivity

As related in chapter four, on May 6, 1763, seventeen-year-old John Rutherfurd was part of a mission under Captain Charles Robertson sent to take soundings in Lake Saint Clair. The party was attacked near present-day Port Huron, Michigan, and Rutherfurd was taken prisoner. He survived many dangerous and thrilling adventures before eventually escaping to rejoin the besieged garrison at Fort Detroit.

At the time of his capture, Rutherfurd was an employee of Detroit trader James Sterling. After his escape, at the urging of his cousin, Sir John Nesbit, he wrote a detailed narrative of his captivity. Rutherfurd was obviously well educated and a keen observer, and through his eyes we get a rare and exciting glimpse of the Indians as real people, with their virtues and vices clearly exposed. As the reader will see, there are numerous times when the author also reveals the prejudices of his own race and class.

During the attack on Robertson's party, Rutherfurd was "laid hold of by one [Indian] whose hideous appearance was enough to have banished any hope of obtaining quarter. . . ."[1]

The Indian dragged him out of the boat and pulled him to shore by his hair, where, "with a rope adorned with trinkets (which they always carry with them to war to bind their prisoners) [he] bound me and delivered me over to in charge of his squaw, and then went back to plunder the boat."[2]

Rutherfurd was taken to the hut of his new master, who was named Peewash. Many of the Indians got drunk on captured shrub, and one, dressed in Captain Robertson's clothing, struck at Rutherfurd with a tomahawk. Fortunately, another Indian intervened and saved him from harm. Peewash's wife then hid Rutherfurd under some skins to protect him from further danger. As the drunkenness continued, Rutherfurd wrote that the Indians "were feasting upon Captain Robertson's body. . .which they do, not for the want of food, but as a religious ceremony, or rather from a superstitious idea that it makes them prosperous in war. They teach their children to be fond of it from their infancy."[3]

The next day, Peewash offered Rutherfurd some of Robertson's flesh, but he refused to eat it. He said that he would obey him in all ways but that one, which satisfied the Indian.

Toward the evening of his second day of captivity, Rutherfurd saw Davers' young Indian slave, who told him that some others in the party had also survived. He and the slave devised a plan where they would sneak out of their huts during the night, meet at a designated spot, and then flee to Detroit together. Rutherfurd estimated that in their captivity they had been taken about eighty miles from the fort. Later that evening, Peewash angrily tied Rutherfurd's leg tightly to a post inside the hut so that he had no chance of getting away. He later learned that the Indian boy had exposed their escape plan in return for his own freedom.

The next day, through an English-speaking Indian, Peewash told him that his plan had been discovered and emphasized that if Rutherfurd had actually made the attempt, it surely would have resulted in death. He told him that Detroit was completely cut off and would soon fall, and then he took him to Davers' grave. He then showed him what remained of Robertson's body and those of the dead soldiers, whose remains the dogs were eating. Rutherfurd agreed that he would not try to escape again and resolved to "put on an air of perfect contentment, which I had often heard was the way to gain the affections of the Indians; whereas a gloomy discontented air irritates them, and always excites worse treatment."[4] That night, Rutherfurd's hands were again tied, but his leg was not bound to the wooden post.

The following day, Rutherfurd's master and his wife left for Detroit, leaving him in the care of Peewash's father. Rutherfurd felt that the old man was genuinely fond of him, but made him dress like an Indian. He gave Rutherfurd a blanket and a breech clout and shaved his hair except for a small tuft on top. He then painted his face and made him a gift of a pipe and a tobacco pouch.

When Peewash returned to the village, he told

Chippewa Indian warrior, by Dirk Gringhuis. Courtesy of Mackinac State Historic Parks.

Rutherfurd about the Indians' success in the war. Soon after, he untied Rutherfurd's hands, telling him that there was no hope of escape. His master was pleased with his Indian dress and seeming happiness, and Rutherfurd noted that "by this behavior, I fared in many respects better than those prisoners who appeared sullen and displeased with their situation, some of them suffering death on that account."[5]

Rutherfurd was now allowed brief meetings with two of the soldiers who had been captured with him, and he was very pleased to "meet and converse with these poor fellows, who a little before I would not suf-

fer to speak to me without the usual marks of respect from an inferior to a superior. Here there was no distinction; nay, we were glad to find three people of our color. We used often to compare notes with regard to the usage we met with from our masters. One of them told me he was obliged to eat of Captain Robertson's body. We would form fifty different ways of making our escape, and immediately reject them as all impracticable."[6]

About mid-May, the Indians found themselves in great need of food, "owing to the indolence of the savages, who ever stir out of their huts to fish or hunt till necessity drives them. . . ."[7]

They were reduced to eating boiled acorns until the weather cleared enough so that they could fish. Rutherfurd described how the Indians fished from their canoes at night. They fixed a pole with a torch to the bow of the canoe, which would attract the fish. The Indian in the stern guided the canoe so that the bow man could spear the fish with a harpoon. In two hours time, Rutherfurd related, the Indians could sometimes take as many fish as the canoe could carry.

When food was plentiful, the Indians "do nothing but eat, smoke their pipe, and sleep. Sometimes they amuse themselves with a game something like our children's diversion of shinty [lacrosse], where the females play against the men, and often come off victorious. It is on this occasion that the beaux and belles make their conquests and dress in their best attire. My Master used to dress me out in the richest manner, putting all the ornaments belonging to the family upon me. . . ."[8]

Toward the end of May, in preparation for returning to Detroit, in two days time, Rutherfurd and Peewash constructed a birchbark canoe large enough to hold the entire family. The night before they left, they killed one of their dogs, and all of the neighbors were invited for a feast. Each guest was given a little painted stick, which they put on a platter when they arrived. Each was then given a double portion, eating one and taking the other home. As a slave, Rutherfurd was not allowed to partake of the feast, but had to sit in the corner and watch.

Before they left the next morning, another dog was killed to appease the evil spirits. They stopped paddling before sunset, and Rutherfurd had to cut firewood and cook fish for dinner. A hut was set up every night, which was described as "about twenty young trees set up in the shape of a sugar loaf, and all covered with a kind of a matting [which is carried in the canoe] excepting a hole in the top to let out the smoke. Everyone carries his or her bed clothes on his back, which is either the skin of a wild beast or a coarse blanket, and all lie down promiscuously, men. women, and children, with their feet to the fire, which is at the center."[9]

On the second day, they stopped at an island where there was an Indian burying ground, and everyone planted a few grains of corn around the grave of Peewash's deceased son.

On the fourth day, they arrived at Detroit, where they constructed a larger hut near the farm of a Frenchman who was a friend of Peewash. Rutherfurd had to do a large share of the work constructing the hut and spent about two hours each day cooking. He also had to help with planting corn, pumpkins, and other vegetables. During this time, he suffered from severe sunburn on his exposed skin.

At times, he was taken to the main Indian encampment, and on several occasions was able to talk with Captain Campbell and Lieutenant McDougall, who had been detained after leaving the fort for a conference with Pontiac. He suggested to Campbell that they try to escape, but Campbell told him that if anyone got away, the Indians would surely kill all those who remained. Every day he saw prisoners and scalps brought in. His description of the practice of scalping is revealing: "The scalp is not, as is commonly believed, the whole skin of the head, but is only the uppermost part of the crown, and must have in it that swirl in the hair that every one has there before it can be approved as a just trophy of the warrior's achievement."[10]

Rutherfurd also commented on Ensign Christopher Pauli, who had been the commandant of Fort Sandusky:

> They at this time brought in Ensign Pauli of the 60th Regiment. . . . The Indians came into his fort as friends, and while some of them were smoking a pipe as a token of pretended friendship the rest were butchering his small garrison, of whom they did not leave one alive. This gentleman made a very good Indian, being of dark complexion, and was much liked by his Master, who soon adopted him into his family, which exempted him from all drudgery.[11]

Rutherfurd noted that with the number of Indians involved in the siege, obtaining enough food was frequently a problem. Sometimes, they had only a handful of corn for an entire day. He sometimes begged for food from the French habitants, but often was turned away. Because of the food shortage, his master eventually

decided to move back up Lake Saint Clair near the spot where Rutherfurd was first captured. On the way, they stopped at the grave of the dead son again. This time, an elaborate ceremony was held, which Rutherfurd learned was to formally adopt him into the family in place of the lost son. He wrote, "my name should no longer be Saganash, or Englishman, but Addick, which signified a white elk. Notwithstanding this, I was generally called by my Master's name, which was Peewash."[12]

Rutherfurd's hope that his workload would diminish with his adoption was not realized. "I flattered myself that my being adopted into the family would have exempted me from this kind of drudgery, as was the case with most of the other prisoners, but Peewash having a particular regard for his wife, chose that I should still assist her on many occasions, and she being fond of ease laid the most of it on my shoulders."[13]

After his adoption, Peewash often took Rutherfurd out hunting, which he greatly enjoyed. Of this endeavor he wrote, "The men think it beneath them to do anything but fish or hunt for the support of their family, and in this they take no more trouble than is absolutely necessary, for they frequently kill the game and leave it till they can send their squaws to carry it home. . . . Having found it she brings home the choicest pieces and dresses them for her Lord and Master, who generally sleeps until he is called to get up and eat. When he has finished his repast he regales himself with a pipe of tobacco mixed with the leaves of the sumac shrub."[14]

As related in chapter four, on July 2, Lieutenant McDougall escaped to the fort, which caused the Indians to guard all of their captives more closely. Rutherfurd often went to visit with Captain Campbell, and, "One evening he told me he felt unwell, and was prepossessed with a notion that he was going to die very soon. . .to my great grief and sorrow the first thing I heard next day was that he had been killed."[15]

The Chippewas had killed Campbell. The Ottawas, who claimed Campbell as their prisoner, were enraged and vowed to kill a prisoner of equal rank that the Chippewas held. They chose Ensign Pauli from Sandusky, "but, he being informed of his danger by a handsome squaw who was in love with him, assisted by her escaped out of the Frenchman's house; from whence with much difficulty he got into the fort after being fired at several times by the sentries, who took him for an Indian."[16]

After Pauli's escape, the Ottawas turned on Rutherfurd for their satisfaction, deeming him next in rank to

an officer. Peewash first hid him in a Frenchman's barn and later marched him as a prisoner again to the main Indian encampment, where he was forced to view a gruesome sight:

> Here in the road was lying a dead body, mangled and scalped, which the dogs were eating. They made me stop for a considerable time, and looked at it with much seeming satisfaction, at the same time, in an exulting tone of voice, telling me that there lay our Chief, our *Great Chief,* Captain Campbell. Indeed, it would not have been possible for me to have recognized that it was the remains of my good friend. He was scalped and his ears, nose, an arm, a leg, and other parts of his body cut off. It was a very shocking spectacle to me, yet however disagreeable, I was obliged to view it.[17]

Rutherfurd was then taken to a Frenchman's house, where Pontiac and several other leading chiefs confronted him. He was given some letters taken from Captain Campbell and told that because he could read English and speak French, he must interpret them fully and accurately, or he would be put to death. They were particularly interested in finding out if peace had really been declared between England and France. There was nothing of any real importance in the letters, which Rutherfurd proceeded to translate. When he was finished, the Indians seemed satisfied and allowed him to return home with Peewash.

This meeting was probably held at the house of Antoine Cuillerier, one of the leading French citizens of Detroit and a friend of Rutherfurd and his employer James Sterling. Cuillerier had offered to buy Rutherfurd from Peewash on several occasions, and it was finally agreed that he would sell him for £40 worth of trade goods and the assurance that Rutherfurd would live with Cuillerier and not return to the English. Rutherfurd's Indian family bid him a very affectionate goodbye and sent him on his way loaded with gifts. He wrote that when he arrived at Cuillerier's:

> I scrubbed myself for two hours with soap and warm water to get the grease and paint off.

Then dressing myself *en Canadien* with a clean French shirt and long ruffles, a new breech clout, with a manlet exactly like our lady's bedgown, and a pair of new leggings, I began to feel somewhat comfortable.

> I got a good supper genteelly served up, went to a good bed which was provided for me, and slept better than I had done for a long while before. I awoke next morning happy in the thought of being out of the hands of the savages. . . .[18]

Rutherfurd's euphoria was not to last long, however. The next afternoon, a party of Ottawas entered the house, roughly seized him, and took him to Pontiac's lodge. After being kept in suspense for several hours, he was informed through a French interpreter that he had been taken because the French had also purchased several other captives, and Pontiac was afraid that if the practice continued, the Indians would have no captives left. Pontiac had ordered all prisoners so purchased reclaimed and told Rutherfurd that he had decided to keep him for himself. The next morning, the Chippewas, to whom he had formerly belonged, sent a party to claim him. This incident nearly resulted in "a war between the two nations." After a lengthy altercation with Wasson, the Chippewa chief, "Pontiac thought it most prudent to deliver me up, and thereby avoid a war with a nation superior in numbers to his own. . .which would have infallibly ruined the common cause for which they were united."[19]

Wasson took Rutherfurd to his lodge, where he was told that he "had plenty of girls in his family to do all the work, so that I should never be asked to do anything, but live as he and his sons did."[20]

Wasson's family treated him extremely well, with every member going out of their way to show kindness. Whenever there was any sign of danger, he was immediately hidden from possible harm.

After about ten days of this, Peewash came to Wasson and said he regretted selling Rutherfurd. He offered to buy him back, and according to Indian etiquette, Wasson was obliged to accept. Peewash's family received Rutherfurd well again, and he also observed,

---

Facing page. *Leaving,* by Robert Griffing. John Rutherfurd's captivity narrative shows that although they were fierce and often ruthless opponents in war, Indians also shared many of the values of the whites. His adopted family's sorrow when he was ransomed was heartfelt and sincere. The need for Indian warriors to provide for their families over the winter was one of the primary reasons why Pontiac's Uprising lost steam in the fall of 1763. This painting by Robert Griffing dramatically illustrates the strong bonds within an Indian family. Courtesy of Robert Griffing and Paramount Press.

"Wasson seemed sorry to part with me and even the princesses showed that they were not indifferent."[21]

The number of Indians prisoners steadily increased, and by the end of July they had more than fifty, as well as many scalps. Some hapless prisoners were murdered every day, even some that had been held as long as he had, Rutherfurd observed. One day he was at a Frenchman's house when eight naked captives were brought in, about to be sacrificed. Rutherfurd sadly noted:

> One little boy in particular, a drummer of the Rangers about twelve years old, was crying bitterly and imploring their mercy, but alas he knew not how vain it was to ask it from wretches whose hearts were steeled against every feeling of humanity.
>
> I saw them lead to the riverside. . .eight of these poor creatures one by one whom they put to death on the spot. Some of them were tomahawked, others they shot with their guns, and some they made little boys shoot with bows and arrows in order to accustom them to cruelty. . . . When they were all dead they scalped them and some of the Indians took the skin off their arms to make tobacco pouches of, as they had formerly done with Captain Robertson and Captain Campbell, leaving the first joints of the fingers by way of tassels.
>
> They then threw the bodies into the river that they might float down to the Fort, where their countrymen might see what they said they should all undergo in a short time.[22]

This and other acts of cruelty toward the captives convinced Rutherfurd that he had to attempt to escape at all costs. He approached a Frenchman named Boileau, who had been friendly toward him and "found that a little money would go a great way with him."[23]

James Sterling, Major Gladwin, and several other officers also promised to reward Boileau if he helped Rutherfurd escape. They devised a plan whereby Boileau would go fishing in his canoe in the evening as he always did, but then wait down river in an area concealed by rushes. After dark, Rutherfurd would sneak away from the village and meet Boileau, who would then carry him to the fort. They had to temporarily delay their plan because of Dalyell's disastrous defeat at Bloody Run, but seeing the fate of some of those captured soldiers, Rutherfurd was more resolved than ever to make his attempt.

Potawatomi Indian warrior, by Dirk Gringhuis. Courtesy of Mackinac State Historic Parks.

On the appointed night, Rutherfurd pretended to go to sleep in the hut as usual. Then when he was sure everyone else was sleeping soundly, he crawled to the doorway on all fours.

Once outside, he waited for five minutes to see if anyone had noticed, and then took off for the woods as fast as he could. He wore only his shirt, not even daring to take moccasins, knowing that if discovered, his captors would immediately know his designs. He covered himself with mud and moss to conceal his white skin. At one point, he had to hide from two Indians who were returning from a feast, fortunately a little intoxicated and engaged in deep conversation. When he reached what he thought was the rendezvous spot, Boileau was nowhere to be seen. He "began to exclaim against the perfidy of the Frenchman, who in my desperate situation, I thought, had deceived me."[24]

Upon closer observation, however, Rutherfurd discovered that he was still about a quarter of a mile upriver from the agreed upon location. When he reached the proper spot, he found the Frenchman asleep in his canoe. They immediately paddled out into the middle of the river and let the current carry them silently past the main Indian camp, where they could "plainly hear them talk, and saw some of them dancing and singing at a feast around a fire."[25]

About an hour before daylight on August 5, they were taken aboard a ship anchored in the river opposite the fort. Rutherfurd could not express his feelings on the occasion, but later he wrote:

> my friends were overjoyed to see me, although I cut a very odd figure among civilized people. The whole town, inhabitants as well as the garrison, turned out to see me. My appearance was sufficient to excite their pity as well as their laughter. I had nothing on but an old greasy, painted shirt, my face was painted red, black, and green, my hair had been cut off, and my body was black with the moss I had put on. My thighs and legs were so torn by the briars and thorns and so affected by the poisoned vines that they were swollen as big as any grenadier's in His Majesty's service.[26]

Boileau left for home immediately, lest the Indians become aware of his part in the escape.

After recovering for about ten days, Rutherfurd sailed for Niagara aboard the *Michigan* to escort a supply of trade goods back to Detroit that Sterling had ordered. They reached Fort Schlosser in four days, and as soon as the ship was loaded, they headed back to Detroit. After only one day of sailing, the ship sprung a leak and was deliberately run aground on the south shore of Lake Erie as described in chapter six. Rutherfurd wrote, "the cries and shrieks of the naval officer's lady with three children affected me much more than

my own condition. It was a pitiful sight indeed. The mother held two of her children in her arms while the other little innocent was making a fruitless attempt with her hands to stop the water from rushing into the cabin, already some three inches deep. She did this, she said, "to prevent the water from drowning her mama."[27]

Even though the ship was eventually brought to rest on a sandbar about fifty yards from shore, the danger was not over. The lifeboat had broken free, and there was still a possibility that the waves would tear the ship apart and drown the passengers before they could get on dry land. Lieutenant Montresor, the engineer, bravely volunteered to swim to shore and retrieve the lifeboat. In spite of the rough water and possible danger from waiting Indians, he was successful, and the rest of the passengers and crew were soon safely ashore. Although he describes the shipwreck and subsequent Indian attack in detail, Montresor omits any mention of this heroic act in his own journal.

Once everyone was ashore, Montresor directed the construction of a makeshift fortification, which proved its worth when the feared Indian attack did come. After waiting three weeks, a rescue party finally reached the group, and they were carried back to Fort Schlosser by bateaux. As they marched down the portage road to Fort Niagara, they passed the victims of the Devil's Hole battle, "about eighty dead bodies, unburied, scalped, and sadly mangled."[28]

From Niagara, Rutherfurd went to New York, where he obtained an ensign's commission in the 42nd Regiment. The next year, he participated in Bouquet's expedition, hoping that "I shall have an opportunity, perhaps, of seeing the savages get a complete drubbing and be instrumental in restoring peace and tranquility to the poor people in the back settlements of this country, where we hear they are committing great ravages and cruelties upon the inhabitants, sparing neither sex nor age."[29]

He was promoted to lieutenant in 1770 and captain in 1778, and he served in North America during the Revolution. After his retirement, he lived in Scotland until his death on January 12, 1830, at eighty-four years of age.

ABBREVIATIONS

Abbreviations

AJ	Amherst Journals
AP	Amherst Papers
BHC	Burton Historical Collection, Detroit Public Library
BP	Bouquet Papers
CISHL	Collections of the Illinois State Historical Library
CL	Clements Library
DRCHSNY	Documents Relating to the Colonial History of the State of New York
GP	Gage Papers
LAC	Library and Archives of Canada (formerly the National Archives of Canada)
LC	Library of Congress
MPHC	Michigan Pioneer and Historical Collections
MSHP	Mackinac State Historic Parks
PHMC	Pennsylvania Historical and Museum Commission
SWJ	Sir William Johnson Papers
TNA	National Archives of England (formerly the Public Records Office)
WHC	Wisconsin Historical Collections

Some Notes on Style

When quoting period sources, for the most part we have left the spelling, punctuation, and grammar as originally written. We believe that this gives the reader a greater appreciation for the flavor of the times. One exception is that we have replaced the 18th century "hard s" (∫) with the modern letter "s."

Readers should also be aware that although today there is a distinct difference between English and British, in the eighteenth century this was not the case. Writers from the period generally used the terms interchangeably, and so have we in this book.

To minimize confusion over the identification of various Indian tribes, except in period quotations, we have used the term Wyandot throughout for both the Wyandot and Huron tribes, and Chippewa for both the Chippewa and Ojibwa tribes.

NOTES

Chapter I
A Bold and Successful Expedition
The British Empire Reaches West
1760

1 Rogers, *Annotated Journals*, p. 208. When citing Rogers' *Journals* in this book, we will use the Purple Mountain Press *Annotated and Illustrated* edition. Rogers' original report of his journey to the west, edited by Victor Patlsits and reprinted in the *Journal of the New York Public Library*, varies only slightly from the version in his published *Journals*. We have chosen to cite the annotated edition of the *Journals* throughout this book, as it is the easiest for interested readers to obtain.

2 Amherst, *Journal*, p. 251.

3 Rogers, *Annotated Journals*, p. 209.

4 The date references in this chapter will be taken from Rogers' *Journals*. Even though they may not be accurate for some specific events, overall they do convey the relative progress of the expedition. In his unpublished personal notes for *Robert Rogers of the Rangers*, John Cuneo speculates that Rogers' original notes may have been lost or damaged during one of the storms that the expedition encountered, and he later had to reconstruct them from memory. This could account for some slight date discrepancies. (Cuneo, *Personal Notes*, p. 88, n. 28).

5 Rogers, *Annotated Journals*, p. 211.

6 BP, Volume V, p. 79.

7 Kirkwood, pp. 80–81.

8 Rogers, *Annotated Journals*, p. 213.

9 Ibid., p. 214.

10 Although Pontiac had not yet achieved the widespread fame that his "uprising" would bring him, he may still have enjoyed stature among his peers. There is a report that he delivered a speech at Fort Duquesne in 1757 saying that a report of the fall of Quebec was false, and he encouraged his listeners to remain loyal to the French. Dowd, *War Under Heaven*, pp. 292–293.

11 Ibid.

12 Peckham, pp. 15–16.

13 Croghan to Johnson, undated letter, November 1763, CISHL, Volume XI, p. 53.

14 Gage to Halifax, April 14, 1764, CISHL, Volume X, Chapter VI, p. 241.

15 Rogers, *Concise Account*, pp. 240–241.

16 Rogers, *Concise Account*, pp. 241–242. The cattle were the oxen that Captain Brewer had been driving overland along the south side of Lake Erie, although it is unclear how the number more than doubled from the forty initially procured.

17 Rogers, *Concise Account*, pp. 242–243.

18 Rogers, *Annotated Journals*, p. 215.

19 Ibid., pp. 215–219.

20 Ibid., p. 219.

21 Ibid.

22 Ibid., p. 220.

23 Ibid., p. 221.

24 Ibid.

25 BP, Volume V, p. 80.

26 John Porteus, November 20, 1763, quoted in Zaboly, *A True Ranger*, p. 311.

27 Dowd, *War Under Heaven*, p. 56–58.

28 Campbell to Bouquet, December 11, 1760, BP, Volume V, pp. 171. Also in MPHC, Volume XXIX, pp. 46–49.

29 Kirkwood, pp. 84–85.

30 Zaboly, *A True Ranger*, p. 314

Chapter II
Peaceable Possession of the Forts—Early Trouble Averted
1761

1 Pitt, Volume II, p. 404.

2 Colonel Thomas Gage originally raised the 80th Regiment of Light Armed Foot during the French and Indian War. On March 29, 1762, Montagu Wilmot became the colonel, but the regiment still often was referred to as "Gage's." Gladwin's illness was probably malaria. Dixon, *Never Come to Peace Again*, p. 90.

3 See Widder, *Mapping the Lakes*, for an interesting account of the discovery and evaluation of this important map.

4 Campbell to Amherst, November 8, 1761, BP, Volume VI, p. 28.

5 Gorrell, *Journal*, entry for October 12, 1761, p. 26.

6 Ibid., entry for October 1, 1761, p. 26.

7 BP, Volume V, p. 816.

8 Campbell to Bouquet, June 16, 1761, BP, Volume V, p. 555–556.

9 Campbell to Walters, June 17, 1761, BP, Volume V, p. 560.

10 Dowd, *War Under Heaven*, pp. 106–107.

11 Campbell to Bouquet. Report of Indian Council Near Detroit, July 3, 1761. Enclosed in Campbell to Bouquet, July 22, 1761, BP, Volume V, pp. 647–650. See also Campbell to Bouquet, July 7, 1763, BP, Volume VI, p. 619, and Peckham, pp.74–75.

12 Armour, *Attack at Michilimackinac*, pp. 25–27.

13 Ibid., p. 29.

14. Ibid., pp. 30–31.

15 Pauli to Bouquet, February 19, 1762, BP, Volume VI, p. 46. For an in-depth study on the history of Fort Sandusky and the British garrison there, see Harburn, "a little Discondent about the Blockhous…"

16 Johnson to Bouquet, September 17, 1761, BP, Volume VI, p. 761, regarding the conference. See also Johnson to Amherst, June 21, 1761, SWJ, Volume X, p. 291. The proceedings of Johnson's council at Detroit, including descriptions of the social events, can be found in SWJ, Volume III, pp. 460–463, and are also described in Peckham, pp. 78–86.

17 Campbell to Bouquet, September 17, 1761, BP, Volume VI, p. 757–758.

Chapter III
Early Signs of Discontent
The Origins of the Uprising
1761–1763

1 Peckham, p. 98; Dowd, *War Under Heaven*, p. 101.

2 Dowd, *War Under Heaven*, pp. 99–101; Dixon, *Never Come to Peace Again*, p. 295.

3 Peckham, p. 99.

4 "Journal of James Kenny," *Pennsylvania Magazine of History and Biography*, Volume XXXVII, 1913, pp. 170–171; quoted in Peckham, pp. 99–100. Also in Dixon, *Never Come to Peace Again*, p. 95.

5 "McCullough's Narrative," in Loudon, Volume I, pp. 321–322. Also in Peckham, pp. 98–99, and Dixon, *Never Come to Peace Again*, p. 95.

6 Dowd, *War Under Heaven*, p. 101.

7 For details of these discussions, see Dixon, *Never Come to Peace Again*, pp. 93–100, 107–109, and Dowd, *War Under Heaven*, pp. 94–105.

8 Trask, p. 10.

9 Campbell to Bouquet, Detroit, June 8, 1761, BP, Volume V, p. 533.

10 Dunn, p. 15.

11 Ibid., p. 8, Amherst to Bouquet, January 11, 1763. Showing that he was still trying to cut expenses, Amherst tells Bouquet to keep costs down by not approving further money for furniture at Fort Pitt. BP, Volume VI, p. 146.

12 Peckham, p. 57.

13 Johnson to Amherst, February 12, 1761, SWJ, Volume III, p. 331–334.

14 Amherst to Johnson, February 1, 1761, SWJ, Volume III, pp. 316–317.

15 Amherst to Johnson, February 22, 1761, SWJ, Volume III, p. 345.

16 Dowd, *War Under Heaven*, p. 70; Peckham, p. 72.

17 Ibid., p. 71.

18 Holmes to Bouquet, March 17, 1762, BP, Volume VI, p. 67.

19 Dowd, *War Under Heaven*, p. 70.

20 Walters to Johnson, April 5, 1762, SWJ, Volume X, p. 427.

21 Hutchins to Croghan, Jenks, pp. 372–373.

22 Campbell to Bouquet, November 8, 1761, BP, Volume VI, p. 26.

23 Campbell to Amherst, November 8, 1761, BP, Volume VI, pp. 28–29.

24 Campbell to Bouquet, November 28, 1761, BP, Volume VI, p. 32.

25 Bouquet to Amherst January 11, 1763, BP, Volume VI, p. 147.

26 Bouquet to Amherst, January 11, 1763, BP, Volume VI, pp. 147–148.

27 John W. Frank, MD, Roland S. Moore, Ph.D., and Genevieve M. Ames, Ph.D., "Historical and Cultural Roots of Drinking Problems Among American Indians," *American Journal of Public Health,* March 2000, Volume 90, Number 3, pp. 344–352; Connie J. Mulligan, Robert W. Robin, Michael V. Osier, Nyamkhishig Sambuughin, Levi G. Goldfarb, Rick A. Kittles, Diane Hesselbrock, David Godlman, and Jeffrey C. Long, "Allelic Variation at Alcohol Metabolism Genes (ADH1B, ADH1C, ALDH2) and Alcohol Dependence in an American Indian Population," *Human Genetics*, July 2003, 113, pp. 325–336; Tamara L. Wall, Ph.D., Lucinda G. Carr, Ph.D., Cindy L. Ehlers, PhD, "Protective Association of Genetic Variation in Alcohol Dehydrogenase with Alcohol Dependence in Native American Mission

Indians," *American Journal of Psychiatry* 160:1, January 2003, pp. 41–46.

28 Onondaga chief to Johnson, May 27, 1761, SWJ, Volume X, p. 683.

29 "Affidavit of Capt. Jacob Klock relative to G: [George] Klock's Proceedings concerning the Lands at Conjaharee," SWJ, Volume X, p. 621, n 1. The exact date of this letter is unknown, but historians have determined it to be between January 19, and March 10, 1763.

30 Bouquet, General Order, Fort Pitt, March 1, 1762: BP, Volume VI, p. 49. The dependent posts were listed as Bedford, Ligonier, Cumberland, Sandusky, Venango, Le Boeuf, Presque Isle, Juniata, Stoney Creek, Bushy Run, Great Crossings, and Burd.

31 Bouquet to Amherst, March 7, 1762, BP, Volume VI, p. 53.

32 Amherst to Johnson, January 16, 1762, Amherst Papers, CL.

33 Gage to Gladwin, July 15, 1764, Gage Papers, CL.

34 Ecuyer to Bouquet, June 16, 1763, and June 24, 1763, BP, Volume VI, pp. 228–33, and Amherst to Gladwin, June 29, 1763, Amherst Papers, Volume 2, Number 3, CL, and Peckham, pp. 226–227.

35 Dowd, *War Under Heaven*, p. 65.

36 Walters to Amherst, April 5, 1762, SWJ, Volume X, p. 427.

37 Carre to Bouquet, November 5, 1761, BP, Volume VI, p. 25.

38 Pauli to Bouquet, February 19, 1762, BP, Volume VI. p. 46.

39 Cochrane, Orders to Dow [Enclosure in Cochrane to Bouquet], Presque 'Isle, September 27, 1761, BP, Volume V, p. 785.

40 Dixon, *Never Come to Peace Again*, pp. 3–41.

41 Anderson, pp. 28–30. For Langlade's involvement in the French and Indian War, see also Todish, *America's FIRST First World War*, pp. 28, 36, 38.

42 Dunn, p. 10.

43 SWJ, Volume XIII, Johnson's Detroit Journal, entry for October 6, 1761, p. 266.

44 Ibid., entry for July 26, 1761, p. 228.

45 Amherst to Johnson, June 3, 1762, DRCHSNY, Book XXXVII, Volume VII, p. 509.

46 Articles for the Western Department, 1760, BP, Volume V, p. 227–228.

47 Bouquet to Amherst, April 1, 1762, BP, Volume VI, p. 72.

48 Bouquet to Creasap, September 10, 1760, BP, Volume V, p. 32.

49 List of Houses and Inhabitants at Fort Pitt, April 14, 1761, BP, Volume V, p. 408; Croghan's house burned, Darlington, p. 90.

50 Croghan to Bouquet, March 30, 1763, BP, Volume VI, p. 169.

51 Johnson to Goldsbrow Banyar, January 7, 1762, SWJ, Volume III, p. 603.

52 Gage to Bouquet, May 14, 1764, BP, Volume VI, p. 539. Also printed in MPHC, Volume XXIX, pp. 257–259. See note in BP, Volume VI, p. 545, for Governor Fauquier's response regarding the Proclamation of 1763.

53 Hay to Bouquet, March 25, 1764, MPHC, Volume XXIX, p. 251.

54 For details of this uprising and the story of Fort Loudoun, see Kelley, *Historic Fort Loudoun*.

55 For more detail see Harburn, "The Post at St. Mary's."

56 Dowd, *War Under Heaven*, p. 90.

57 Primm, pp. 17–18.

58 The Gladwin Manuscripts, MPHC, Volume XXVII, p. 637.

59 Sterling to MacAdams, August 7, 1763, *Sterling Letter Book*, CL. See also Gladwin to Amherst, July 28, 1764, enclosed in Bradstreet to Gage, August 5, 1764, Gage Papers, Volume 22, CL.

60 Bouquet to Gage, November, 30, 1764, BP, Volume VI, p. 713.

Chapter IV
The Whole World Is on Fire
The War Begins in the West
1763

1 Holmes, Copy of Speech of Miami Chiefs, Fort Miamis, March 30, 1763, BP, Volume VI, p. 173.

2 Amherst, *Journal*, entry of May 28, 1763, p. 305.

3 Rutherfurd, p. 220.

4 Ibid., p. 225.

5 Amherst Papers, Volume 7, CL. Quoted in Peckham, p. 124.

6 Peckham, p. 127.

7 Hay, p. 203.

8 Rogers, *Annotated Journals*, Detroit Journal, pp. 273–274. Some authors have claimed that the journal attributed to Rogers was actually the work of Lieutenant Jehu Hay. Hay did indeed keep a journal of the siege, but his known account and this one are two decidedly different documents. This journal begins on May 6, and ends on July 4, before Rogers arrived at Detroit. The introduction clearly

states that the account was "taken from the Officers who were then in the Fort, and wrote in their Words in the following Manner. . . ." (p. 273). In his French and Indian War *Journals,* Rogers mentions a future second volume that would include "An Account of the Indian Wars in America subsequent to 1760." A likely explanation is that he was accumulating information about events before his arrival at Detroit to be combined with his own observations during his service there. The second portion may have been lost or may never have been written. At any rate, in this book, Rogers will be accepted as the author of this journal, and Hay will be credited with the account known to be his.

9 MacDonald to Bouquet, July 12, 1763, MPHC, Volume XX1X, p. 216.

10 Harburn, "a little Discondent about the Blockhous. . .Fort Sandusky," p. 12, p. 18, n. 44. See also MacDonald to Bouquet, July 12, 1763, MPHC, Volume XXIX, p. 218, and Peckham, pp. 194–195.

11 "Extract of a Court of Enquiry Held by Order of Major Henry Gladwin to Enquire Into the Manner of the Taking of the Forts Sandusky, St. Josephs, Miamis and Presque'Isle, Detroit, July 6, 1763," The Gladwin Manuscripts, MPHC, Volume XXVII, p. 636. See alsoMacDonald to Bouquet, July 12, 1763,The Gladwin Manuscripts, MPHC, Volume XXVII, p. 217.

12 Sergeant Steiner of Captain Donald Campbell's company of the 60th Regiment was in the initial garrison stationed at Fort Saint Joseph in 1761. He apparently was in poor health as well as near the end of his enlistment period. In April 1762, he applied to Campbell for an early discharge. Bouquet could not honor the request because he had "no Serjeant to spare to relive Stenier . . . ," but promised to have him discharged as soon as a replacement was available. No further information has been found to date to show if Steiner was relieved, so he may very well have been there at the time of the attack. Campbell to Bouquet, April 26, 1762, MPHC, Volume XXIX, p. 138, and Bouquet to Campbell, May 25, 1763, MPHC, Volume XXIX, p. 147.

13 "Extract of a Court of Enquiry Held by Order of Major Henry Gladwin to Enquire Into the Manner of the Taking of the Forts Sandusky, St. Josephs, Miamis and Presque'Isle, Detroit, July 6, 1763," The Gladwin Manuscripts, MPHC, Volume XXVII, p. 636.

14 Winston to the English merchants at Detroit, June 10, 1763, The Gladwin Manuscripts, MPHC, Volume XXVII, pp. 634–635.

15 Hay, pp. 212–213.

16 MacDonald to Bouquet, July 12, 1763, MPHC, Volume XXIX, p. 217.

17 Morris, p. 17.

18 Jenkins to Gladwin, June 1, 1763, The Gladwin Manuscripts, MPHC, Volume XXIX, p. 636.

19 MHPC, Volume XXIX, p. 686 Also WHC, Volume XVII, p. 240 and Gage to Loftus, March 29, 1764, in the Gage Papers, Volume 16, CL.

20 Armour, *Attack at Michilimackinac,* p. 45. Also Harburn, "The King's Quiet Commandant," p. 7.

21 Armour, *Attack at Michilimackinac,* pp. 49–50

22 Henry Bostwick, Deposition to Daniel Disney, Montreal, August 13, 1763, The Gladwin Manuscripts, MPHC, Volume XXVII, pp. 666–667.

23 Armour, *Attack at Michilimackinac,* p. 51.

24 We thank our friend Bob Andrews for discovering and sharing Tracy's long-unknown first name.

25 Hay, pp. 213–214.

26 Etherington to Gladwin, June 12, 1763, The Gladwin Manuscripts, MPHC, Volume XXVII, pp. 631–632. In an extensively researched study, Harburn discusses the garrison's numbers and the casualties, even documenting some names of the survivors. For further details, see *In Defense of the Red Ensign.*

27 Father Francois Philibert Watrin, S. J., September 3, 1764, *Jesuit Relations,* Volume LXX, pp. 251–253. Also cited in Boynton, p. 45.

28 Armour, *Attack at Michilimackinac,* p. 61.

29 Etherington to Gladwin, June 12, 1763, quoted in Boynton, p. 45.

30 Etherington to Gorrell, Michilimackinac, June 11, 1763, in Gorrell, p. 39. Gorrell's original journal is in the Maryland Historical Library, while a shorter version is in the Clements Library at the University of Michigan.

31 Gorrell, *Journal,* entry for July 13, 1763, p. 46.

32 Etherington to Gorrell, June 11, 1763, p. 39.

33 Gorrell, *Journal,* entry for July 13, 1763, pp. 46–47.

34 For further discussion of this paradox, see Harburn, *In Defense of the Red Ensign,* p. 8. See also Burton to Gage, September 18, 1764, Gage Papers, CL.

35 Gorrell, *Journal,* entry for August 16, 1763, p. 47.

36 Amherst, *Journal,* entry for July 29, 1763, p. 315.

37 Gorrell, *Journal,* entry for June 11, 1763, p. 39.

38 Ibid.

39 Ibid., pp. 40–42.
40 Amherst to Gladwin, August 28, 1763, Amherst Papers, CL.
41 Rogers, *Annotated Journals*, Detroit Journal, p. 274.
42 Ibid.
43 Hay, p. 205.
44 Rogers, *Annotated Journals*, Detroit Journal, p. 275.
45 Howard Peckham, whose 1947 *Pontiac and the Indian Uprising* is still considered one of the classic works on the subject, states that Hopkins "deserves almost as much credit as Major Gladwin for the valiant defense of Fort Detroit" (p. 142). While he may have been a brave soldier in combat, Hopkins certainly lacked character and moral scruples, going over to the French shortly after the siege because he felt his efforts were not sufficiently rewarded. He is believed to be the author of the mysterious letter attempting to lure Robert Rogers into the French service while he was commandant of Fort Michilimackinac. Brave or not, even during the siege, Hopkins incurred the disdain of his fellow officers. On November 12, a group of the fort's officers sent Gladwin a letter that read as follows: "As Captain Hopkins has been accused by Lieutenant Cuyler of ungentleman like behavior in selling rum & c. at a Profit and over charging the men of his Company for Necessary's furnished by him—The Officers of the Garrison whose names are undermentioned do therefore refuse to do duty with him till such times as he Cleares his Character" The list of the signers reads like a who's who of the fort's garrison. First and in the largest script, much like John Hancock on the Declaration of Independence, is Robert Rogers. He is followed in order by John Montresor and Dederich Brehm, the engineers; Lieutenant Edward Abbott of the Royal Artillery; Lieutenants Jehu Hay and George McDougall of the 60th; Ensign Garrett Fisher of the 55th Regiment; Lieutenant Samuel Williams of the 17th Regiment; Lieutenants James Blane and Abraham Cuyler and Ensign Mervin Perry, all of the Queen's Rangers; as well as Ensign Christopher Pauli, Ensign Francis Schlosser, and Ensign John Christie, all of the 60th Regiment. The original of this letter is included in correspondence Gladwin sent to Amherst on December 12, 1763, now in the Amherst Papers at the Clements Library.
46 Navarre, p. 70.
47 Ibid., pp. 71–72.
48 Ibid., p. 91.
49 Ibid., p. 97.
50 Ibid., p. 98.
51 Ibid., p. 100.
52 Hay, p. 208.
53 Amherst, *Journal*, entry for June 16, 1763, pp. 306–307.
54 Navarre, pp. 114–115.
55 Ibid., pp. 128–129.
56 Hay, p. 211.
57 Navarre, pp. 143–144.
58 Ibid., pp. 153–154.
59 Rogers, *Concise Account*, p. 244
60 Amherst to Hamilton, June 19, 1763, BP, Volume VI, p. 242.
61 Amherst to Bouquet, June 29, 1763, BP, Volume VI, p. 277.
62 Amherst to Bouquet, July 2, 1763, BP, Volume VI. p. 283.
63 Navarre, p. 159.
64 Ibid., p. 161.
65 Ibid., p. 164, n. 82.
66 Hay, p. 215.
67 Ibid., p. 216.
68 Navarre, p. 191.
69 Rogers to Lord Hillsborough, November 17, 1771, quoted in Zaboly, p. 339.
70 Rogers, *Concise Account*, p. 244.
71 Robert Rogers wrote to his wife from Fort Ontario, "Capt Rogers [James Rogers, who was a captain in the French and Indian War] has got a company of Rangers and goes forward with me his company was recruited out of the boto [bateau] men of this place and at Niagra—I shall set out in two days for Niagra with two hundred and fifty of the fifty fifth regiment and Capt Rogers company of Rangers. . . ." Robert to Elizabeth Rogers, June 29, 1763, Rogers/Roche Papers, CL.
72 Zaboly, p. 341.
73 Amherst to Johnson, August 14, 1763, SWJ, Volume IV, pp. 186–187; quoted in Zaboly, p. 341.
74 *Gentleman's Magazine*, October 1763, p. 486.
75 As predicted, the Indians had heard of the planned British attack. Navarre (p. 204) claims that word was carried from some French inside the fort to their countrymen on the outside, and from there it was passed on to Pontiac. Whether this is the exact means that the word traveled by or not will never be known, but the fact is that the Indians did have time to prepare.
76 Cuneo, *Robert Rogers*, p. 166.

77 Rogers, *Journals*, p. 283.

78 Hay, p. 219.

79 Ibid., and MacDonald to Gates, August 8, 1763. Original in the Clements Library; quoted in Peckham, p. 208. For Peewash, see Rutherfurd, p. 263.

80 Amherst, *Journal*, p. 320.   After the battle, the water of Parent's Creek ran red with the blood of the fallen soldiers, and ever since, it has been known as Bloody Run. Until it was cut down in 1886, a huge tree along the line of march, measured at sixteen feet in circumference by historian Benjamin Lossing in 1860, still bore bullet scars from that fateful day. Today, the modern metropolis of Detroit has obliterated virtually all traces of the desperate fight.

Chapter V
The Uprising Spreads East
The Siege of Fort Pitt and the Pennsylvania Posts
Summer 1763

1 For extensive biographies of George Croghan and Alexander McKee, see Wainwright, *George Croghan: Wilderness Diplomat*, and Nelson, *A Man of Distinction among Them: Alexander McKee and the British-Indian Affairs along the Ohio Country Frontier, 1754–1799.*

2 Croghan to Bouquet, December 10, 1762, BP, Volume VI, p. 137–138.

3 Ecuyer to Bouquet, "Indian Intelligence From Fort Pitt," January 30, 1763, BP, Volume VI, p. 155–156.

4 McKee to Croghan, Fort Pitt, April 12, 1763, and McKee: Indian Conference Minutes, Fort Pitt, April 16–18, 1763, BP, Volume VI, pp. 180–186.

5 Ecuyer's description of the damage is interesting and provides a glimpse at the powerful force of nature at the juncture of the Allegheny and Monongahela Rivers. For details, see Ecuyer to Bouquet, March 11, 1763, BP, Volume VI, pp. 165–166. Bouquet's description of the extensive damage to Fort Pitt is contained in BP, Volume VI, pp. 36–37; for Amherst's assessment, see Amherst to Bouquet, New York, April 5, 1763, BP, Volume VI, p. 17.

6 Ecuyer to Bouquet, May 29, 1763, BP. Volume VI, p. 193. Andrew Byerly, a former sergeant in the 60th Regiment ran a way station at Bushy Run to host travelers between Fort Pitt and the eastern posts.

7 Trent's Journal was originally attributed to Ecuyer and first published in 1892 by Mary C. Darlington, however, later historians show Trent to have written it. It has been reprinted in *Fort Pitt and Letters from the Frontier*, Mary C. Darlington, editor. The above incident is noted on p. 85; for further information on Trent, see BP, Volume V, p. 282, n. 3 and Volume VI, pp. 203–204, n. 3.

8 Ecuyer to Bouquet, May 30, 1763, BP, Volume VI, pp. 195–196. See also Darlington, Trent Journal, p. 85.

9 Ecuyer to Bouquet, June 2, 1763, BP, Volume VI, pp. 202–203.

10 Ourry to Amherst, June 10, 1763, BP, Volume VI, p. 248.

11 Blane to Bouquet, June 4, 1763, BP, Volume VI, p. 206.

12 Ibid., June 28, 1763, BP, Volume VI, pp. 268–269.

13 Ourry to Amherst, June 10, 1763, BP, Volume VI, p. 246.

14 Ourry to Bouquet, Fort Bedford, June 3, 1763, BP, Volume VI, p. 204.

15 Ibid., June 9, 1763, BP, Volume VI, p. 213.

16 Amherst to Bouquet, June 6, 1763, BP, Volume VI, pp. 209–210.

17 SWJ, Volume IV, pp. 137–138.

18 Price to Bouquet, June 26, 1763, BP, Volume VI, pp. 266–267.

19 Darlington, Trent Journal, entries for June 25, and 26, 1763, pp. 93–94.

20 Ibid., Entry for June 27, 1763, p. 96. Benjamin Gray, from garrison at Presque Isle, escaped during the surrender of that post and met up with the Le Boeuf survivors along the route back to Fort Pitt. His account of the fall of Presque Isle later corroborated that of the Ensign John Christie, the commandant there. For a brief biographical sketch of Grey, see BP, Volume VI, p. 301, n. 1. Regarding the discrepancies in the number of survivors of the attack, apparently, either the Indians killed those missing (perhaps accounting for the shots heard upon their initial escape) or they died from the elements.

21 Johnson to Amherst, July 11, 1763, DRCHSNY, Volume VII, pp. 532–533.

22 Amherst to Bouquet, June 25, 1763, BP, Volume VI, p. 256.

23 Christie to Bouquet, July 10, 1763, BP, Volume VI, pp. 301–303. Also Court of Enquiry at Detroit July 9, 1763, AP. W.O. 34/49, f. 212, TNA.

24 Ecuyer to Bouquet, June 26, 1763, BP, Volume VI, p. 260.

25 Court of Enquiry at Detroit, July 9, 1763, AP, W.O. 34/49, f. 212, TNA. In this deposition, Christie stated that the Englishman he mentioned in his

account had been a captive of the Indians for seven years and had identified the tribes involved. Christie also stated that during negotiations two Indian chiefs had promised him that he and his garrison would be unharmed and allowed to go either to the *Huron* or to Fort Pitt.

26 Court of Enquiry at Detroit, July 6, 1763, The Gladwin Manuscripts, MPHC, Volume XXVII, 1896, pp. 637–639.

27 Bouquet to Ecuyer, July 4, 1763, BP, Volume VI, p. 293.

28 Bouquet to Ourry, July 4, 1763, BP, Volume VI, p. 296.

29 Amherst, *Journal*, entry for July 7, 1763, p. 310.

30 Amherst to Bouquet, July 7, 1763, BP, Volume VI, p. 300.

31 Amherst to Gage, July 12, 1763, Amherst Papers, CL.

32 Amherst to Campbell, TNA, W.O. 34/97, June 6, 1763, University of Michigan Graduate Library microfilm copies. Also contained in Amherst to Bouquet, June 6, 1763, BP, Volume VI, p. 209.

33 Amherst, *Journal*, entries for June 12, and 13, 1763, p. 306, and Amherst to Bouquet, June 12, 1763, BP, Volume VI, p. 220.

34 Amherst to Bouquet, June 16, 1763, BP, Volume VI, p. 227.

35 Ibid., June 18, 1763, BP, Volume VI, p. 235. The Royal Artillery contingent consisted of "Lieutenant Mitchjelson [Walter Mitchelson]. . .with One Corporal, One Bombardier, One Gunner, & Seven Mattrosses. . . ."

36 Amherst to Bouquet, June 19, BP, Volume VI, p. 240.

37 Amherst to Bouquet, June 23, 1763, MPHC, Volume XXIX, p. 197.

38 Hamilton to Bouquet, July 12, 1763, BP, Volume VI, p. 305–307. See also Bouquet to Amherst, June 13, 1763, BP, Volume VI, p. 222, n. 2. This entire sequence of events is outlined in a series of letters between Bouquet, Amherst, and Hamilton during June and July 1763. These can be seen in the Bouquet Papers for further details.

39 Bouquet to Amherst, June 16, 1763, BP, Volume VI, p. 226.

40 Bouquet to Callender, Carlisle, June 29, 1763, BP, Volume VI, p. 272. An interesting note: Callender was a trader who had been conducting business at both Fort Pitt and Fort Sandusky. He was initially thought to be among the victims of the attack at

Sandusky. However, he was not in the area at that time. See Harburn, "a little Discondent about the Blockhous. . . Fort Sandusky"

41 Bouquet to Slough and Simon, June 29, 1763, BP, Volume VI, p. 275.

42 Bouquet to Amherst, June 19, 1763, BP, Volume VI, p. 239.

43 Ibid., June 29, 1763, BP. Volume VI, p. 271.

44 Campbell to Bouquet, June 24, 1763, BP, Volume VI, p. 255. In his troop return, Campbell listed 17 officers, 19 sergeants, 7 drummers, and 171 rank and file for the 42nd. He listed 29 officers, 23 sergeants, 11 drummers, and 102 rank & file respectively for the 77th Regiment.

45 Bouquet to Amherst, June 25, 1763, BP, Volume VI, p. 255.

46 Ibid., July 7, 1973, BP, Volume VI, p. 299–300.

47 Bouquet to D. Campbell and J. McIntosh, June 29, 1763, BP, Volume VI, p. 273.

48 Ourry to Bouquet, July 13, 1763, BP, Volume VI, p. 309, and J. Robertson to Bouquet, July 13, 1763, BP, Volume VI, p. 311.

49 Bouquet to Amherst, June 29, 1763, BP, Volume VI, p. 271.

50 Ourry to Bouquet, July 2, 1763, BP, Volume VI, p. 286.

51 Ecuyer to Bouquet, June 26, 1763, in Darlington, p. 136. Also contained in BP, Volume VI, pp. 259–260. The military garrison consisted of companies of the 60th or Royal American Regiment and militia. A muster list of the militia at Fort Pitt is contained in the Gage Papers/Warrants of the Clements Library, University of Michigan.

52 For multiple examples of this dispersal, see Ecuyer's Fort Pitt Orderly Book in Darlington, pp. 153–171.

53 Ecuyer, Fort Pitt Orderly Book, Darlington, Entry for June 18, 1763, p. 135.

54 Ecuyer, Reply to Indians, July 27, 1763. Enclosure in Ecuyer to Bouquet, August 2, 1763, BP, Volume VI, p. 336–337. Also described by Trent in Darlington, Trent Journal, p. 103–104.

55 Bouquet to Amherst, June 23, 1763, BP, Volume VI, p. 251 tells of the establishment of the smallpox hospital, and Darlington, Trent Journal, entry for June 24, 1763, describes giving the Indians the infected items.

56 For an extensive discussion on these theories, see Dixon, *Never Come to Peace Again*, pp. 152–155; Bernard Knollenberg, "General Amherst and Germ

Warfare," Mississippi Valley Historical Review, 41 (1954–1955); and Dowd, *War Under Heaven*, p. 190. Regarding the use of dogs in warfare with the Indians, John Hughes, a Quaker Pennsylvania assemblyman suggested a theoretical plan to Bouquet. See Hughes to Bouquet, July 11, 1763, BP. Volume VI, pp. 304–305. Bouquet notes this in his "Reflections on the War With the Savages of North-America," in Smith, p. 117. For Amherst's smallpox statements, see also Amherst to Bouquet, July 7, 1763, BP, Volume VI, p. 301, and Amherst to Bouquet, July 16, 1763, BP, Volume VI, p. 315.

57 Kenny, Journal, p. 19. Also mentioned in Dixon, *Never Come to Peace Again*, pp. 72 and 153.

58 Bouquet to Robertson, July 19, 1763, BP, Volume VI, p. 321.

59 Darlington, Trent Journal, pp. 105–106.

60 Darlington, Fort Pitt Orderly Book, July 31, 1763, p. 167.

61 Ecuyer to Bouquet, August 2, 1763, BP, Volume VI, pp. 332–333.

62 Ibid., p. 333.

63 Bouquet to Amherst, August 5, 1763, BP, Volume VI, pp. 338–339. Additionally in MPHC, XXIX, pp. 219–222, and TNA, W.O. 34: 40, ff. 322, 324. This account has been published in a variety of other works. An additional and important primary account is that of Robert Kirkwood, a soldier in the 42nd Royal Highland Regiment who fought in the battle. His eyewitness account adds further details and has been reprinted with extensive annotation and new research by Ian M. McCulloch and Timothy J. Todish, in *Through So Many Dangers*, pp. 90–95.

64 Bouquet to Amherst, Camp at Bushy Run, August 6, 1763, BP, Volume VI, pp. 342–344. See also McCulloch and Todish, *Through So Many Dangers*, pp. 90–95.

65 McCulloch and Todish, *Through So Many Dangers*, p. 94.

66 Bouquet to McDonald, August 28, 1763, quoted in McCulloch and Todish, *Through So Many Dangers*, p. 95, and Dixon, *Never Come to Peace Again*, p.195.

67 Specific totals are listed in the Casualty Return: Battle of Bushy Run, Enclosure in Bouquet to Amherst, August 6, 1763, BP, Volume VI, p. 345. The 42nd or Royal Highlanders are listed as having twenty-five killed and twenty-seven wounded; the 60th or Royal Americans are listed as having six killed and four wounded; the 77th or Mont-

gomery's Highlanders are noted as having five killed and seven wounded; the Volunteers, Rangers, and Pack Horse Men had seven killed, eight wounded, and five missing.

68 McCulloch and Todish, *Through So Many Dangers*, p. 95.

69 Quoted in Stephen Brumwell, "A Service Truly Critical," pp. 173–174. For additional discussion of the Battle of Bushy Run see Dowd, *War Under Heaven*, p. 145, and Dixon, *Never Come to Peace Again*, pp. 197–198.

70 Darlington, Trent Journal, entry for August 10, 1763, p. 109.

71 Bouquet to Amherst, August 11, 1763, BP, Volume VI, p. 361.

72 Bouquet to Campbell, August 12, 1763, BP, Volume VI, p. 363. See also Darlington, Trent Journal, p. 108.

73 Amherst to Bouquet, August 31, 1763, BP, Volume VI, p. 377.

74 Bouquet to Amherst, August 11, 1763, BP, Volume VI, p. 361.

75 Ourry to Bouquet, August 27, 1763, BP, Volume VI, p. 371.

76 Ourry to Bouquet, August 27, 1763, BP, Volume VI, p. 372. As one example, a skirmish occurred between a small detachment of the Pennsylvania militia and the Delaware Indians on the west branch of the Susquehanna River on August 26. For an excellent description of this and other later engagements, see Dixon, *Never Come to Peace Again*, pp. 199–202. William Trent's Journal also describes small Indian attacks.

77 Bouquet to Amherst, August 11, 1763, BP, Volume VI, p. 362.

78 Bouquet to Amherst, Sept 7, 1763, BP, Volume VI, p. 385.

Chapter VI
The Platoons:"The Unknown Campaign" and the Battle of Buffalo Creek
Autumn 1763

1 Amherst, *Journal*, entry for June 16, 1763, p. 306. Also in Amherst to Bouquet, June 19, 1763, BP, Volume VI, p. 240.

2 Amherst to Bouquet, New York, June 23, 1763, MPHC, Volume XIX, pp. 197–198.

3 Amherst to Bouquet, July 7, 1763, BP, Volume VI, pp. 299–300.

4 Gardner's Orders, Amherst to Johnson, New York, August 10, 1763, SWJ, pp. 182–183.

5 15th Regiment Succession Books, TNA, W.O. 25/209, p. 103. Gamble, formerly of the 43rd Regiment, purchased the Lieutenancy of Edmund Worth of the 15th Regiment.

6 This is the same Patrick Sinclair who later commanded a naval vessel and founded Fort Sinclair north of Detroit the following year, and still later became lieutenant governor, commandant, and the builder of Fort Mackinac for the British during the American Revolution. This recently discovered information showing Sinclair's involvement in the Platoons solves the mystery of the gap in his career during 1763–1764. Gage Warrants, Box 7:38, CL. "Subsistence of 5 Platoons from the 25th Augt to the 12 Decr 1763 Dated New York 13th Febry 1764." For biographical information on Sinclair, see Armour/Widder, *At the Crossroads, Michilimackinac During the American Revolution*, Hamish Bain Eaton, *Patrick Sinclair: Builder of Mackinac*, and Eugene John Mayhew, *Fort Sinclair, The British Roots of St. Clair, Michigan*. See also 15th Regiment Succession Books, W.O. 25/209, p. 102.

7 Return of the Platoons included in "General Return of the Troops at the Detroit, Presque'Isle, and Niagara; & of those that are orderd Hither, New York, September 2, 1763," Amherst Papers, CL. Also, pay bills for five of the Platoons, with complete listings of the soldiers' names in each detachment and their disposition, are contained in the Gage Warrants, Clements Library, and are reprinted here in Appendix D. See Gage Warrants, Box 7:38, CL. "Warrant from Gage, for order for payment to Sutherland by Abraham Mortier, Deputy Paymaster General of the British Army." This document is reprinted in Appendix D. Gardner was promoted from captain lieutenant to captain on June 15, 1763. TNA, W.O., 25/209. Lieutenant Andrew Cathcart of the 15th Regiment was to be Gardner's second in command. Amherst to Gardner, W.O. 34/97, p. 65. For Cathcart's commission dates, see 15th Regiment Succession Book, W.0., 25/209, p. 101. The authors thank our friends, historians Bob Andrews, Brian L. Dunnigan, John Houlding, and Ian McCulloch for their unselfish assistance in understanding the often-confusing organization and history of the Platoons.

8 After serving as a lieutenant in the 15th Regiment, Erving purchased a captaincy in the 77th Regiment on November 29, 1762. For biographical notes on Mante, see Amherst to Bouquet, September 18, 1763, BP, Volume VI, p. 396, n. 4.

9 Amherst to Gardner TNA, W.O. 34/97 p. 67, August 10, 1763, University of Michigan Graduate Library microfilm collections.

10 Amherst to Gamble (and likewise for Sinclair), August 15, 1763, TNA, W.O. 34/95, p. 2, University of Michigan Graduate Library microfilm collections.

11 Amherst to Gamble, "Instruction for your proceeding with the Platoon under your Command," August 15, 1763, Amherst Papers, TNA, W.O. 34/35, University of Michigan Graduate Library microfilm collection. For further information on clothing and accouterments Light Infantry troops utilized during the French and Indian War and Pontiac eras, see McCulloch and Todish, *British Light Infantryman of the Seven Years' War*.

12 Amherst to Bouquet, September 7, 1763, BP, Volume VI, p. 388.

13 Ibid., See also Amherst to Bouquet September 18, 1763, BP, Volume VI, p. 396 n. 2. The return showed that seventeen of the forty men had already left under Captain Gardner, while the remaining twenty-three were waiting to depart under Capt. Erving. The return, which was included in Amherst to Bouquet, September 7, 1763 above, (WO 34/41: ff. 138-129, and f. 130) reads as follows:

> Return of the Men of the 42nd & 77th Regiments already gone, & that are to go by the way of Niagara, New York, 7 September, 1763.
> 42nd Regt. Gone with Captain Gardiner: 1 Sjt. 6 Pvts. = 7
> 42nd Regt. To go with Captain Erving: 1 Sjt. 1 Corp. 1 Drum. 14 Pvts. = 17
> 77th Regt. Gone with Captain Gardiner: 10 Pvts. = 10
> 77th Regt. To go with Captain Erving: 6 Pvts. = 6
> Total = 40

14 Bouquet to Amherst, August 11, and 12, 1763, BP, Volume VI, pp. 362–363.

15 Amherst to Bouquet, September 18, 1763, MPHC, Volume XIX, pp. 231–233. Also in BP, Volume VI, p. 395.

16 Amherst to Bouquet, September 25, 1763, BP, Volume VI, p. 397.

17 Peckham, pp. 222–224. For more on the amazing adventures of the shipwrecked crew of the *Michigan*, see the essay on John Rutherfurd in Appendix E.

18 Gardner to Amherst, September 26, 1763, Amherst

Papers, TNA, W.O. 34/95, p. 162–163, University of Michigan Graduate Library microfilm collection.

19 Ahrens, *The Devil's Hole Massacre*, pp. 66–67, 115–116, and 118.

20 SWJ, Journal of Indian Affairs, entry for October 6, 1763, Volume X, pp. 892–893, and Johnson to Amherst, October 6, 1763, SWJ, Volume X, p. 869.

21 Etherington to Johnson, September 17, 1763, SWJ, Volume X, pp. 817–818. For other accounts of the Devil's Hole Massacre, see De Couagne to Johnson, September 16, 1763, SWJ, Volume X, p. 815; Browning to Johnson, September 17, 1763, SWJ, Volume X, pp. 816–817, Johnson to Amherst, October 6, 1763, SWJ, Volume X, pp. 867–668; *The London Gazette*, Tuesday, November 8, to Saturday, November 12, 1763, copy in Clements Library. Accounts on the final death toll vary. From the reports noted above and official correspondence, it appears that about eighty soldiers were killed, plus two sutler's servants. The *London Gazette* reports, in addition to the officers mentioned, there were three rank and file of the 60th and sixty-three rank and file and six sergeants of the 80th killed, with eight rank and file wounded, along with two rank and file each of the New Jersey and New York Provincials. Johnson's October 6, letter states that Kanadasegey, a friendly Seneca chief, claims 309 Senecas were involved in the attack, and they suffered only one casualty.

22 Rutherfurd, p. 273

23 Amherst to Erving, September 9, 1763, WO, 34/97, University of Michigan Graduate Library microfilm collections.

24 "Return of the Troops Encamped at the Lower Landing under the Command of Major Wilkins the 24th September, 1763." W.O. 34/22 pp. 185–189. The second return, entitled "Return of His majesty's Troops Encamped on the Portage of Niagara under the Command of Major Wilkins, 12 October 1763," notes that sixteen privates were sick at Niagara, one at Fort Schlosser. W.O. 34/95, p. 218.

25 Browning to Gage, November 1, 1763, Gage Papers, CL, Volume 9.

26 Ibid..

27 *New York Mercury*, Dec 5, 1763, p. 3; copy of original in CL. See also Browning to Gage, November 1, 1763, Gage Papers, CL; and Browning to Johnson, October 22, 1763, SWJ, Volume X, p. 926. A warrant to pay monies due Mrs. Joyce Johnson, the widow of Lieutenant James Johnston of the platoons, who

was killed in the Battle of Buffalo Creek, is in the Gage Warrants, CL, Document 7:39.

28 Wilkins to Amherst, November 27, 1763, Amherst Papers, CL, Volume 7.

29 Browning to Gage, October 31, 1763, Gage Papers, CL, Volume 9.

30 Browning to Gage, October 31, 1763, second letter, Gage Papers, CL, Volume 9.

31 Browning to Gage, November 1, 1763, Gage Papers, CL, Volume 9.

32 Gage to Bouquet, December 22, 1763, Gage Papers, CL. Also in BP, Volume VI, pp. 481–482. The warrant for pay due Major Wilkins and officers of the 60th for this expedition is in the Clements Library: "John Wilkins, Esqr; of His Majesty's Sityth or Royal American Regiment of Foot. . .being for "Batt & forrage Money for the Officers of the First Battn: of Said Regiment: Employd on an Expedition Intended for the Detroit in the Campaign 1763. . . ." Gage Warrants, Box 6, Jan 1763–Dec 1763, CL. The names of men in Lieutenant Paynter's Platoon who drowned (along with others) are contained in the pay bills of the Gage Warrants. See Appendix

33 Browning to Amherst, November 19, 1763, Amherst Papers, CL, Volume 7.

34 Gladwin to Amherst, November 19, 1763, Amherst Papers, CL, Volume 7.

35 Gladwin to Amherst, Nov 1, 1763, received by Gage, BP, Volume VI, p. 447.

36 Gladwin would soon hear of this. Gladwin to Amherst, November 1, 1763, Amherst Papers, CL, Volume 7.

37 Bouquet to Amherst, October 24, 1763, Amherst Papers, CL. See also BP, Volume VI, pp. 436–439, and Hamilton to Bouquet, July 12, 1763, BP, Volume VI, pp. 305–307.

38 Halifax to Amherst, October 19, 1763, Amherst Papers, CL.

39 Bouquet to Amherst, October 24, 1763, Amherst Papers, CL.

40 Gage to Bouquet, November 18, 1763, Gage Papers, CL. Also in BP, Volume VI, pp. 460–462.

41 Stephen to Bouquet, November 7, 1763, BP, Volume VI, pp. 451–452. See also Bouquet to Stephen, October 23, 1763, BP, Volume VI, pp. 434–436.

42 The orders for these disbursement plans include the following: Amherst to Gage, November 17, 1763, Amherst Papers, CL; Gage to Bouquet, November 18, 1763, Gage Papers, CL (also in BP, Volume VI, p. 460–462); Amherst to Bouquet,

August 7, 1763, Amherst Papers, CL, (also in BP, Volume VI, pp. 346–360); Amherst to Bouquet, September 7, 1763, BP, Volume VI, pp. 387–389; Amherst to Bouquet, September 18, 1763, BP, Volume VI, p. 395; Bouquet to Amherst, September 30, 1763, enclosures contain the disbursements of the 60th Regiment, including officers sent to South Carolina, BP, Volume VI, pp. 414–416; Bouquet to Amherst, October 24, 1763, Amherst Papers, CL, (also in BP, Volume VI, p. 436); Amherst to Bouquet, January 11, 1763, BP, Volume VI, pp. 142–143, n. 1; and Dow to Bouquet, July 22, 1764, BP, Volume VI, pp. 596–597. For the detailed regulations of the New Military Establishment, see Amherst to Bouquet, New York, August 7, 1763, including enclosures, Amherst Papers, CL, (also in BP, Volume VI, pp. 346–360).

Chapter VII
The Uprising Loses Momentum
and the Changing of the Guard
Fall 1763 toWinter 1764

1 Amherst, *Journal*, entry for October 5, 1763, p. 323.
2 Gladwin to Johnson, October 7, 1763. Original in the BHC; quoted in Peckham, p. 233.
3 Gladwin to Bouquet, November 1, 1763, in BP, Volume VI, p. 445. Lieutenant Colonel William Amherst served as an aide to his brother Jeffery.
4 Pontiac to Gladwin, November 1, 1763, in BP, Volume VI, p. 449. The original is in the Amherst Papers, Volume 7, CL. Also quoted in Peckham, p. 238.
5 Gladwin to Amherst, November 1, 1763, in BP, Volume VI, pp. 446–447. The original is in the Amherst Papers, Volume 7, CL. Also quoted in Peckham, pp. 238–239.
6 Amherst, *Journal*, entry for October 24, 1764, p. 325.
7 Croghan to Bouquet, October 11, 1763, BP, Volume VI, p. 430–431; and Amherst to Bouquet, September 25, 1763, BP, Volume VI, pp. 397–399. Croghan was not entirely honest about his reasons for wanting to go to England. He told the general that his main reason was to "request compensation for his losses in goods at the beginning of the war." Croghan to Amherst, September 26, 1763, SWJ, Volume X, pp. 823–825. While in England, he actually lobbied for expanded powers for the Indian Department at the expense of the British military. See further discussion in the Epilogue.
8 Gage to Bouquet, November 18, 1763, Gage Papers, CL. Also in BP, Volume VI, pp. 460–462.

9 This analysis of Amherst's return to England is based on the work of his three biographers, Cognets, Long, and Mayo, and personal communication with Mr. Robert Andrews, whose very thorough and up-to-date study is soon to be published by the Michigan State University Press.

Chapter VIII
The "Forgotten" Campaign
The British Attempt to Take Possession of the
Illinois Posts and the Ambush at Roche a Davion
Winter toSpring 1764

1 Ekberg, pp. 32–33. This book provides a comprehensive study of the settlement, socioeconomic, and cultural history of this region.
2 Primm, p. 8.
3 Ibid., pp. 7–18.
4 SWJ, Volume X, p. 819.
5 For a discussion of the founding and history of Vincennes, see Ekberg, pp. 82–88; for Kaskaskia, see Belting, *Kaskaskia Under the French Regime*.
6 Wright, p. 2. The 9th Regiment arrived in Saint Augustine on July 30, 1763.
7 BP, Volume VI, p. 394, n. 2.
8 Gage Warrants, Box 7:130 and 131, October 20, 1763, "Colonel A. Prevost bo[ugh]t of William Satterthwaite," CL.
9 Ibid., Box 8:48, May 22, 1764, CL.
10 Ibid., Box 8:2, "Warrant per order of General Gage for payment to Robertson by Abraham Mortier, Deputy Paymaster General of the British Army," May 2, 1764, CL.
11 Ibid., Box 8:57, Gage to Mortier, July 3, 1764, including "Memorial of Robertson re: Loftus," CL.
12 Abbadie, *Journal*, CISHL, Volume X, January 1764, pp. 166–167.
13 Abbadie to de Villiers, January 30, 1764, CISHL, Volume X, p. 234.
14 Ekberg, pp. 151–155 and also Belting, pp. 39–40. Both Ekberg and Belting note that the French census is slightly incomplete, yet it's the most reliable source from the period. Both studies elaborate on the specifics of the population, for example, noting that in the 1752 census, Negro slaves accounted for thirty-two percent of the region's population. During his tours of the region in 1766 and in 1771, Captain Phillip Pittman estimated the population at "about 2000 of all ages and sexes." Lieutenant Thomas Hutchins estimated that it was about one

thousand, including slaves. From *A Topographical Description of Virginia, Pennsylvania, Maryland and North Carolina*, (Hicks Edition), p. 100 and p. 111.

15 Abbadie, *Journal*, CISHL, Volume X, pp. 174–175.
16 Abbadie, *Journal*, CISHL, Volume X, pp. 166–167.
17 CISHL, Volume X, p. 227.
18 Gordon, p. 32.
19 CISHL, Chapter X, p. 233.
20 Gage Warrants, Box 8:57, "Robertson Memorial," CL.
21 Primm, p. 10–11.
22 Abbadie, *Journal*, February 15, 1764, CISHL, Volume X, p. 172.
23 CISHL Volume X, p. 334.
24 Abbadie, *Journal*, CISHL, Volume X, p. 172.
25 CISHL, Volume X, p. 227.
26 Abbadie, *Journal*, CISHL, Volume X, p. 228.
27 Gordon, p. 29.
28 CISHL, Volume X, pp. 229-230.
29 Loftus to Gage, April 9, 1764, p. 237 CISHL, Volume X, p. 237–239.
30 Abbadie, letter, June 29, 1764, CISHL, Volume X, pp. 230–233.
31 Abbadie, *Journal*, entry for August 1763, CISHL, Volume X, p. 162.
32 Abbadie to Desmazellieres, March 14, 1764, CISHL, Volume X, p. 235–236.
33 De Villiers to Abbadie, April 20, 1764, CISHL, p. 242.
34 Loftus to Gage, April 9, 1764, CISHL, Volume X, p. 237–239; Gage to Halifax, April 14, 1764, CISHL, Volume X, p. 240; de Villliers to d'Abbadie, April 14, 1764, CISHL, Volume X, p. 242; and de Villiers to Loftus, April 20, 1764, CISHL, Volume X, p. 244.
35 Gage to Johnson, July 2, 1764, Gage Papers, Volume 21, CL. Gage also wrote the same to Colonel John Bradstreet in a letter dated the same day; the original is contained in the same collection.
36 Abbadie *Journal*, entry for July 1764, CISHL, Volume X, p. 189 and p. 200.
37 "Thomas Gage Proclamation" re: Disallowing granting of lands in the Illinois country, February 9, 1771, original in the CISHL.
38 Kirkwood, *Through So Many Dangers*, p. 110. The 34th Regiment later relieved the 42nd on December 1, of the same year.
39 Abbadie, *Journal*, CISHL, Volume X, p. 200.
40 Ibid., p. 245.

Chapter IX
End of the Uprising
Summer toFall 1764

1 Gage to Bouquet, June 5, 1764, Gage Papers, CL. Also printed in BP, Volume VI, pp. 556–558.
2 Gage to Bouquet, April 4, 1764, BP, Volume VI, p. 507. Undated, unsigned copy in the Gage Papers, CL.
3 Bradstreet to Gage, July 12, 1764, Gage Papers, CL.
4 Mante, p. 508.
5 Montresor, entry for April 18, 1764, pp. 253–254.
6 Dunnigan, *A History and Guide to Old Fort Niagara*, pp. 63–64.
7 Mante, p. 507.
8 Montresor, entry for May 17, 1764, p. 257.
9 Ibid., p. 275.
10 Morris, p. 7.
11 Ibid., pp. 9–10.
12 Ibid., p. 10.
13 This is the same Godfroy who had been arrested at Detroit for aiding the Indians at Fort Miami. He was allowed to accompany Morris to prove his loyalty to the British, and he served very honorably.
14 Morris, p. 22.
15 Mante, pp. 517—518.
16 Ibid., p. 519.
17 Montresor, entry for September 6, 1764, p. 289.
18 Ibid., entry for September 1, 1764, p. 287.
19 Ibid., entry for September 13, 1764, p. 291.
20 Ibid., entry for September 19, 1764, p. 294.
21 Bouquet to Gage, August 27, 1764, BP, Volume VI, p. 621.
22 Gage to Bouquet, September 2, 1764, BP, Volume VI, p. 626.
23 Gage to Bradstreet, September 2, 1764 (enclosed in Bouquet to Bradstreet, September 12, 1764) BP, vol VI, pp. 637–638; the original letter is in the Gage Papers, CL.
24 Gage to Bradstreet, October 15, 1764, quoted in Parkman, Volume II, pp. 191–192.
25 Montresor, entry for September 27, 1764, p. 301.
26 Ibid., October 9, 1764, p. 306.
27 Ibid., October 31, 1764, p. 318.
28 Ibid., entries for October 18, 19, and 21, 1764, pp. 312—314.
29 Ibid., entry for August 12, 1764, p. 280.
30 Mante, p. 527.
31 Ibid., p. 528.
32 Ibid., p. 528.

33 Ibid., p. 529.

34 Gage to Bradstreet, August 16, 1764. *Gage Papers*, CL.

35 Mante, p. 528.

36 Ibid., p. 529.

37 Montresor, September 25, 1764, pp. 298–299.

38 Gage to Bradstreet, September 2, 1764. *Gage Papers*, CL.

39 Bouquet to Johnson, May 31, 1764, BP, Volume VI, p. 551–552.

40 Bouquet to Gage, Philadelphia, June 21, 1764, BP, Volume VI, p. 575.

41 Bouquet to Gage, June 21, 1764, BP, Volume VI, p. 575.

42 Bouquet to Harris, July 19, 1764, BP, Volume. VI, p. 594.

43 For details on the Paxton Boys incident, see BP, Volume VI, p. 513, n. 2.

44 Bouquet to Franklin, August 10, 1764, BP, Volume VI, p. 600; and Bouquet to Gage, August 15, 1764, Gage Papers, CL. Also in BP, Volume VI, p. 607.

45 Bouquet to Gage, August, 15, 1764, p. 607.

46 Gage to Bouquet, September 2, 1764, Gage Papers, Volume 24, CL. Also in BP, Volume VI, pp. 626–627, and MPHC, Volume XIX, pp. 272–273.

47 Johnson to Bouquet, September 1, 1764, BP, Volume VI, p. 625.

48 Bouquet to Gage, August 27, 1764, BP, Volume VI, p. 621. See also Reid to Bouquet, September 16, 1764, p. 640–641, and Bouquet: Speech to the Delawares, Shawnees, and Ohio Senecas, October 17, 1764, pp. 673–675, n. 9.

49 Copy of "Preliminary Articles of Peace, Friendship & Alliance entered into between the English and the Deputys sent from the whole Seneca Nation by Sir William Johnson, Bart his Majestys Sole Agent and Superintendant of Indian Affairs for the Northern Parts of North America, & Colonel of the Six united Nations, their Allies and dependants &c, at Johnson Hall,"April 3, 1764, Gage Papers, CL, Volume 16. Throughout the spring, Gage and Johnson corresponded about the Senecas concessions. The peace articles, including the Niagara Portage concessions, were finalized and signed on August 6, 1764, at Niagara. DRCHSNY, Book XXXVII, Volume VII, pp. 652–653.

50 "Return of the Effectives in Colonel Bouquet's Army," November 5, 1764, Henry Bouquet Papers, typescripts (British Library Add. MSS. 21651: f.35). There is also an extensive list of vouchers for the militia contained in the Gage Warrants, CL. The list of men from the Fort Pitt 1763 militia who served in the campaign are contained in a microfiche supplement of the Bouquet Papers, dates of February 15, and April 25, 1765, photostat copies in the Library of Congress. Among the Pennsylvania troops, the companies were to be formed "of 50 each, Serjeants, Drimmers & Corporals included" and "50 Men [more] to be employed as light Horse Men." See Bouquet to Reid, June 15, 1764, BP, Volume VI, pp. 570–571. Prevost's and William Murray's appointments for brevet majors (temporary for the campaign only) are noted in Bouquet to Gage, June 21, 1764, Gage Papers, CL, and also in BP, Volume VI, p. 577. Apparently, John Small who was major of the brigade for Bouquet's Department (Bouquet, General Orders: Staff Appointments, BP, Volume VI, p. 599) served as acting major on the campaign in place of Murray. Personal correspondence with Lieutenant Colonel Ian McCulloch, former commanding officer of the Canadian Battalion of the 42nd Highland Regiment.

51 Bouquet, speech to the Delawares, September 20, 1764, enclosed in Bouquet to Gage, September 26, 1764, BP, Volume VI, pp. 649–650.

52 Bouquet, reply to Onondaga and Oneida Indians, October 2, 1764, enclosed in Bouquet to Bradstreet, October 2, 1764, Gage Papers, CL. Also in BP, Volume VI, pp. 651–654.

53 Smith, pp. 41–44.

54 The journal traditionally had been attributed to Lieutenant Thomas Hutchins of the 60th Regiment, known for his previous expedition maps and journals of 1762. Hutchins drew the now famous maps of Bouquet's expedition, and while the daily entries were most likely derived from his notes, it has been shown that Father William Smith, Provost of the College of Philadelphia, penned the first published account of this expedition. It was published in 1765 as *An Historical Account of Bouquet's Expedition Against the Ohio Indians in 1764*.

55 Smith, p. 48.

56 Ibid., pp. 48–49.

57 Ibid., p. 50

58 Ibid.

59 Gage to Bouquet, October 1, 1764, BP, Volume VI, p. 651.

60 Bouquet to Gage, October 2, 1764, Gage Papers, CL. Also in BP, Volume. VI, pp. 651–652.

61 Smith, p. 51.

62 Ibid., p. 52. The site of this small stockaded fort, referred to as Bouquet's Blockhouse, is believed to be the site of Fort Laurens, built by the Americans in 1778 during the American Revolution; personal communication with Mr. Chris Matheney of the Ohio Historical Society. See also Bradley T. Lepper, *Archeological Investigations At the Fort Laurens Site, Lawrence Township, Tuscarawas County, Ohio,* Ohio Historical Society, Columbus, Ohio.

63 Speeches of Seneca and Delaware Chiefs, October 17, 1764, BP, Volume VI, p. 669.

64 Bouquet, speech to Delawares, Shawnees, and Ohio Senecas, Camp at Tuscarawas, October 20, 1764, BP, Volume VI. pp. 671–674.

65 Bouquet to Gage, October 21, 1764, BP, Volume VI, p. 677.

66 Smith, p. 60.

67 Bouquet: "Notes on an Agreement with the Ohio Indians, November 5, 1764," BP, Volume VI, p. 686. The names of the Indian hostages and deputies for both the Delaware and Shawnee are listed in Minutes: Conference with the Delaware Chiefs, November 11, 1764, BP, Volume VI, p. 692, and Minutes: Conference with Shawnees, November 14, 1764, BP, Volume VI, p. 701.

68 Bouquet to Gage, November 15, 1764, Gage Papers, CL. Also in BP, Volume VI, pp. 703–707, and Smith, p. 64. A comprehensive list of prisoners returned is in SWJ, Volume XI, pp. 484–-491. The Indian delegates were the Delaware chief King Beaver and 20 Warriors, Chief Kelipama and 25 Warriors, Chief Custaloga, and Chief Keyashuta of the Senecas, the Shawnee tribes, including Chiefs Keissinautchtha Nimisha, Lawissimo, Binsivasicca, Ewenccunnee, Red Hawk and Keightughque (Cornstalk) and 40 warriors.

69 Bouquet to Gage, November 15, 1764, BP, Volume VI, p. 704, Smith, pp. 76, 80.

70 Red Hawk to Bouqet, November 8, 1764, BP. Volume VI, p. 687.

71 Smith, p. 65; Red Hawk to Bouquet, November 8, 1764, BP, p. 687, n. 3.

72 Bouquet, Orders, November 18, 1764, BP. Volume, VI, p. 697.

73 Bouquet to Gage, November 15, 1764, Gage Papers, CL. Also in BP, Volume VI, pp. 703–706.

74 Gage to Bouquet, October 21, 1764, BP, Volume VI, p. 680, and Gage to Bouquet, December 7, 1764, BP, Volume VI, p. 717–179. Gage seems to have had a propensity for favoritism and only listening to one side of a situation during his career. He clearly was supportive of Sir William Johnson, but toward several of his other fellow officers, he showed ambiguity and hypocrisy. Among those were Robert Rogers, George Etherington, and John Bradstreet, whose situation is discussed at length in this book. For further details on Rogers, see David Armour, *Treason? At Michilimackinac,* and the Introduction to the Annotated and Illustrated edition of his *Journals.* For Etherington, see *A Vindication of My Conduct,* by Dr. Todd E. Harburn and Rodger Durham.

75 Bouquet to Gage, November 30, 1764, Gage Papers, CL. Also in BP, Volume VI, pp. 711–715.

76 "Murray to Bouquet, January 31, 1765, with "Enclosure of Prisoners Delivered By Shawnees, at Fort Pitt," January 5, 1765, BP, Volume VI, pp. 751–754. Murray, commandant at Fort Pitt, commended Chief Bowisicas for his assistance and noted that all the captives suffered from frostbite and one women captive died shortly after arrival. The remaining captives were mostly "old women and young children" who would not be able to travel to Fort Pitt until the spring. Bouquet wrote to Gage, "there remains only in the Indian Country Six Virginia Voluntiers, who went at their own request to the Lower Shawanese Town; to bring some of their Relations from thence." Bouquet to Gage, January 5, 1765, BP, Volume VI, p. 744.

77 Bouquet to Gage, December 22, 1764, BP, Volume VI, p. 737.

78 Bouquet to Gage, December 22, 1764, Volume VI, pp. 736–738. Also Bouquet to Sharpe, December 20, 1764, BP, Volume VI, pp. 738–739.

79 Murray to Bouquet, December 24, 1764, BP, Volume VI, p. 741.

80 Bouquet to Gage, November 30, 1764, Gage Papers, CL. See also Bouquet to Johnson, November 30, 1764, BP, Volume VI, p. 716. Bouquet appears to have referred to the Mingoes and Ohio Senecas as the same tribe in most of his campaign letters.

81 Ibid.

82 Gage to Bouquet, December 7, 1764, BP, Volume VI, p. 718.

83 Etherington to Bouquet, April 19, 1765, BP, Volume VI, pp. 783–784. Etherington was referring to the Stamp Bill that was recently passed in the House of Commons, the precursor to the infamous Stamp Act that would be a major cause of the American Revolution. Etherington later commanded at Fort

George (also known as Patterson's Fort, now Mexico, Pennsylvania). See Etherington to Bradstreet, May 23, 1765, in "The Col. John Bradstreet Manuscripts—Manuscript Records of the French and Indian War" in the Library of the American Antiquarian Society; facsimile reprint by Heritage Books, Bowie, MD, 1992, p. 83. Originally published by the Society, Worcester, MA, 1909.

84 Gage to Bouquet, May 15, 1765, BP, Volume VI, pp. 789–793.Original in the Gage Papers, CL. This lengthy letter from Gage outlines Bouquet's orders, powers, and policies for the command of the Floridas.

85 BP, Volume I, p. xxvii.

Epilogue

1 Dixon nicely tells the details of this rebellion, which contributed to the outbreak of the American Revolution, in *Never Come to Peace Again*, pp. 254–258. Additional details of the rebellion are related in a series of original letters. See Grant to Bouquet, March 9, 1765, BP, Volume VI, pp. 763–764; Callender to Bouquet, March 11, 1765, BP, Volume VI, pp. 764–765; Croghan to Bouquet, March 12, 1765, BP, Volume VI, pp. 766–767; McCulloch to Croghan, March 7, 1765, BP, Volume VI, pp. 767–768; Bouquet to Gage, March 16, 1765, Gage Papers, CL, (also in BP, Volume VI, pp. 768–769); Bouquet to Gage, March 20, 1765; Gage Papers, CL (also in BP, Volume VI, p. 771); Gage to Bouquet, March 21, 1765, Gage Papers, CL, (also in BP, Volume VI. pp. 772–773); Grant to Bouquet, March 30, 1765, BP, Volume VI, p. 777; Petition: Cumberland County Inhabitants to Governor John Penn, March 1765, BP, Volume VI, pp. 777–779; Gage to Bouquet, April 4, 1765, Gage Papers, CL (also in BP, Volume VI, pp. 779–780); and Bouquet to Gage, Philadelphia, April 10, 1765, Gage Papers, CL.

2 Bouquet to Gage, March 4, 1765, Gage Papers, CL. Also in BP, Volume VI, pp. 758–759.

3 For further details regarding the Stamp Act, see Anderson, pp. 641–652

4 Nelson, p. 52. See also Johnson to the Lord of Trade: Plan for Future Management of Indian Affairs, October 8, 1764, DRCHSNY, Book XXXVI, Volume VII, pp. 657–666.

5 Bouquet to Gage, December 22, 1765, Gage Papers, CL. See also Bouquet to Murray, January 12, 1765, BP, Volume VI, p. 747.

6 Bouquet to Gage, Dec 22, 1764, BP, Volume VI, p. 737.

7 Callender to Bouquet, March 11, 1765, BP, Volume VI, pp. 764–766, n. 2; and Gage to Bouquet, March 21, 1765, Gage Papers, CL. Also printed in BP, Volume VI, pp. 772–773. John Baynton, Samuel Wharton, and George Morgan formed their trading partnership in Philadelphia in 1763. Callender was a partner with Croghan and is the same Robert Callender who was initially thought to have been killed by the Indians during the attack on Fort Sandusky. For further details see Harburn, "a little Discondent about the Blockhous."

8 Smith, p. 89; Croghan to Bouquet, May 12, 1765, BP. Volume VI, p. 789; Croghan to Gage, May 12, 1765, Gage Papers, CL. See also Nelson, pp. 53–54.

9 Dixon, *Never Come To Peace Again*, p. 323, n. 28.

10 Fraser to Gage, Intelligence from Kyashuta, March 21, 1765, Gage Papers, CL. See also Peckham, p. 232. For further details on Fraser's expedition, see CISHL, pp. 491–497. Formal proceedings of the final peace agreements of this July 4–13, 1765, conference are contained in DRCHSNY, Book XXXVIII, Volume VII, pp. 750–755.

11 Kirkwood, p. 110. Editors McCulloch and Todish present a detailed account of the Stirling Expedition based on the original memoirs of Robert Kirkwood, a Highland private who accompanied the expedition.

12 Croghan to Murray, July 12, 1765, Gage Papers, CL. Also in CISHL, pp. 58–59, and Peckham, p. 280. See also Johnson to the Lord of Trade, September 28, 1765, DRCHSNY, BOOK XXXVIII, Volume VII, pp. 765–767.

13 Peckham, p. 282.

14 Ibid., p. 285. For more details on the Ross, Fraser, and Croghan expeditions and the associated Indian conferences, see Peckham, pp. 269–287. CISHL, Dowd, and Dixon also have accounts and analyze these; all are based on the original correspondence in the Gage Papers and Croghan's Journal.

15 Cuneo, *Personal Notes*, p. 113, n. 20.

16 Cuneo, *Robert Rogers*, pp. 179–180.

17 Quoted in Cuneo, *Robert Rogers*, p.184.

18 Ibid., p.184.

19 Peckham, pp. 288–289, and Dowd, *War Under Heaven*, pp. 260–261.

20 Rogers to Johnson, June 28, 1766, quoted in Zaboly, *A True Ranger*, p. 371.

21 Quoted in Cuneo, *Personal Notes*, pp. 133–134, n. 9.

The original letter is now believed to be in a private collection.

22 Armour, *Treason? At Michilimackinac*, p. 50.

23 Cuneo, *Personal Notes*, p. 117, n. 40.

24 *New Hampshire Gazette*, December 12, 1766, quoted in Zaboly, *A True Ranger*, p. 378.

25 Gage to Shelburne, October 10, 1766, Gage, *Correspondence*, p. 110.

26 Ibid., p.114.

27 Kenneth Roberts, whose magnificent novel *Northwest Passage* has inspired interest in Rogers for several generations, had this to say about Roberts: "The facts that are known about Roberts. . .indicate that he was thoroughly unprincipled: that he would stoop to anything to accomplish his ends: that he was petulant, hot-headed, unreliable, a sycophant, a tale-bearer, devoid of good judgement, and a liar, in addition to having other grave faults." Roberts, Volume II, pp. 76–77, n. 4.

28 Gage to Bouquet, May 14, 1764, BP, Volume VI, p. 539. This is discussed in more detail in chapter three.

29 Gorrell, *Journal*, entry for March 1, 1763, pp. 36–37. It is obvious that Gorrell wrote or at least augmented his journal after the fact, as a number of events that he talks about had not occurred yet as of the date of the entry.

30 Robert J. Rogers, p. 157.

31 For the complete text of the letter, see Armour, pp. 44–46.

32 Zaboly, *A True Ranger*, pp. 380–381.

33 Gage to Spiesmaker, October 19, 1767, quoted in Armour, p. 26.

34 Gage to Hillsborough, August 17, 1768, Gage, *Correspondence*, p. 184.

35 Armour, *Treason? At Michilimackinac*, pp. 94–95.

36 Gage to Shelburne, March 12, 1768, Gage, *Correspondence*, p. 165. See also Gage to Hillsborough, June 18, 1768, p. 181.

37 Armour, *Treason? At Michilimackinac*, p. 98. The transcript of the court-martial is also reprinted in Volume II of the special edition of Kenneth Roberts' *Northwest Passage*.

38 Cuneo, *Personal Notes*, p. 137, n. 28.

39 Robert J. Rogers, p. 160.

40 Gage to Hillsborough, September 9, 1769, Gage, *Correspondence*, p. 237

41 Peckham, pp. 306–307. The original of this letter is in the Gage Papers at the Clements Library, enclosed with Turnbull to Gage, June 14, 1768.

42 The details of this incident are not fully known. For more discussion, see Roberts to Johnson, June 3, 1766; Cole to Johnson, June 23, 1766, SWJ, Volume V, pp. 278–279; McLeod to Johnson, Aug 4, 1766, SWJ, Volume. II, p. 279; Peckham, pp. 288–289 and 310.

43 Peckham, p. 314, n. 7. Special thanks to Tim's friend and Grand Rapids Police Department classmate Robert "Buffy" Price for passing down additional information from his family tradition about this legend.

Appendix E

1 Rutherfurd, p. 226.

2 Ibid., p. 227.

3 Ibid., p. 229.

4 Ibid., p. 232.

5 Ibid., p. 235.

6 Ibid., p. 235.

7 Ibid., p. 237.

8 Ibid., pp. 238–239.

9 Ibid., p. 241.

10 Ibid.

11 Ibid.

12 Ibid., p. 243.

13 Ibid., pp. 244–245.

14 Ibid., p. 245.

15 Ibid., pp. 246–247.

16 Ibid., p. 247.

17 Ibid., p. 248.

18 Ibid., pp. 252–253.

19 Ibid., pp. 255–256.

20 Ibid., p. 256.

21 Ibid., p. 257.

22 Ibid., pp. 258–259.

23 Ibid., p. 261.

24 Ibid., p. 266.

25 Ibid., p. 268.

26 Ibid., pp. 267–268.

27 Ibid., p. 270.

28 Ibid., p. 273.

29 Ibid.

Bibliography

NOTE: In addition to citing the sources used in the preparation of this book, this bibliography is intended to assist our readers in identifying and locating important books and documents. In some cases, more than one edition of an entry is cited. This is to document its publishing history and help our readers who might want to locate a copy of the entry.

****

Abbadie, Jean-Jacques-Blaise d'. *Journal*. Contained in Alvord, Clarence Walworth and Clarence Edwin Carter, editors. *Collections of the Illinois State Historical Library—The British Series, the Critical Period 1763–1764*. Springfield, Illinois: Illinois State Historical Library, 1915.

Ahrens, Edward W. *The Devil's Hole Massacre—A True Story*. Sanborn, New York: Rissa Productions, 2004.

Alvord, Clarence Walworth and Clarence Edwin Carter, editors. *Collections of the Illinois State Historical Library—The British Series 1763–1764*. (CISHL) Springfield, Illinois: Illinois State Historical Library, 1915.

Amherst, Jeffery. *The Journal of Jeffery Amherst, Recording the Military Career of General Amherst in America from 1758 to 1763*. Edited and with an introduction and notes by J. Clarence Webster, MD Toronto: The Ryerson Press and Chicago: the University of Chicago Press, 1931.

Amherst, Jeffery. "The Journal of Jeffery Amherst." Robert Andrews, editor. Michigan State University Press, not yet published. Although not yet in print at the time of our book's publication, our Canadian friend Bob Andrews has been working for many years on a magnificent new edition of Amherst's "Journal" and papers. When eventually published it will be *the* definitive work on Amherst for years to come, and we want our readers to be aware that it is forthcoming.

Amherst, Jeffery. *War Office Manuscripts*. Originals in the National Archives of England (formerly the Public Records Office); microfilm copies in the University of Michigan Hatcher Graduate Library, Ann Arbor, Michigan. All records cited in this book are from WO 34, and the complete reference is included with every endnote. (Cited in endnotes as *Journal*.)

Anderson, Fred. *Crucible of War: The Seven Years' War and the Fate of Empire in British North America 1754–1766*. New York: Alfred A. Knopf, 2000.

Armour, David A., editor. *Attack at Michilimackinac: Alexander Henry's Travels and Adventures in Canada and the Indian Territories Between the Years 1760 and 1764*. Mackinac Island, Michigan: Mackinac Island State Park Commission, 1971.

_____. and Keith Widder. *At the Crossroads, Michilimackinac During the American Revolution*. Mackinac Island, Michigan: Mackinac State Historic Parks, 1978

_____. *Colonial Michilimackinac.*, Mackinac Island, Michigan: Mackinac State Historic Parks, 2000.

_____. editor. *Treason? At Michilimackinac: The Proceedings of a General Court Martial held at Montreal in October 1768 for the Trial of Major Robert Rogers*. Mackinac Island, Michigan: The Mackinac Island State Park Commission, (now Mackinac State Historic Parks), 1967, revised 1972.

Belting, Natalia Maree. *Kaskaskia Under the French Regime*. Carbondale, Illinois, Southern Illinois University Press, 2003.

Bouquet, Henry. *The Papers of Henry Bouquet, December 11, 1755–August 31, 1759*. BP Edited by Donald H. Kent, Louis M. Waddell, and Autumn L. Leonard. Harrisburg: The Pennsylvania Historical and Museum Commission.Published in six volumes: 1951, 1972, 1976, 1978, 1984, and 1994. (Cited in endnotes as BP.)

_____. *The Papers of Henry Bouquet*. Typescripts. Harrisburg: The Pennsylvania Historical and Museum Commission.

Boynton, Brother James, S. J. *Fishers of Men: The Jesuit Mission of Mackinac 1670–1765*. Mackinac Island, Michigan: Sainte Anne's Church, 1996.

BP. *The Papers of Henry Bouquet*. See Bouquet.

Brumwell, Stephen. "A Service Truly Critical: The British Army and Warfare with the North American Indians, 1755–1764," in *War in History*, vol. 5, no. 2, (April 1988): 146–175.

_____. *Redcoats: The British Soldier in the War in the Americas 1755–1763*. Cambridge, England: Cambridge University Press, 2002.

Carver, Jonathan. *Travels Through the Interior Parts of North America in the Years 1766, 1767, and 1768*. London: 1781; facsimile reprint Minneapolis, Minnesota: Ross & Haines, Inc., 1956.

CISHL. *Collections of the Illinois State Historical Library.* See Alvord.

Cognets, Louis des, Jr. *Amherst and Canada.* Princeton, New Jersey: Privately published by the author, 1962.

Cuneo, John R. *Robert Rogers of the Rangers.* (Cited in endnotes as *Robert Rogers.*) New York: Oxford University Press, 1959; reprint New York: Richardson & Steirman,1987; reprint Ticonderoga, New York: Fort Ticonderoga Museum, 1988.

_____. Unpublished personal research notes for *Robert Rogers of the Rangers.* Original in the collections of the William L. Clements Library, the University of Michigan, Ann Arbor, Michigan. (Cited in endnotes as *Cuneo: Personal Notes).* Copy in the author's collection. There are no page numbers in the original manuscript. Therefore, for the purposes of my citations, I have added my own numbers. The page titled "Abbreviations in Notes and Bibliography" is page number one, and each page is numbered sequentially thereafter.

Dann, John C., ed. "North West Passage Revisited." In *American Magazine and Historical Chronicle, ,* vol. 2, no. 1, Ann Arbor, Michigan: William L. Clements Library, University of Michigan, (Spring–Summer 1986): 18–35.

Darlington, Mary C., editor. *Fort Pitt and Letters from the Frontier.* Pittsburgh:Weldon and Company, 1892; reprint New York, Arno Press, 1971.

Dixon, David. *Bushy Run Battlefield: Pennsylvania Trail of History Guide.* Mechanicsburg, Pennsylvania: Stackpole Books, 2003.

_____. *Fort Pitt Museum. Pennsylvania Trail of History Guide.* Mechanicsburg, Pennsylvania: Stackpole Books, 2004.

_____. *Never Come to Peace Again: Pontiac's Uprising and the Fate of the British Empire in North America.* Norman, Oklahoma: University of Oklahoma Press, 2005.

DHSNY *Documentary History of the State of New York.* See O'Callaghan

Dowd, Gregory Evans. "The French King Wakes Up in Detroit: Pontiac's War in Rumor and History." *Ethnohistory,* vol. 37, no. 3, (Summer 1990): 255–278

_____. *War Under Heaven: Pontiac, the Indian Nations, & the British Empire.* Baltimore & London: Johns Hopkins University Press, 2002.

DRCHSNY *Documents Relating to the Colonial History of the State of New York.* See O'Callaghan

Dunn, Walter S. Jr. *Frontier Profit and Loss: The British Army and the Fur Traders, 1760?1764.* Westport, Connecticut: Greenwood Press, 1998.

Dunnigan, Brian Leigh. *Frontier Metropolis: Picturing Early Detroit.* Detroit: Wayne State University Press, 2001.

_____. *A History and Guide to Old Fort Niagara.* Youngstown, New York: Old Fort Niagara Association, Inc., 1985.

Ekberg, Carl J. *French Roots in the Illinois Country, the Mississippi Frontier in Colonial Times.* Urbana and Chicago: Illinois State University, 2000. Originally published by the University of Illinois Press, 1998.

Fifteenth Regiment Succession Books (1755–1763), TNA, W.O. 25/209.

Ford, Worthington Chauncey. *British Officers Serving in North America 1754–1774.* Compiled from the "Army Lists." Originally published in the *New England Historical and Genealogical Register for 1894.* Boston: David Clapp & Son, 1894; facsimile reprint Oldwick, New Jersey: Kings Arms Press & Bindery, 1999.

Fowler, William M. Jr. *Empires at War: The French and Indian War and the Struggle for North America 1754–1763.* New York: Walker & Company, 2005.

Gage, Thomas et al. *The Gage Papers, American Series.* Original manuscripts in the collections of the William L. Clements Library Ann Arbor, Michigan: University of Michigan. (Cited in endnotes as *Gage Papers,* CL)

_____. *The Gage Papers.* Original manuscripts in the collections of the Illinois State Historical Library, Springfield, Illinois.

_____. *The Gage Warrants.* Original manuscripts in the collections of the William L. Clements Library. Ann Arbor, Michigan: University of Michigan..

Gage, Thomas and Clarence Edwin Carter, editor. *The Correspondence of General Thomas Gage with the Secretaries of State.* (Cited in the endnotes as *Correspondence).* New Haven, Connecticut: Yale University Press, 1931. Archon Books edition, 1969.

Gentleman's Magazine, London: (October 1763). Copy of quoted material in the author's collection.

Gladwin, Henry and Charles Moore, editor. "The Gladwin Manuscripts." In the *Michigan Pioneer and Historical Collections,* Volume XXVII Lansing, Michigan: Robert Smith Printing Company,1896.

Gorrell, James. *Journal.* Reuben G. Thwaites and Lyman C. Draper, editors. Collections of the State Historical Society of Wisconsin, vol. I (1855; reprint edition

1903): 25–48. The original is in the collections of the Maryland Historical Library, and a shorter version is in the Clements Library in Ann Arbor, Michigan.

Gordon, Harry [Henry]. *Diary of Captain Harry Gordon, June–Dec 1766.* Original manuscript is in the Illinois State Historical Library, Springfield, Illinois.

Harburn, Dr. Todd. "A Most Unfortunate Officer: Lieutenant John Jamet of the 60th Royal American Regiment." *Michigan History,* (March/April 1988): 44–48.

_____. "British Folly on the St. Joseph: Ensign Francis Schlosser of the 60th Regiment—Massacre at Fort St. Joseph During Pontiac's Uprising May 25, 1763." Okemos, Michigan: The Michilimackinac Society Press, 2002.

_____. "In Defense of the Red Ensign at Michilimackinac 1763: The British Garrison at Michilimackinac During Pontiac's Uprising and Captain George Etherington's Company." Okemos, Michigan: The Michilimackinac Society Press, 2000.

_____. "The King's Quiet Commandant at Michilimackinac: a Biographical Sketch of Captain George Etherington of the 60th Royal American Regiment." Okemos, Michigan: The Michilimackinac Society Press, 1999.

_____. "The Post at St. Mary's: Fort de Repentingy (1750–1762): The French and the British Fort at Sault Ste. Marie, Michigan." Okemos, Michigan: The Michilimackinac Society Press, 2001.

_____. "'a little Discondent about the Blockhous. . . Fort Sandusky' British Fort Sandusky 1761–1763, Lieutenant Elias Meyer, Ensign Christopher Pauli and the Massacre at Fort Sandusky During Pontiac's Uprising May 22, 1763." Okemos, Michigan: Michilimackinac Society Press, 2005.

_____. *A Vindication of My Conduct, the General Court-Martial Trial of Lieutenant Colonel George Etherington of the 60th or Royal American Regiment Held on the Island of St. Lucia in the West Indies, October 1781 and the Extraordinary Story Regarding the Surrender of the Island of St. Vincent in the British Caribbean During the American Revolution.* Bowie, Maryland: Heritage Books, 2002.

Hay, Jehu. *Lieut. Jehu Hay's Diary: Under Siege in Detroit, 1763.* Reprinted in *The Lakeside Classics: Narratives of Colonial America 1704–1765.* Edited by Howard H. Peckham. Chicago: The Lakeside Press, R.R. Donnelley & Sons Company, 1971. Original manuscript in the Clements Library. Ann Arbor, Michigan: University of Michigan. Page references for endnotes in this book are from the Lakeside Classics edition.

Henry, Alexander. *Travels of.* See Armour, *Attack at Michilimackinac.*

Hibernian Magazine: or, Compendium of Entertaining Knowledge. Original in the William L. Clements Library, Ann Arbor, Michigan: University of Michigan, (September 1776). Copy of quoted material in the author's collection.

Houlding, J. A. *Fit for Service: The Training of the British Army, 1715–1795.* Oxford: Clarendon Press, 1981.

Hutchins, Lieutenant Thomas. *A Topographical Description of Virginia, Pennsylvania, Maryland and North Carolina.* Frederick C. Hicks, editor. Cleveland, Ohio: Arthur H. Clark,1904.

Jenks, William. "The Hutchins Map of Michigan." Michigan Historical, vol. 10 (1926): 358-373.

Johnson, Sir William. *The Papers of Sir William Johnson, Volumes I-XIV.* Multiple editors. Albany, New York: The University of the State of New York, 1921-1965.

Kelley, Paul. *Historic Fort Loudoun.* Vonore, Tennessee: Fort Loudoun Association, , 1958.

"James Kenny's Journal, 1761–1763."Edited by Kenny, James and John W. Jordan. *Pennsylvania Magazine of History and Biography,* vol. 37 (1913).

Kirkwood, Robert, Lt. Col. Ian McCulloch, and Timothy J. Todish, editors. *Through So Many Dangers: The Memoirs and Adventures of Robert Kirk, Late of the Royal Highland Regiment.* Fleischmanns, New York: Purple Mountain Press, 2004. Originally published in Limerick, Ireland, 1775.

Kubiak, William J. *Great Lakes Indians: A Pictorial Guide.* Grand Rapids, Michigan: Baker Book House, 1970; reprint New York: Bonanza Books (undated).

Lepper, Bradley T. "Archaeological Investigations at the Fort Laurens Site (33TU193), Lawrence Township, Tuscarawas County, Ohio, 1997." Manuscript on file at the Ohio Historical Society, Columbus, Ohio.

Loescher, Burt Garfield. *The History of Rogers' Rangers, Volume I: The Beginnings: January 1755–April 6, 1758.* San Francisco, California: Published by the author, 1946.

_____. *The History of Rogers' Rangers, Volume II: Genesis: Rogers' Rangers—The First Green Berets, The Corps and the Revivals: April 6, 1758–December 24, 1783.* San Mateo, California: Published by the author, 1969.

_____. *The History of Rogers' Rangers, Volume III: Officers and Non-Commissioned Officers.* Burlingame, California: Published by the author, 1957.

Long, J. C. *Lord Jeffery Amherst: A Soldier of the King.* New York: The MacMillan Company, 1933.

Lossing, Benson J. *The Pictorial Field-Book of the Revolu-*

tion; or, Illustrations, by Pen and Pencil, of the History, Biography, Scenery, Relics, and Traditions of the War for Independence. Two volumes. New York: Harper & Brothers, Publishers, 1859.

Loudon, Archibald. A Selection of Some of the Most Interesting Narratives of Outrages, Committed by the Indians in their Wars with the White People, Carlisle, Pennsylvania: privately printed, 1808; reprint New York: Arno Press, 1971.

Mante, Thomas. The History of the Late War in North-America and the Islands of the West-Indies, Including the Campaigns of MDCCLXIII and MDCCLXIV Against His Majesty's Indian Enemies. London: W. Strahan and T. Cadell, 1772; reprint New York: Research Reprints, Inc., 1970.

Mayo, Lawrence Shaw. Jeffery Amherst. New York: Longmans, Green and Company, 1916.

McCoy, Raymond. The Massacre of Old Fort Mackinac (Michilimackinac). Saginaw, Michigan: Published by the author, eighth edition, 1956.

McCulloch, Lt. Col. Ian and Timothy J. Todish. British Light Infantryman of the Seven Years' War 1757–63. Oxford, England: Osprey Publishing, 2004.

Michigan Pioneer and Historical Collections, Volume XXIX. (MPHC) Lansing, Michigan: Michigan Pioneer and Historical Commission, Robert Smith Printing Company, 1891.

Moerman, Daniel E., ed. "Herbs, Plants, and Shrubs that possess uncommon Virtues: Robert Rogers on the Dyes and Medicines of the American Indian." In American Magazine and Historical Chronicle, vol. 2, no. 1, The William L. Clements Library, Ann Arbor, Michigan: University of Michigan, (Spring–Summer 1986): 36–44.

Montresor, Colonel James and Captain John, The Montresor Journals. Edited by G. D. Skull. New York: The New-York Historical Society, 1881.

Morris, Thomas. Journal of Captain Thomas Morris, from Miscellanies in Prose and Verse., New Canaan, Connecticut: Readex Microprint Corporation, 1966. Originally published in London, 1791.

Navarre, Robert. The Journal of Pontiac's Conspiracy. Reprinted in The Lakeside Classics: The Siege of Detroit in 1763, Chicago: The Lakeside Press, R.R. Donnelley & Sons Company, 1958. An anonymous journal generally attributed to Detroit habitant Robert Navarre. For a thorough discussion of the provenance of this important journal, see Milo Quaife's "Historical Introduction" and Clarence Burton's "Preface" to the Lakeside Classics edition.

Nelson, Larry L. A Man of Distinction Among Them: Alexander McKee and the British Indian Affairs Along the Ohio Country Frontier, 1754–1799. Kent, Ohio: Kent State University Press, 2001.

O'Callaghan, Edmund Bailey, editor. The Documentary History of the State of New York. (DHSNY) Albany: Weed, Parsons & Company, 1849–1851. The entire four volume series is published on CD-Rom. Abilene, Texas: Fine Books Company.

O'Callaghan, Edmund Bailey, editor. Documents Relating to the Colonial History of the State of New York, Procured by John Romeyn Brodhead. (DRCHSNY) Albany: Weed, Parsons & Company, 1856. The full fifteen volumes published on CD-Rom by LeGrand J. Weller, Abilene, Texas:

Owen, David A. Fort Erie (1764–1823) An Historical Guide. The Niagara Parks Commission, 1986.

Pargellis, Stanley, editor. Military Affairs in North America 1748–1765: Selected Documents from the Cumberland Papers in Windsor Castle. Hamden, Connecticut: Archon Books, 1969. Originally published by the American Historical Association, 1936.

Parker, John. "New Light on Jonathan Carver." American Magazine and Historical Chronicle, vol. 2, no. 1. The William L. Clements Library, Ann Arbor, Michigan: University of Michigan, (Spring–Summer 1986), 4–17.

Parkman, Francis. The Conspiracy of Pontiac and the Indian War after the Conquest of Canada. Two volumes. Boston: Little, Brown, and Company, 1910. First published in 1870.

Peckham, Howard H. Pontiac and the Indian Uprising. Chicago and London: University of Chicago Press, 1947. Phoenix Books edition, 1961.

Pitt, William and Gertrude Selwyn Kimball, editor. Correspondence of William Pitt When Secretary of State with Colonial Governors and Military and Naval Commissioners in America. Two volumes New York & London: The MacMillan Company, 1906; reprint New York Kraus Reprint Co., 1969.

Primm, James Neal. The Lion of the Valley: St. Louis, Missouri 1764–1980. Saint Louis: Missouri Historical Society Press, third edition, 1998.

Roberts, Kenneth. Northwest Passage. Special two volume, limited edition of 1,050 copies. Volume I is the novel itself. Volume II is an appendix containing research material that Roberts compiled while working on this famous book. Garden City, New York: Doubleday, Doran & Company, Inc., 1937.

Rogers, Robert. A Concise Account of North America. New

York: Johnson Reprint Corporation, 1966. First published in London, 1765.

_____. with annotations by Timothy J. Todish and illustrations by Gary S. Zaboly. *The Annotated and Illustrated Journals of Major Robert Rogers.* Fleischmanns, New York: Purple Mountain Press, 2002. Orignal edition published in London, 1765.

_____. *Journal of Robert Rogers the Ranger on His Expedition for Receiving the Capitulation of Western French Posts (October 20, 1760 to February 14, 1761).* Edited by Victor Hugo Patlsits. Reprinted in the *Journal New York Public Library,* (April 1933): 261–276.

_____. "Journal of the Siege of Detroit." In *Diary of the Siege of Detroit in the War with Pontiac,.* edited and with notes by Franklin B. Hough, 123–135. Albany, New York: 1860. Reprinted in *The Annotated and Illustrated Journals of Major Robert Rogers,* with annotations by Timothy J. Todish and illustrations by Gary S. Zaboly.

_____. "Michilimackinac Journal." In the *Proceedings of the American Antiquarian Society,* edited and with an introduction by William L. Clements: 3-52. Worcester, Massachusetts: The Davis Press,1918.

_____. *Ponteach, or the Savages of America: A Tragedy.* New York: Lenox Hill Publishing and Distributing Company, 1971. First published in London, 1766.

Rogers, Robert J., U. E. *Rising Above Circumstances: The Rogers Family in Colonial America.* Bedford, Quebec, Canada: Sheltus & Picard Inc., 1999.

Rutherfurd, John. *John Rutherfurd's Captivity Narrative.* Reprinted in *The Lakeside Classics: The Siege of Detroit in 1763,* Chicago: The Lakeside Press, R.R. Donnelley & Sons Company, 1958. Originally contained in a letter to Sir John Nesbet in New York, 1763. Also reprinted in the April 1958 issue of *American Heritage.*

Smith, William, Rev. *An Historical Account of the Expedition Against the Ohio Indians in the Year 1764, Under the Command of Henry Bouquet, Esq.* Cincinnati: Robert Clarke & Company, 1868; reprint New Canaan, Connecticut: Readex Microprint Corporation, 1966. Originally published in Philadelphia, 1765.

Steele, Ian K. *Warpaths: Invasions of North America.* New York: Oxford University Press, 1994.

Sterling, James. *Letterbook 1761–1763.* Original in the William L. Clements Library, Ann Arbor, Michigan.

Stirling, James et al. *Broadswords and Bayonets: The Journals of the Expedition Under the Command of Captain Thomas Stirling, Royal Highland Regiment (The Black Watch) to Occupy Fort Chartres in the Illinois Country, August 1765 to January 1766,* edited by Robert G. Carroon. Illinois: The Society of Colonial Wars in the State of Illinois, 1984.

Todish, Timothy J. *America's FIRST First World War: The French & Indian War 1754–1763.* Grand Rapids, Michigan: Dickinson Press, 1982; Ogden, Utah: Eagle's View Press, 1988; Fleischmanns, New York: Purple Mountain Press, , 2001.

_____. "Michilimackinac: Land of the Great Turtle." *Muzzleloader,* (March/April 1983): 16–20.

_____. "Rendezvous on the Ouabache: Fort Ouiatenon and the Feast of the Hunter's Moon." *Muzzleloader,* September/October 1991): 39–42.

Trask, Kerry A. "In the Name of the Father: Paternalism and the 1763 Indian Uprising at Michilimackinac." *The Old Northwest,* vol.9, no 1 (Spring 1983): 3-–19.

Trent, William. "William Trent's Journal at Fort Pitt." In *Fort Pitt and Letters from the Frontier,* edited by Trent, William and Mary C. Darlington (84-110). New York: Arno Press, 1971. Originally published by J. R. Weldon, Pittsburgh, 1892. Also reprinted in *The Mississippi Valley Historical Review,* vol. 11, no. 3 (December 1924): 390–413, A. T. Volwiler, editor. Page references in this book are from the Darlington edition.

Wainwriight, Nicholas B. *George Croghan: Wilderness Diplomat.* Chapel Hill, North Carolina: University of North Carolina Press, 1959.

Way, Peter. "Rebellion of the Regulars: Working Soldiers and the Mutiny of 1763–1764," *The William and Mary Quarterly,* vol. 57, no. 4 (October 2000): 761–792.

West, Martin, editor. *War for Empire in Western Pennsylvania.* Ligonier, Pennsylvania: Fort Ligonier Association, 1993.

Widder, Keith. "Mapping the Lakes: The 1761 Balfour Expedition Maps." *Michigan History,* (May/June 1991): 24–31.

Wright, J. Leitch. *British St. Augustine.* Saint Augustine, Florida: Historic Saint Augustine Preservation Board , 1975.

Zaboly, Gary S. *A True Ranger: The Life and Many Wars of Major Robert Rogers.* Garden City Park, New York: Royal Blockhouse LLC, 2004.

Index

About the Authors

TIM J. TODISH is a native of Grand Rapids, Michigan, and a graduate of Michigan State University with a degree in Management. He has had a nearly lifelong interest in Rogers' Rangers and the French and Indian War.

Now retired from the Grand Rapids Police Department after over twenty-seven years of service, Todish works as an independent historical writer and consultant, specializing in the French and Indian War and Alamo periods. He provided background information and worked as an extra in the 1992 movie *The Last of the Mohicans*, and also served as the Technical Advisor and appeared as an extra in the award-winning History Channel documentary *Frontier: Legends of the Old Northwest*. He has also been a consultant for such productions as the Learning Channel show *Archaeology*, and the PBS series *Anyplace Wild*. Todish has written articles for a number of historical publications, and is a staff writer for *Muzzleloader Magazine*. In addition to his books, he has written a number of historical articles for such magazines as *The Journal of the Forces of Montcalm & Wolfe*, *Living History*, *Smoke & Fire News*, and *F&I War*.

While still in college, Todish became interested in black powder shooting and historical reenacting, and this still occupies much of his time. He is the Adjutant of the French and Indian War reenactment group Jaeger's Battalion, Rogers' Rangers. His next project will be writing the text for the second book of historical artist Robert Griffing's paintings.

Todish's published works include: *America's FIRST First World War: the French & Indian War 1754-1763*, *The Annotated and Illustrated Journals of Major Robert Rogers*, with art by Gary Zaboly, *Through So Many Dangers: The Memoirs and Adventures of Robert Kirk* with Ian McCulloch and art by Robert Griffing, *British Light Infantryman of the Seven Years' War, 1757-1767* with Ian McCulloch, *Alamo Sourcebook 1836: A Comprehensive Guide to the Alamo and the Texas Revolution* with Terry Todish and art by Ted Spring.

DR. TODD E. HARBURN is a man of many talents and interests. A native of Flint, Michigan, he attended Hope College, where he majored in pre-med and earned all conference honors in football. He graduated from the Chicago College of Osteopathic Medicine and now has an orthopedic surgery and sports medicine practice. He is also the football team physician for his alma mater Hope College.

Todd has nearly a lifelong interest in the British 60th or Royal American Regiment and its service in North America. He has done extensive research on the officers and garrisons of the 60th Regiment in the Great Lakes region, and has authored several publications on these topics in recent years. His biography of Captain/Lt. Col. George Etherington, *A Vindication of My Conduct*, relates the officer's Revolutionary War career and the fascinating story of the 1779 surrender of St. Vincent's Island in the Caribbean during that conflict. In addition to coauthoring this current book on the Pontiac Uprising with his longtime friend Tim J. Todish, he has also co-authored two books on college football history. He was a consultant and an extra in the History Channel's 1997 award-winning *Frontier: Legends of the Old Northwest*. He has also portrayed Captain Etherington for several years in the annual Fort Michilimackinac Pageant in Mackinaw City, Michigan.

Todd currently resides in Okemos, Michigan with his wife Shirley and daughters Shannon and Stacey. He enjoys spending time at their "Commandant's Cottage," a modern version of the Commandant's Quarters at Michilimackinac, not far from the reconstructed fort.

His published works include: *A Vindication of My Conduct: The General Court Martial Trial of Lieutenant Colonel George Etherington. . .* with Rodger Durham, *MIAA FOOTBALL: The Gridiron History of the Michigan Intercollegiate Athletic Association* with Gerald E. Harburn, *A Tradition of Excellence—A Salute to the Champions: The Centennial History of Alma College Football, 1894-1994* with Dr. Charles A. Gray, and numerous vignettes.